for Emma,

G000167631

I trust this will give you some helpful pointers on your journey of discovery.

Have fun!

Craig

DISCIPLEMAKER

© Copyright 2015 by Craig Millward

All rights reserved. No part of this book may be reproduced without written permission, except for brief quotations in books and critical reviews. This book has been published in collaboration with 3DM Publishing. For information, write to 3 Dimension Ministries, PO Box 719, Pawleys Island, SC, 29585.

All Scripture quotations, unless otherwise noted, are taken from the Holy Bible, New International Version®, NIV® Copyright ©1973, 1978, 1984, 2011 by Biblica, Inc. Used by permission of Zondervan Publishing House. All rights reserved worldwide.

Some scriptures quoted are from the Good News Bible © 1994 published by the Bible Societies/HarperCollins Publishers Ltd UK, Good News Bible© American Bible Society 1966, 1971, 1976, 1992. Used with permission.

Some scripture quotations are from the Contemporary English Version © American Bible Society 1991, 1992, 1995. To find out more about the Contemporary English Version translation and the work of Bible Society visit www.biblesociety.org.uk.

All PEANUTS cartoons reprinted with permission from UNIVERSAL UCLICK. . All rights reserved.

Published by 3DM Publishing
3dmpublishing.com

First Edition

First printing 2015

1 2 3 4 5 6 7 8 9 10 Printing/Year 25 24 23 22 21 20 19 18 17 16 15

Artwork & Illustrations: John Rainford

Layout & Design: Shaun Millward

Cover: Blake Berg

ISBN: 978-0-9907775-9-5

Acknowledgements

I am one of those people who is always asking questions. I believe we are known as 'divergent thinkers', but the phrase feels like it expresses a little too much frustration with people like us! I am, therefore, always thinking, always reading, always connecting ideas in new ways. It also means that books that have stimulated me have become good friends. It will therefore not surprise you that I draw from a wider range of sources than might be expected of a Christian who considers himself a charismatic evangelical. As a Plant/Shaper[1] I have become grateful for my God-given ability to unearth creative and unorthodox dimensions of well-known texts and I hope you find my reflections stimulating.

There have also been many individuals who have contributed thoughts and ideas that find their way into this book. From the moment John Davis, my lecturer in Missiology at Moorlands College, unpacked Genesis 12 in a way I had never heard before, I was hooked. I am also grateful to Rob Bell whose book Velvet Elvis was my launch pad to studying the Hebrew background to the life and times of Jesus. I also thank the line of Russian-speaking Messianic Rabbis who hugged me so tightly after I shared my early reflections on first century Jewish culture in a church basement in Minsk. You gave me such confidence that I was on to something important. So many more people have encouraged me as I tested out many of these ideas in a variety of settings. I thank every one of you, together with my family for allowing me so much writing time.

I am also grateful to Paul Maconachie who first floated the idea of turning my notes into a book, and to my friends and colleagues at 3DM Europe for their assistance in so many ways. It should be understood that many of the ideas that follow may flow from my interaction with 3DM material but do not carry a 3DM imprimatur. That is not how we work! Thanks to John White and Helen Bearn for reading the manuscript and for your suggestions and to numerous individuals who have read sections and chapters at various stages and given me encouragement to keep on writing. Thanks also to my wonderful son Shaun for helping with the technical aspects of preparing this book for publication, to Si Ford and Libby Culmer from 3DM publishing, and to John Rainford for providing the unique artwork and Blake Berg who designed the cover and offered his advice so freely.

1   See www.belbin.com for an explanation of what these roles bring to a team.

Table of Contents

Chapter 2:

The Call to Follow Jesus

John 1:35-51

- Every rabbi had disciples
Jesus uses a different set of selection criteria to Gamaliel
Open-system and closed-system thinkers
Why we tend to define discipleship in terms that suit us
The dangers of Christendom thinking
Seven things discipleship is not
Reflecting on God's call to you

Chapter 3:

The First Miracle

John 2:1-12

Growth-minded and fixed-minded people
Spotting learning opportunities: The Learning Circle
Being dropped in it by your mum may be God's leading
Jesus is fully present in the most ordinary scenarios
Learning to see God in every detail

Chapter 4:

Turning the Tables

John 2:13-25

Jesus prepares himself for his first confrontation with authority
The fig tree did nothing to make Jesus angry
The empty temple courtyard was a symbol of unfruitful religion
Tests of Jesus' messiah-ship
The reasons Jesus maintained his distance from those who would follow
Learning to see as Jesus saw

Part Two: Themes from John's Gospel

Part Three: Jesus' Commission

Chapter 14:

John 20:19 – 21:25

John's great commission
How easy it is to miss God's presence
We need frequent reminders to do God's work his way
Each healing journey is as unique as our failures
How to feed the sheep food they don't want to eat
How to lead sheep that have become fat or suspicious
Creating a culture of permission
Jesus' global mission fulfilled through us

A note on the Illustrations

A number of years ago, whilst on a trip to Belarus, I recall walking through an open-air market full of stalls containing thousands of beautifully painted matryoshkas: Russian nesting dolls. As I was selecting a doll to take home for my daughter it struck me that they illustrated the relationship between Father, Son and Holy Spirit: each resembled the other, were truly one and yet could also be experienced independently of each other.

As we wrestled with the creative task of preparing the graphics for this book we saw the matryoshka as an equally powerful symbol of the relationship between a disciple and Christ. Paul loves to remind us that we are each 'In Christ', in the sense that our life and our future are wrapped up in his work on the cross and his resurrected life.

The New Testament also teaches that, as we imitate Christ and the character of Christ we see in others, we are becoming formed into a likeness that is his. This is represented by the distinctive shape and the similar images on the body of each doll. But our becoming like Christ happens in such a way that none of our story or our individual identity becomes lost. Thus we add our own faces to a doll that looks like Jesus - as the drawings at the beginning of each chapter illustrate so beautifully.

Bethany's doll holds just six smaller representations of itself inside it. Christ has made many more copies of himself and he continues to do so. Each of us bear the shape of Christ whilst also telling our own story and it is God's will that we also become filled with the radiant life that is his.

INTRODUCTION
A Personal Journey

Back in the summer of 2008 I asked my church to try and recall what they were doing in June 1984 and gave them a list of events from that month to jog the memory:

- A famine in Ethiopia kills hundreds of thousands of people.

- Over 1,000 are killed when Prime Minister Indira Gandhi sends troops to the Sikh Golden Temple in India.

- Madonna has her first hit with "Like a Virgin," and Prince releases his album Purple Rain.

- The Olympic Games take place in Los Angeles and are boycotted by fourteen countries from the Soviet bloc.

- John McEnroe wins both the Wimbledon and the U.S. Open tennis championships.

- Shimon Peres becomes Prime Minister of Israel.

- Apple releases the Macintosh.

- British Prime Minister Margaret Thatcher privatizes the telephone service.

- Incumbent Ronald Reagan wins re-election to the U.S. presidency. His Democrat opponents are Walter Mondale and Geraldine Ferraro, who is the first woman to run for vice-president from a major political party.

I then asked them how they would feel if in June 1984 they had made a huge, life-altering, promise to someone they cared about deeply but now, 24 years later, they had still not kept their word. What's more, for the whole of that time they had it in their power to do what they had promised and had never explained why they were delaying. I was reading through the book of Genesis at the time and it had hit me with great force that Abram was being forced to face this exact dilemma.

Follow the story with me: in Genesis 12 we discover God inviting Abram into a major covenant. As far as we know Abram was content. He was a successful God-fearing man with a loving and devoted wife and a large extended family who honoured him as its patriarch. But then God intervenes and makes a promise that is almost too good to be true:

> The Lord had said to Abram, "Go from your country, your people and your father's household to the land I will show you. I will make you into a great nation, and I will bless you; I will make your name great, and you will be a blessing. I will bless those who bless you, and whoever curses you I will curse; and all peoples on earth will be blessed through you."

To the more cynical modern day reader this may sound too much like the no-strings offer promised by a cold-caller who has randomly generated our phone number and is now speaking to us like a long-lost friend in order to persuade us to buy something we don't want. But Abram believed God. He signed on the line. By chapter 15 we read that Abram is becoming disillusioned and he asks God about his promise and why he still has no children. God answers him by giving him an even more enticing picture of a sky full of stars. This seems to have satisfied Abram but clearly didn't impress Sarai since in the following chapter she suggests Abram takes matters into his own hands by trying to secure God's promise through Hagar.

By the time we get to chapter 17 at least 24 years have passed. For all that time Abram had been waiting for his first generation of descendants – and in the meantime his brother Nahor had fathered twelve children with two wives! This is the way God reintroduces himself to his servant who has been waiting so long for some activity on the promise-keeping front:

> When Abram was ninety-nine years old, the Lord appeared to him and said, "I am God Almighty; walk before me faithfully and be blameless. Then I will make my covenant between me and you

and will greatly increase your numbers." Abram fell facedown, and God said to him, "As for me, this is my covenant with you: You will be the father of many nations. No longer will you be called Abram; your name will be Abraham, for I have made you a father of many nations. I will make you very fruitful; I will make nations of you, and kings will come from you. I will establish my covenant as an everlasting covenant between me and you and your descendants after you for the generations to come, to be your God and the God of your descendants after you. The whole land of Canaan, where you now reside as a foreigner, I will give as an everlasting possession to you and your descendants after you; and I will be their God." Then God said to Abraham, "As for you, you must keep my covenant, you and your descendants after you for the generations to come. This is my covenant with you and your descendants after you, the covenant you are to keep: Every male among you shall be circumcised. You are to undergo circumcision, and it will be the sign of the covenant between me and you.

My most frequently repeated mistake as far as understanding the ways of God goes is to submit to frustration and then to try and do God's work myself. I have often said that if I were outside of time I would use it as a reason for getting more things done in a given time-span whereas God seems to do the opposite. My walk with God has included many occasions when God has made promises and then delayed in keeping them and each time I have found this a confusing experience. In the passage we find revealed a God who is so unlike me – a God who is deeply respectful of Abraham's faith whilst also being so secure in himself that he feels no need to prove himself or explain his actions even to the one he has chosen to follow his lead. Despite not yet delivering on his promise, God is clearly confident enough in Abraham's faith that he makes the further demand that this 99 year old man cut off his own foreskin as a further commitment to a covenant he himself had not yet kept.

The Scandalon

The truth is that the two years prior to June 2008 had been very dark for me. My brother had died in deeply distressing circumstances and this had led to an internal collapse of the coping mechanisms I had been using to function as a physically disabled person in a world that, despite a great deal of equality legislation, still treats people on the basis of first impressions. Back in January 2008 I took a three month sabbatical during which time I had set myself the task of discovering why, despite 15 years of hard work, the church I was leading was still not producing the kind of disciples Jesus had said would be such compelling signs of the Kingdom. Back then it felt to me like God had not kept a whole host of his promises and I was depressed. In the few weeks before Christmas 2007 I had come across a set of Peanuts cartoons around which I wrote a personal statement to God explaining how I was feeling. It went something like this:

As I reflect on 18 years in local church ministry I find the following cartoon series uncannily helpful. It goes without saying that these years have seen a measure of success, growth, development and accomplishment. But, like Linus, I have also have had to shed my naivety as certain Kingdom breakthroughs I was eagerly expecting have not happened and some core convictions that were once so clear and straightforward are now replaced by unnerving questions.[2]

® UFS, Inc.

Coping with the loss of certainty is often necessary in order to appreciate the fact that any living faith in a God who can never be fully

2   PEANUTS ©1960 Peanuts Worldwide LLC. Dist. By UNIVERSAL UCLICK. Reprinted with permission. All rights reserved. Applies to all PEANUTS cartoons in this chapter.

known is a journey through unknown terrain. Thankfully, each loss has been more than counterbalanced by pleasant surprises. However, since much disillusion is rooted in some kind of illusion, and the best thing to do to illusions is to dispel them. It seems important to mark the fact that some revisions can be painful, especially when they touch upon deeply held convictions, hopes or dreams. As the cartoon series unfolds we will see the effect this mounting disillusionment has upon Linus and others around him – and it presents some very poignant images:

Christian history and experience testifies to the truth of Christ's promise that following him would never be a straightforward issue. As we are invited to help build his church under his direction the first thing we discover is that God is willing to build using very imperfect people.[3] He also takes us on journeys that make little sense except in hindsight. We know to expect struggles against the world, the flesh and the devil, but are maybe less expectant that there will also be times when it seems that God himself appears to put stumbling blocks in our way. I am thinking of occasions when I have prayed for something in response to words I have believed were from God or occasions I have tried to act in obedience only to meet with a closed door at the end of a hopeful process.

I am reminded of Paul's conviction that God is an expert at using stumbling blocks designed to prevent people following him on their terms. Jesus also talked about narrow gates, presumably restricting our ability to bring along previously accumulated theories, ideas and methods. We know that entry into the Kingdom begins with repentance – which is a kind of stumbling - and that this humbling start paves the way for a call to the kind of diligent obedience which can be so inconvenient that it upsets our whole lives! It seems that humility is the necessary prerequisite if we are to walk the journey of faith with a sensitivity to the Spirit which can seem illogical to the rationalist and foolish to those who prefer various forms of man-made

....

3   I think the title "Building with Bananas" (by Derek Copley) is a fine choice for a book about people problems in the church.

religion that can be tamed and thereby controlled.[4]

Not only do the cartoons above hint at the dangers of bringing our own ideas into a life in Christ that we frequently struggle to understand,[5] they also reveal how even in the most devout believer, both a selfish and a legalistic streak often runs hidden and deep, suggesting that the stumbling stone put in place by God will always be a means by which we will learn most about him and his ways.[6] Michael Card demonstrates the way this works in his powerful song Scandalon:

> *The seers and the prophets had foretold it long ago*
> *That the long awaited one would make men stumble*
> *But they were looking for a king to conquer and to kill*
>
> *Who'd have ever thought He'd be so meek and humble*
> *He will be the truth that will offend them one and all*
> *A stone that makes men stumble*
> *And a rock that makes them fall*
> *Many will be broken so that He can make them whole*
> *And many will be crushed and lose their own soul*
>
> *Along the path of life there lies a stubborn Scandalon*
> *And all who come this way must be offended*
> *To some He is a barrier, to others He's the way*
> *For all should know the scandal of believing*
>
> *It seems today the Scandalon offends no one at all*
> *The image we present can be stepped over*
> *Could it be that we are like the others long ago*
> *Will we ever learn that all who come must stumble.*[7]

A God who chooses to offend rather than flatter as a means of calling potential followers is always going to be a God who is hard to follow – both

....

4   1 Cor 2:13-15.

5   It is not that life in Christ is irrational or makes no sense. It has a level of rationality that is perhaps best described as supra-rational, making sense to God in advance and at the time, but only to us in hindsight if we are granted the benefit of being able to see the bigger picture.

6   The Greek word Skandalon is used in this way in Rom 9:33, 1 Pet 2:8, 1 Cor 1:23 and Gal 5:11.

7   Michael Card – Scandalon (Dv&a music, 2009).

in personal terms and as we engage in any attempt to share him with others.

Yet Linus' promise "if you are a good little girl Sally, he'll bring you something too" sounds so similar to the kind of message that drew me to Christ. What a shock as we realise that the Gospel turns out to be truer than we thought it was but not half as comfortable! What a disappointment to discover that God is less committed to giving me what I want than I am to getting it.

In my own experience it is my growing understanding of God's grace that has debunked the link between my goodness and God's gift. And it is dealing with questions and disappointments that have exposed the fraudulent connection between Jesus and Santa (not to mention the Great Pumpkin!). But Linus is yet to discover the limitations of his belief system and, in his many attempts to fend off this moment of inevitable crisis, he attempts to build an ever more impressive theological system...

whilst getting as many friends onside as he can as a way of bolstering his belief that it is working...

and ignoring the doubts of those who think they can see the flaws...

thus entrenching him even more firmly into his system of untenable beliefs.

But Linus' deep conviction simply turns what was designed to be an attractive proposition into a defensive mindset that alienates his potential converts...

Sadly, everything that is founded upon illusion will inevitably fail...

Poor old Linus has just discovered that any theological system based upon fixed views that are not open to revision runs the risk of producing the kind of disillusion that will eventually overbalance the whole belief system, necessitating the need to rethink the whole thing from the ground upwards.

In my case this was just the moment the God of the stumbling block had been waiting for!

It is healthy to ask questions

During this period of questioning I had a conversation with a friend who is also a highly skilled therapist. He explained to me his understanding that an honest and diligent leader of any faith community will always be living in a place of tension. Thus, whilst the people may expect comfort, a wise leader knows the importance of the occasional provocation if we are to be true to our calling. Although a church may be designed to be a place to learn and have fellowship, the careful discipler knows that a lesson has not been truly learned until it is lived and so she seeks to help this to happen. Denominational structures may be built around a certain set of recovered truths, but the prophet senses the need to go further than his forefathers ever went and that every truth needs to be reinterpreted for a new age.

So a Sunday congregation may feel the need to be persuaded of the inherent truth of scripture on a weekly basis but the wise teacher eventually suspects that the reason for this might be that they are not seeing the reality of it lived out in their own lives. The sensitive worship leader knows they can draw a crowd and generate a certain feel good factor through the careful choice of songs but is also aware of the ease with which people become addicted to an emotional high that may or may not be linked with the moving of the Spirit. The list could go on and on.

I experienced all these tensions and more, but none of them came close to the BIG ONE which I frequently expressed in the form of a question: Why is the church I'm leading not producing quality disciples who are seen by others as living symbols of the Kingdom of God? Long ago I developed the habit of asking not only why we did the things we do but also how we think the things we do will attract others to Jesus. In the 20+ years I have been in local church leadership I have met and got to know countless individuals who are fascinated by Jesus but totally confused by church in all its forms. And so many of these people began by encountering the church with an open mind but found nothing there that would help them live better lives, let alone lives that were becoming more like Jesus. It is recalling these faces that draws me back to the uncomfortable questions.

Let me be specific in order to guard against exaggeration and also to ensure that I am not misunderstood. There were many things I witnessed in the life of the church I led which convinced me of the wisdom of God and the genuine commitment to Christ exhibited by my fellow believers. These included such things as commitment to meeting regularly, welcoming newcomers, serving in many ways, allowing change to happen, being creative, giving of themselves and sharing life together in such a way that grace and mercy formed the bedrock of our fellowship. We certainly weren't lacking in sincerity:

© UFS, Inc.

Despite our hard work, there were times when I was tempted to wonder to what degree we did these things any differently to other groups or societies that weren't founded upon faith in God. Whenever I expressed these feelings they were inevitably misunderstood but I could not be satisfied. My goals were so high because any plain reading of the New Testament is so wonderfully compelling. I read, for example, that our calling is to become disciples of Christ and that our meetings should be places where all manner of spiritual gifts are operating on a fairly regular basis. I also felt that we should be encountering more response than we were and

I longed for our church community to be demonstrating the signs of the Kingdom amongst the lost of our wider community. Not only did we rarely witness such things, we also seemed to have become so used to them not happening that we didn't seem to yearn for them.

On my sabbatical I discovered more disillusioned Christian leaders whose reserves of faith had dwindled because they too were concluding that the life they were living with as much conviction as they could muster wasn't producing the result that they were told to expect. I also encountered other leaders who were willing to share my conviction that the chief failure within our churches was that all our church services and programmes are not geared to producing fruitful disciples. The more people I spoke to, the greater encouragement I found to persist with my theory:

...to which the answer must be sought with great diligence:

The church I was leading in January 2008 was winning new converts and attracting existing Christians. It was lively, creative and relatively healthy. And yet I began my three-month sabbatical with a deep sense that it wasn't working as it should. I knew it had something to do with my lack of awareness of what a true disciple of Jesus looked like and therefore how they were formed. I knew I could not continue summoning up the energy to lead this church – or any church for that matter – until I had some answers. I began my period of study and reflection with the desire to examine the way Jesus formed disciples. I also possessed an intuitive drive to study the culture of the New Testament in greater detail.

One of the first things I realised was that the brokenness I had experienced over the previous two years was an opportunity – a personal scandalon. There are certain questions which, when asked, break our lives open in such a way that things can never be the same again. It wasn't that God hadn't kept his promises, as I had feared. Rather, he was doing everything he could to point me towards the questions and the resources that would answer my deepest longings. He was helping me to put the pieces back into a shape and form that matched my calling.

The right questions yield answers – eventually

My own journey began with a period of significant crisis. There may be times when reading my reflections brings about a strong emotional response within you. It is my intention to be both positive and honest but there may be times when it seems that my desire to tell it like I believe it is provokes a reaction. Disagree with me by all means, but please try and resist stuffing the uncomfortable questions back into the boxes in which they were previously hidden. I trust you are aware that we all have well-practised ways of deflecting things we fear may be true when we are afraid of the consequences. It is my hope that you have enough self-awareness to spot the difference between a well-embedded defence mechanism and a genuine disagreement. Having said this, I am self-aware enough to concede that there are occasions when I overstate my case to make a point or when my own rawness may still show through. Please bear with me where this may be the case whilst remembering that sometimes it takes a big jolt to push us away from the familiar – even when we have become disillusioned with it.

It was a few years before I realised that the reflections I recorded at length during my sabbatical could be fitted around the various accounts and encounters recorded by John in his gospel. As I began to receive invitations to work with churches that were also asking the 'discipleship' question I found myself returning to this gospel time and again, each time discovering that familiar texts were speaking fresh insights to me. This is especially true of the narrative passages which became gold mines once I began exploring them from a Jewish cultural perspective. This gave me the courage to return to my notes.

Previously I had felt that my reflections read too much like a how-to manual and were rather self-indulgent. John's Gospel gave me a loose framework that made sense, although the fact that I have allowed John to dictate when each theme arises does mean that this book cannot be used as a step-by-step guide. This is no bad thing since this there is no one size-fits-all disciple-making blueprint but I am aware that some readers will still be hoping there is so they can build a church program around it! I hope that the way I have ordered the contents section helps you return to what you are looking for.

I do not claim that what follows is a traditional Commentary on John's gospel. Instead it is best read as a reflection on parts of the Gospel from a missional perspective. The book is divided into three sections. The first section covers the first four chapters of John's Gospel, illustrating the way each event has been selected by the author to present Jesus as the perfect restatement of God's mission to bless the whole earth. The second section is an attempt to separate a number of key strands that are woven through the Gospel and explore what these themes teach us about engaging with God's mission in our current context. I close with a final chapter that covers John's version of Jesus' commission to the Twelve. In each chapter I have sought to balance my own theological reflection with practical insights for personal reflection.

Let's Get Started

I hope it is already clear that this book emerged from a journey. I am a church leader, an ordained Baptist, who found myself captivated by the way Jesus worked with people and wanted to learn how to follow him like his disciples did. Like the Apostle Paul, whilst I do not consider myself yet to have fully taken hold of this lifestyle, I believe I am now pressing on in the right direction toward the eternal prize.

I have found it important to write in such a way that feels like a cross between a commentary, a theological reflection and a journal. This is because I find why people think as they do as fascinating as what they actually believe. This also explains the numerous references which I always enjoy since they provide an endless number of potential tangents.

I have come to believe that there is much to learn from the Gospel of John as we approach it in faith that Jesus Christ is calling his church back to its core purpose: to make disciples and teach them to do all the things he taught those who walked with him in the flesh to do. It is my hope and prayer that you are able to identify closely enough with my journey to walk with me in an adventure which I trust will help us all to become far more effective disciples of Jesus Christ.

PART 1

John 1-4

CHAPTER 1
A Gospel for Everyone

We know that John wrote his gospel quite some time after Matthew, Mark and Luke had completed theirs. Although there is evidence that John makes use of a small amount of material from Mark and Luke, and uses these sources imaginatively, 96% of John's gospel is unique. John also draws on familiar Old Testament imagery – such as the vine and the shepherd – but, unlike the other gospel writers, he avoids the Old Testament 'proof texts' that point to Jesus as Messiah. I take this to imply that John is confident that the earlier writers have done their job and that Jesus' credentials are, by now, firmly established. John's intention is to argue Jesus' claims to a wider audience than Jews who were waiting for God to come amongst them.

All this suggests to me that the disciples Jesus trained and sent out had done what they had been prepared and sent to do. Second-generation followers of *The Way*[9] were causing a stir wherever they were being scattered and John clearly saw the need to write a universally pitched account of the life and teaching of Jesus in popular middle Greek, drawing

9   The beginning of Acts 9 seems to suggest that this was the original term used by followers of Christ to describe themselves.

on current themes and teachings from oral Torah, the *Targums*, [10] Greek philosophy and a variety of mystery religions.

"In the beginning was the Word, and the Word was with God and the Word was God." The structure of this opening verse immediately invites a comparison with the first verses of Genesis. What is more, the use of the potent image of 'light' alongside its opposite 'darkness' and the enigmatic and versatile concept of *logos* serve as a clear implication that John sees Jesus as a powerfully creative and potentially global revelation of God.

The Greek word '*logos*' had wide and varied currency in the first century. Jews had become used to the phrase '*the word of God*' from its frequent use in Wisdom Literature and the *Targums*, by writers who had become wary about writing definitively about, or even using the name of, God. Writing from Ephesus, John would also have been aware that the designation *Logos* had been taken by Heraclitus, a native of that city, half a millennium earlier and used to describe the principle by which constant change could be said to have an underlying order. Heraclitus understood the *logos* to be the very essence of wisdom by which truth could be recognised. More recently Philo, a Jew who studied both Jewish scripture and Greek philosophy at great depth, had taught that the *Logos* was the oldest thing in the world and the instrument through which God made the world. He said that the *Logos* was the thought of God stamped upon the universe; he talked about the *Logos* by which God made the world and all things; he said that God, the pilot of the universe, held the *Logos* as a tiller and with it steered all things. He said that man's mind was stamped also with the *Logos*, that the *Logos* was what gave man reason, the power to think and the power to know. To Philo, the *Logos* was the intermediary between men and God and was also the priest who prepared the soul before God.[11]

As if such claims weren't bold enough, John introduces a second character to his opening verses. The figure of John the Baptist seems to walk straight off the pages of the Old Testament in order to become Jesus' sponsor. Which, of course, is the point. There were many messianic figures in the first century but Jesus comes with references from the ideal person:

....

10   The Targums were Aramaic translations of the original Hebrew scriptures for common people who no longer spoke classical Hebrew.

11   William Barclay – *The Gospel of John, Volume 1. Revised Edition* (Edinburgh: Saint Andrew Press, 1982), 36.

an ascetic who has honed his spiritual senses in the desert. And, what's more, this referee needed no asking. The Baptist volunteers his services as a witness and, as he baptises Jesus, his testimony is echoed by the Father as he baptises his own Son with the Holy Spirit.

At this point I need to remind myself that I am not writing a commentary. My intention is to illuminate the gospel in such a way that a missional light shines through the portals John has designed for that purpose. I therefore jump to verses 6 and 9 which unashamedly declare that Jesus, this man who is the *Logos* and is from God, came so that all may believe and was thus sent as a light for all people everywhere. This too is a throwback to the first book in Jewish scripture and from there to the entirety of God's dealings with the Jewish people.

God's Global Mission

I have already referred to Genesis 12 in which we read of an encounter which forms the essential bedrock of all there is to understand about the missional purposes of God:

> *The LORD had said to Abram, "Go from your country, your people and your father's household to the land I will show you. I will make you into a great nation, and I will bless you; I will make your name great, and you will be a blessing. I will bless those who bless you, and whoever curses you I will curse; and all peoples on earth will be blessed through you."*[12]

This first covenant with the first Patriarch is clear. God chose one man originating from the great Chaldean city of Ur, but now living in Haran after his father had decided to join the throngs who had been attracted by the fertile land of Canaan. The tense of the first verse makes it very clear that Abram has already heard God's voice and obeyed the simple command to leave – thus explaining why, according to Hebrews 11:8, Abram has already delighted God by his faith. So it is while Abram is already on the move to an unknown destination that God declares his intention to make him the father of a great nation and, as if that wasn't enough, to bless and honour him.

The first thing to remind ourselves is that the nation of Israel did not exist at this point except in God's imagination. God has no favourites. It

12 Genesis 12:1-3.

wasn't as if he scoured the earth and chose a people group to bless above all others. He makes a decision to create a people for his purposes and decides that the founding parents are going to be two infertile people who are not going to have their first child until well beyond normal child-bearing age. What is more, there's a reason for all this. God's larger intention is to bless all peoples on earth through this not-yet-begun nation. We've already hinted at the manner in which God drew Abram into this relationship and upon the fact that he took a long time to keep his promise and here we need to reflect on the reason the covenant was necessary.

If we flick back to Genesis 1 we encounter a passage that describes what humans were created for:

> Then God said, "Let us make mankind in our image, in our likeness, so that they may rule over the fish in the sea and the birds in the sky, over the livestock and all the wild animals, and over all the creatures that move along the ground." So God created mankind in his own image, in the image of God he created them; male and female he created them. God blessed them and said to them, "Be fruitful and increase in number; fill the earth and subdue it. Rule over the fish in the sea and the birds in the sky and over every living creature that moves on the ground." Then God said, "I give you every seed-bearing plant on the face of the whole earth and every tree that has fruit with seed in it. They will be yours for food. And to all the beasts of the earth and all the birds in the sky and all the creatures that move along the ground—everything that has the breath of life in it—I give every green plant for food." And it was so. God saw all that he had made, and it was very good. And there was evening, and there was morning—the sixth day.[13]

Humans had been given security, significance and purpose by our creator. Security was derived from our place at the pinnacle of a creation brought into being by a perfect God. Significance naturally followed from being made in the creator's image - meaning that we each have the capacity to relate to God, each other and the creation and possess the capacity to think, reflect, choose and enjoy our privileges. We find purpose in ruling as tenants of the created order under God's general direction. Things were, as God rightly says, ideal.

....

13   Genesis 1:26-31.

But the story has a twist to it and things didn't go quite as planned. An event occurs which is described in chapter 3 and which we know as the Fall. Genesis 2:16 reveals that God had issued humans both with freewill and a warning:

"You are free to eat from any tree in the garden; but you must not eat from the tree of the knowledge of good and evil, for when you eat from it you will certainly die."

In the first verse of Genesis 3 we encounter a serpent who immediately begins sowing seeds of doubt in Eve's mind. A simple question - "Did God really say, 'You must not eat from any tree in the garden'?" - provokes an over-reaction as she recounts God's prohibition. The original instruction hadn't said anything about not touching the tree of the knowledge of good and evil and the overstatement now makes God's command seem harsh. How quickly she forgets that every tree in the garden except one is freely available to them and she has now been sufficiently distracted to swallow the lie that follows. "You will not certainly die," the serpent said to the woman. "For God knows that when you eat from it your eyes will be opened, and you will be like God, knowing good and evil."

Eve evaluates her options and is lured by the attractiveness of the one act that has been prohibited. She eats and immediately discovers that the serpent seems to have told the truth. She remains alive. But she realises, by stages, that something far worse has happened – the snake was also truthful about God with-holding knowledge, but for a very good reason. Eve soon discovers that she has brought upon herself the horror of being made aware of complexities she is unable to cope with.

Three modern day images help us to connect this ancient story to our own lives. The first two come from Tolkien's *Lord of the Rings*. In *The Two Towers* we encounter Theoden, a pale shadow of a King as a result of Wormtongue's treachery and lies. On seeing the film for the first time I recall being struck by the way Peter Jackson portrays Theoden as an ashen-faced puppet, thus illustrating sin's deadening effect. The manner in which Gandalf releases Theoden from his mental prison by declaring truth and resisting the source of the lies that kept the spell in place is equally powerful.

The opening to *The Return of the King* begins in a serene and pastoral setting. Sméagol and his friend Déagol are fishing from a boat on a lake and Déagol dives in, only to find a ring on the lake bed. Sméagol is immediately overtaken by the power of the ring and kills his friend in order to steal it. Gradually he becomes possessed by his "precious" and his mind is warped to the extent that he even forgets his name. This is the point we discover that the noise "Gollum", by which we have known him, is the sound of a choking noise brought about by the corrupting effect of the ring he has stolen. Sin hides us from our true identity.

The final picture demonstrates the way sin blinds us to the source of our life and is found in C. S. Lewis' *The Last Battle*. We find a group of dwarves sitting in Aslan's kingdom without the ability to appreciate their surroundings:

> "Well, at any rate there's no Humbug here. We haven't let anyone take us in. The Dwarfs are for the Dwarfs."... "You see, " said Aslan. "They will not let us help them. They have chosen cunning instead of belief. Their prison is only in their own minds, yet they are in that prison; and so afraid of being taken in that they cannot be taken out. But come, children. I have other work to do."

The Genesis story demonstrates how the effects of the Fall are evidenced in a number of broken relationships. The first is between humans and God and we witness the pitiful scene of humans created in God's image hiding from their creator. Such alienation leads to a doubting of God's character: is God only good because we obeyed him? We then note how the resulting fear, guilt and shame affected their sense of self. Adam and Eve experience angst for the very first time and this results in the first unresolved argument, which symbolises the third broken relationship - division between humans. This lack of harmony is then worked out across the whole of the creation as we read of work being experienced as a curse. Animals become defined as meat and are accordingly afraid of the very individuals who have previously named them and thereby affirmed their uniqueness and intrinsic value. The breakdown in the relationship with God thus leads to a loss of the corresponding security, significance and purpose and the descent towards the judgement wrought by the great flood.

The Fall: A Loss or a Gain?

Before we move on I want to ask a more fundamental question about what happened to humans after that first transgression. Although Christian theology talks freely of *the Fall*, the phrase is never used in the account itself. This is important since the very word 'Fall' implies we lost something: we are less than we were. Viewed from one angle this is indeed the case. We were gifted with a relationship with our creator from which everything that made us fully human was derived. We have become so used to living this pale shadow of a life (the Genesis story refers to our current existence as a living death) that we can barely imagine what complete intimacy with God will look like when we will, at some point in the future, experience it once again.

Nevertheless, Genesis 3 teaches clearly that our transgression was not a result of losing something but gaining knowledge which blurred the boundary between God and humanity:

> And the Lord God said, "The man has now become like one of us, knowing good and evil. He must not be allowed to reach out his hand and take also from the tree of life and eat, and live for ever.[14]

The temptation which looked good to Eve was to 'become like God'. And, once again, the serpent wasn't lying. This is exactly what she gained and it presumably felt like such a positive experience that she shared the fruit with Adam. It was once both of them had eaten that the curse of the new knowledge became increasingly evident as it affected both their relationship and their call. Adam and Eve now had more knowledge than they could cope with and their new awareness began acting to obscure their true nature from themselves.

This may feel like playing with words until we ask a further question: how do we experience the renewed life which we believe Christ has restored to us? Well, if we have so imbibed the idea that we have fallen, it may seem to us that the solution is to regain what we have lost, perhaps by effort, study, attending church, living morally or serving others. One significant branch of the church teaches that doing such things gives us access to a store of grace that keeps us in the way of life. Other sectors of the church are implacably opposed to this doctrine but often seem, to my eyes at least, to have little to offer in its place. We have doctrines that tell us our guilt has been atoned for and that we have been fully restored to a God who can be experienced as a loving Father, but many of the models of discipleship we encounter imply that we still need to try harder if we are to live for God.

---

14   Genesis 3:22.

If it is true that our sin had its root in gaining a knowledge that was too much for us to bear and has resulted in us forgetting who we were, surely the way we live out our salvation must begin by rejecting lies about ourselves that masquerade as truth. Ephesians 2 tells us that God initiated the process of salvation by encountering us while we were dead in our sins. Our death was in relation to God and this was our experience because of the thick layer of dark matter that has been added to lives that were not intended to bear the weight. In trying to live life our way we have felt the need to take upon ourselves all kinds of scripts and coping mechanisms which may seem to quell our fears, angst and pain but only drive us further into ourselves. We have become so used to meeting our needs with our own resources within a self-contained system that has no place for God.

Paul describes this experience as being made alive even whilst our spirits were dead towards God.[15] And this encounter with new life refuses to allow us to return to our unilateral, self defining, self serving existence because it is not just our life that has been restored to us in Christ but also a true understanding of what that life means and how it is best lived. God breaks through the dark layer of suffocating matter and demands that we begin throwing off all false identities in order that the being that has been created in the image of God can come forth into the light.[16] Paul tells the Colossians to put all sins of the flesh to death in recognition that this old nature has been shed.[17] The result is that we will then be able to recognise the new nature that is already our true identity. Paul links this new nature to the image of God that is at the core of every human being and is clearly capable of being renewed.[18]

My mind is drawn to my cousin who farms a piece of ancient woodland that a previous owner had ruined by planting fast-growing trees as a cash crop. I was told that the best way to restore the woodland after the trees had been removed was to introduce a herd of pigs and let them burrow through the feet of tree litter that covered the floor of the woodland. She has known wild flower roots that had lain dormant for up to 30 years to germinate and sprout new growth as they feel the warmth of the sun once again.

....

15   Ephesians 4:2.

16   Maybe this helps us to read Hebrews 12:1 with fresh eyes.

17   Colossians 3:5-9.

18   Colossians 3:10.

When Paul tells the Galatians that he has been 'crucified with Christ' and that the life he now lives is best defined as 'Christ in me' he is taking this concept one step further. Discipleship has to be founded on a regained understanding of our new identity in Christ but it is not an identity that comes from our own efforts.[19] We are called to make room for the personality of Christ to be formed within us and channel the desires that spring from this new nature down new pathways. This is the kind of life Jesus teaches his disciples to live and we will learn how he teaches them as we proceed. According to Paul, our ongoing battle is then one of 'renewing the mind' to the fact that we are now held securely in a relationship with a merciful God who, having paid the price our sins deserve, now accepts the offering of ourselves to him and deals with us in ways that will inevitably be judged by us to be good, pleasing and perfect.[20]

God's Response to Sin

Back to Genesis 3. In verse 21 we read that God makes clothes for his renegades, thus mitigating their alienation from him and each other. I take this to be the creator declaring: "I'm going to work with this". Nevertheless, sin has consequences and God has no choice but to banish Adam and Eve from the garden, thus cutting them off from the quality and length of life they were created for. They are on their own in a world that has changed and, unsurprisingly, the story takes a series of dark turns. Cain kills his brother Abel and refuses even to acknowledge that the blood tie between them implies an obligation to watch over him. Genesis 5 begins with a reminder that God created humans in his own likeness but the final name in the short genealogy that follows is that of the individual God chooses to halt the rapid decline of human depravity that has followed this loss of awareness of what it means to be human. The judgement that follows gives way to a new covenant, not with the earth as previously, but with Noah and his descendants and, through them, all living things. Which returns us to Genesis 12. We can now appreciate that God's covenant with Abram has a precedent.

It is worth reminding ourselves of the huge theological leaps that Abram was being required to make. Rob Bell helpfully reminds us that the gods of the land Abram and Sarai had left and the gods of the surrounding nations

19   Galatians 2:20.

20   Romans 12:1-2.

were thought to be unpredictable deities who needed placating in order to ensure the most basic of daily needs.[21] The most detestable gods of the surrounding nations were even thought to demand human sacrifices which, evidently, is the reason Abraham didn't flinch as he took Isaac to Mt Moriah a few chapters later. It also explains the questions he didn't ask God: Why? and How?

It is as we appreciate the context in which this biblical narrative was set that we begin to appreciate the degree of re-training that was necessary before Abraham could shed the patterns and images he had imbibed within his father's household. So, although the God of Abraham gradually reveals himself to be entirely different to his familial gods, Abraham shows no sign of being shocked at the command to sacrifice Isaac. God allows Abraham to go this far in order that he may say "'stop Abraham. You are used to gods that demand the thing most valuable to you'... Then this God says 'offer an animal instead'... The story does not end with the greatness of Abraham. It ends with a statement about God: This God provides."[22]

We can now see the extent to which the promise recorded in Genesis 12 is such a departure. Maybe it also explains why Abraham needed to walk with God for such a long time before he could take this new revelation on board. The focus of the promise is to bless Abraham, the nation that is formed from those who were to become his descendants, and the world. The magnitude of this choice means that Abraham needs to learn deep truths about the character of the God who has called him. Before he can create a people who can become a blessing it is necessary for God to lead Abraham on a journey of discovery during which his inherited ideas about angry and capricious deities are replaced by numerous experiences of a God who makes and keeps promises. Twenty-four years may have seemed like an eternity to Abraham. It can take this long for humans with a damaged capacity to relate to the divine to learn God's character sufficiently well in order that they may mediate it to others. Little has changed.

There is so much to learn from the story of Abraham but we need to move on. Abraham responds in faith time and again. Isaac, Jacob and Joseph also learn their own lessons about God. All the time the Lord is building a nation, establishing a dynasty, developing a shared history. But

....

21   View the first 30 minutes of the DVD *The Gods Aren't Angry* by Rob Bell.

22   Ibid. 32–33 minutes.

they are not yet a free people. Enter Moses, the man God uses to deliver his people. One of the most significant early lessons God teaches Moses comes in Exodus 6:2-3:

> God said to Moses, "I am the Lord. I appeared to Abraham, to Isaac and to Jacob as God Almighty, but by my name the Lord I did not make myself fully known to them.

Almighty God is an ideal title for a Deliverer but God wants to be known as a great deal more than a national talisman and so he reveals that he is also to be known and experienced as the *Holy One*. This can be seen as an invitation to worship him for who he is, not just what he does. This is the first of many occasions in which God gives himself a new name. To his people it must have seemed as if each time they became used to one particular image of God, they were forced to experience a mini-revolution as the object of their gaze morphs himself into something else before their eyes.

This progressive revelation brings to my mind the kaleidoscope I was given as a young boy. Each slight twist of the end of the kaleidoscope reveals a new image. Same toy, same beautifully coloured pieces, different picture. At times the new image looked so different to the previous one and it seemed impossible to believe that it was made up of the same pieces. It was also impossible to go back and recreate the previous image once the new one had emerged, precisely because parts of the last image were being used to make up the present one. In a similar way, followers of God find ourselves stretched as we attempt to hold apparently competing or contradictory images of God in our minds. God will not allow our vision of him to remain static, and who are we to dare to choose which image we prefer if God has many more facets of himself to disclose to us?

Back to Moses. God continues to reveal more of himself, firstly through the law which is best seen as a set of commands that reveal the nature of God and can therefore be the only basis of a true and honest relationship with him. God then initiates the construction of the tabernacle which establishes the theological basis for atonement through sacrifice. I have heard many Christians dismiss the Old Testament revelation of God, and thereby the whole of Judaism, by insisting that it teaches salvation by law keeping. This is rubbish.[23] Moses receives the promise from God that he

---

23   See chapter 2 of Lois Tverberg – *Walking in the Dust of Rabbi Jesus: How the Jewish Words of Jesus can Change your Life* (Grand Rapids: Zondervan, 2012).

has chosen to accept the blood of an innocent creature as atonement for the sins of a nation, thereby deepening their understanding of both the seriousness of sin and God's merciful nature.

As the Old Testament unfolds we notice that God chooses a variety of people to be his representatives. Patriarchs (Abraham, Moses...) give way to judges who administer justice by interpreting the written codes given to Moses by God. The judges are a mixed bunch and we never get the impression that they win the hearts of the nation. Even the best are only heeded for the duration of their lifetime.[24] At the end of this period we read that "everyone did as he saw fit"[25] and this is the spirit in which the people issue their demand that God allow them to be led by a human king. The roller-coaster ride continues as many of the kings exhibit little desire to honour God and he is forced to speak to his people at intervals through prophets. This sad state of affairs was never God's plan. If we cast our mind back to Exodus 19:4-6 we are reminded of God's original intention:

> 'You yourselves have seen what I did to Egypt, and how I carried you on eagles' wings and brought you to myself. Now if you obey me fully and keep my covenant, then out of all nations **you will be my treasured possession**. Although the whole earth is mine, **you will be for me a kingdom of priests** and a holy nation.' These are the words you are to speak to the Israelites.

God wanted the whole nation to become priests. What do priests do? Represent God. Before whom? The nations. God really was serious when he said in Genesis 12 that he wanted to win the world back to himself by showing favour to one group, thereby provoking the interest and jealousy of the other nations God loved with an equal passion. The astute reader may be thinking ahead to the last part of Paul's letter to the Romans but that is for later.

Returning to the account in Exodus 19-20, Moses is called up the mountain and God places a boundary around it. Moses is called into God's presence and receives the law. As Moses descends we read:

> When the people saw the thunder and lightning and heard the trumpet and saw the mountain in smoke, they trembled with fear.

....

24 See, for example, Judges 13:13-13:1.

25 Judges 21:25.

They stayed at a distance and said to Moses, "Speak to us yourself and we will listen. But do not have God speak to us or we will die." Moses said to the people, "Do not be afraid. God has come to test you, so that the fear of God will be with you to keep you from sinning." **The people remained at a distance,** while Moses approached the thick darkness where God was. [26]

How can you be a priest of God if you won't come near him? Note how, in verse 20, God speaks of two types of fear. There is a fear that provokes awe in humans and the fear that terrifies and paralyses. God cannot help instilling fear in humans whenever they draw near to him but it is our choice which kind of fear predominates. The people made the wrong choice and stood at a distance - "Don't let God speak directly to us" they cowered.

It is not only the people who are afraid of drawing near to God. Their representatives are too. As we read the Old Testament it is clear that the patriarchs knew God because they had walked with him, often for a whole lifetime. Judges were appointed to help Moses interpret God's laws but reading and interpreting someone's instructions is a big step from knowing them. Some of the kings did their best to represent God, others were a national disaster, but even the most celebrated leaders were unable to prepare the whole nation to become priests of God. During the era of the Prophets God found himself restricted to the occasional comment, either warning his people of impending disaster, pronouncing judgement or announcing that God hadn't given up on his people. The Prophets were largely ignored.

Notice one thing: as God's dealings with his people moved from patriarch to judge to king, the intermediaries' intimate knowledge of God's character becomes increasingly remote. Once the Lord has only a prophet to speak on his behalf it is a sure sign that the whole community had become deaf to his call. How are such people going to become priests before a waiting world? So God's chosen people are taken into exile and find themselves excluded from his greater purposes because they would not draw near to him. The whole story I have just recounted can be visualised in the diagram on the next page.

Proximity to God was to have been the key to Israel's success. As God's people thrived under his care, he knew the world would sit up and watch

---

26   Exodus 20:18-21.

as a nation of priests ministered gladly to him, doing only those things that delighted him and brought them peace. This is the extent to which Israel fell short: the priestly representatives of God became alienated from their source of life and grace. They thus had nothing to mediate to others. "Return to me", pleads God through the prophets[27] who are the only people unable to let go of the ultimate vision:

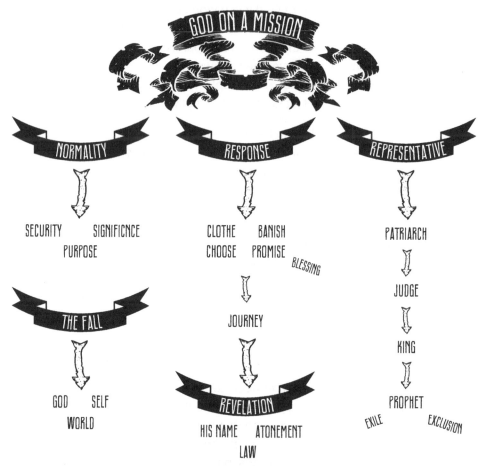

*In the last days the mountain of the Lord's temple will be established as the highest of the mountains; it will be exalted above the hills, and **all nations will stream to it. Many peoples will come** and say, "Come, let us go up to the mountain of the Lord, to the temple of the God of Jacob. He will teach us his ways, so that we may walk in his paths." The law will go out from*

27   For example – Isaiah 44:22; Jeremiah 3:1,7,10,12; 4:1; 24:7.

Zion, the word of the Lord from Jerusalem. He will judge between the nations and will settle disputes for many peoples. They will beat their swords into ploughshares and their spears into pruning hooks. Nation will not take up sword against nation, nor will they train for war anymore. Come, descendants of Jacob, let us walk in the light of the Lord..[28]

Jesus redefines the Law

I have inserted this brief survey of the Old Testament at John's invitation:

The true light... was in the world, and though the world was made through him, the world did not recognise him. He came to that which was his own, but his own did not receive him.[29]

As we consider the first few chapters of the Gospel we'll see that this is one of the key questions John is addressing: how can a people who define themselves as chosen by God become increasingly unlike him until they eventually forget the purpose for which they were called? And how can they do this so completely that they are unable to recognise their God when he stands before them in human form? First Century Jews knew they were living within "a story in search of an ending"[30] but were blind to the fact that it was they who had driven God's plan into the sand, thus causing their own exile.

The Jews of Jesus' time had completely lost sight of the ultimate intention behind God's relationship with their nation. Despite the repetition of his intention to use them to reach the Gentiles,[31] they had become more attracted by the belief that the Messiah would deliver a decisive blow to their opponents and thus had no desire or wish to be instruments of God's blessing to them.[32]

John was therefore stirring a hornets' nest in verses 14-17:

....

28   Isaiah 2:2-5 .See also Isaiah 11:9, 25:6-8 and 54-55 and 1 Kings 8.

29   John 1:9-11.

30   N. T. Wright – *The New Testament and the People of God: Christian Origins and the Question of God v. 1* (Minneapolis: Fortress Press, 1992) see chapter 10.

31   See Isaiah 2:1-5, 19:18-25.

32   Wright – The New Testament... op. cit, 267-8.

*The Word became flesh and made his dwelling among us. We have seen his glory, the glory of the one and only Son, who came from the Father, full of grace and truth. (John testified concerning him. He cried out, saying, "This is the one I spoke about when I said, 'He who comes after me has surpassed me because he was before me.'") Out of his fullness **we have all** received grace in place of grace already given. For the law was given through Moses; grace and truth came through Jesus Christ.*

When he contrasts the grace that was mediated through Jesus with the grace that came through the Law given through Moses John is not suggesting that the two are opposed to each other but that, by the time Jesus walked the earth, God's grace demonstrated in the Old Testament had become perverted by a religious system that was deaf to God.

What we now call the "Commandments" or "Laws" were known by the Jews as *"The Teachings"* and were well understood to be God's gift to his people, underpinning and maintaining the gracious covenant God had initiated between them. These were the standards by which God's people were to judge their own shortcomings and the provisions made by God in the Tabernacle and Temple were his means of restoring right relationship. The phrase 'works of the law', used by Paul and frequently misunderstood by Christians, "indicated those prized badges of identity that were understood as marking out the true members of the people of God who could one day be expected to be restored by him".[33]

By the time of Jesus *"The Teachings"* had been added to by a 'hedge' of minor laws which, although they seemed like an ingenious way of helping people to keep the core laws sacred, only succeeded in putting too much attention upon a list of practises that were forbidden. Whenever Jesus declared "You have heard it said... but I am telling you... he was referring to these hedge laws, or *'oral torah'* and was pointing out that the heart, or intentions, of his Father had been lost amidst the added detail.[34]

The trouble is that simply adding more laws to the Torah as a way of trying to take it more seriously only ends up drawing attention away from its very purpose. God wants relationship and real relationships have boundaries within which they can flourish. Simply focusing on a list of 'dos'

33   Stephen Kuhrt – *Tom Wright for Everyone* (London: SPCK, 2011) 39.

34   Chapter Four discusses Jesus' relationship with the law in more detail.

and 'don'ts' risks turning a lively Covenant relationship into a conveniently distant arrangement governed by the mechanical application of a series of formulae. As such an attitude took root, Israel began to see themselves as preferential creditors of a god who bound himself to them by means of an irrevocable covenant. What they missed was the sad fact that the relationship the law and covenant were intended to serve had died.

Writing his gospel so many years after his compatriots, John knew that Jesus had stirred up a great deal of controversy over whether or not he was an upholder of the law. Right at the beginning of his account he attempts to nail this question by describing the Christ as 'full of grace and truth' as opposed to a stickler for the letter of the law – both written (from God) and oral (man-made) Torah. Surely this is also the reason Jesus' encounter with Nicodemus is inserted so early into John's Gospel. Here we have a Pharisee, one who knows the Torah like the back of his hand but cannot see the author of the law who is standing in front of him! "No one can SEE the present activity of God unless he is born again" says Jesus.

In Jesus, John insists, God was throwing off the shackles of an increasingly complex religious system and the first person to recognise him was a prophet. How fitting in the light of the downward Patriarch – Judge – King – Prophet trajectory we noted above. And the first metaphor this prophet chooses to ascribe to Jesus is a lamb. More innocent, but similar in kind, to the ram God provided Abraham with and deliberately reminiscent of the means by which people are put right with God. This choice of image is thus a deliberate attempt by God to re-engage the memory of his chosen people.[35] That this is God's initiative is underlined by the fact that even John did not recognise his second cousin as the Messiah until the voice from heaven identified him as God's son.[36]

Which box constrains you?

When I began asking God to renew my vision and his will for the church I was called to lead I was quickly taken back to the text that had inspired me many years previously. I longed to be part of a church that looked something like the picture I found in Acts 2:42-47:

They devoted themselves to the apostles' teaching and to

35   John 1:31.

36   John 1:33.

fellowship, to the breaking of bread and to prayer. Everyone was filled with awe at the many wonders and signs performed by the apostles. All the believers were together and had everything in common. They sold property and possessions to give to anyone who had need. Every day they continued to meet together in the temple courts. They broke bread in their homes and ate together with glad and sincere hearts, praising God and enjoying the favour of all the people. And the Lord added to their number daily those who were being saved.

I was converted into a church that put a lot of energy into trying to persuade non-believers to believe as they did but to little effect. In Acts we read of converts from all races wanting to be part of Christ not just because they heard a sermon in their own language but because they witnessed the activity of God in the church. The deaths of Ananias and Sapphira put fear amongst the unsaved but crowds of them continued to flock to faith in Christ.[37] What better illustration of the vision within Genesis 12 is there in scripture?

How did these "priests of the human race"[38] miss their calling so spectacularly? The answer is found in an amalgam of many factors. Priests are only able to represent a God they know intimately. The story we have just recounted is a sorry account of a gradually deteriorating relationship between Israel and her God. Once God's people began to lose sight of their true identity and calling, the religion that had once set them apart for God became seen by them as the reason they were superior to those nations they were sent to bless. The reception given to Jesus by his own people is illustrative of the extent to which humans, once they have lost sight of what God has bestowed upon them, can become hardened in their blindness and utterly committed to their own folly.

As I sat nursing what I believed was my call alongside the job that was earning me a living I was forced to admit that I no longer knew how to pursue both at the same time. As I looked at the church I knew that the missing key was a true understanding and commitment to forming disciples in a manner similar to the one Jesus employed. I knew I had to make a

37   Acts 5:13-14.

38   N T Wright – *Following Jesus: Biblical Reflections on Discipleship* (London: SPCK, 1994), 9.

choice.

Wendell Berry, in his novel *Jayber Crow*, shows great insight in the way he describes Jayber's feelings as he allowed his questions to surface and push out the limiting and restrictive denominationally correct world-view he had lived in for so long. "The main thing", he says "is that it made me feel excluded from it, even while I was in it."[39] Jayber's professor of Greek offers him wise advice: "You have been given questions to which you have not been given answers. You will have to live them out – perhaps a little at a time."[40]

I described in the Introduction to this book how I began my sabbatical a few years earlier with the suspicion that the God who is the expert at deploying stumbling blocks was at work in the questions he had planted within me. It felt, to use a delightful description borrowed from another of my favourite novels, like a dog "having...pups in my brain."[41] I had a sense that God was not afraid to dispel illusions, wanted me to question my usual assumptions and was ready to open my eyes to hidden truths that had not been visible whilst I was doggedly committed to making the old model work better.

However, as an ordained minister within an established denomination, I returned from sabbatical feeling like I had learned a new language whilst I'd been away. It felt like no one understood me and it was ultimately necessary to step out of the box that constrained me from becoming what I knew I wanted to be. This is not to condemn other people as less obedient or denominational structures as inherently wrong. Nevertheless, I can't help but ask: are there any patterns of thinking and behaving you know need to change? Are there structures within which you are insisting you must serve God that are unhelpful to you and are thus preventing you from fulfilling your calling? If any of these ring bells for you I ask God to show you how to submit yourself to him. I believe God is in the process of turning his church inside out for the sake of the lost and it would be a great mistake to hang on to structures that are resistant to his missional agenda.

---

39   Wendell Berry – *Jayber Crow* (Washington, Counterpoint; 2000), 49.

40   Ibid. P 54.

41   John Steinbeck – *East of Eden* (New York: Penguin, 1992), 271.

CHAPTER 2
The Call to Follow Jesus

Every rabbi in Jesus' day would have had disciples. The prophet John clearly had followers and it was one of his, Andrew, who became Jesus' first disciple. Simon Peter is added to the list not at Jesus' initiative but at the invitation of Andrew. Jesus immediately affirms Andrew's choice both by mentioning that he had noticed Simon earlier, and by indicating his future potential: "'You are Simon son of John. You will be called Cephas' (which, when translated, is Peter)."[42]

> The name "Simon" means "to hear" and it is a reasonable name for the man who so quickly heard and responded to Christ's call, but Jesus sees a different future for Simon. Jesus sees him becoming a loyal, immovable force – a brick. So he renames him "Peter", meaning "rock". The new name is like a new set of spectacles by which Peter can look at the world.[43]

The next day Philip is added and he seems to take encouragement from

---

42   John 1:42.

43   Michael Frost – *Exiles: Living Missionally in a Post Christian Culture* (Peabody: Hendrickson, 2006), 194.

Andrew's initiative since he seeks out Nathanael. This choice also receives special affirmation by Jesus who tells Nathanael he'd had his eye on him before Philip made his move. According to Matthew's gospel Jesus also calls John and his brother James at some point between these two pairs but John is characteristically reticent about naming himself. He lets us guess how the other six were recruited.

Delving deeper, it seems that Andrew chooses to follow Jesus after hearing his previous master call him 'the Lamb of God'. Simon Peter believes the testimony of his brother. Philip is challenged to 'follow me' and tells Nathanael that he believes Jesus to be the one both the law and the prophets spoke about (it is easy to miss this further appeal to the Old Testament but John knows what he is doing). In his selection of the Twelve, Jesus was making a decisive statement. Tom Wright is correct to note that he is making a deliberate allusion to the twelve tribes of Israel, thus reconstituting the people of God around himself and his kingdom agenda.[44]

Jesus was therefore doing something that was expected of any first century rabbi, but going about it in an unorthodox way. Compare his methods, for example, to Gamaliel who offered his counsel to the assembly of Jewish elders in Acts 5. Gamaliel is described as "a teacher of the law held in honour by all the people" and was clearly highly respected by the Sanhedrin. It is also said that Gamaliel was called upon to advise those in positions of power. We also discover later in the New Testament that Paul was "educated at the feet of Gamaliel".[45]

According to accounts of the day, a rabbi such as Gamaliel would have chosen only the most outstanding candidates to become part of his entourage. And the reasons for this were obvious. In Luke 6:40 Jesus declares: "A disciple is not greater than his teacher, but everyone when fully trained will be like his teacher." Gamaliel chose Paul to be his disciple because he saw potential in him and could visualise himself basking in reflected glory. In effect he was declaring: "You are smart enough to become like me." In the video *Jewish Disciple*, Rabbi Barney Kasdian of the Kehilat Ariel Messianic Synagogue explains the meaning of the call to follow a rabbi in Jesus' day. To be invited to follow would have been understood as an

....

44   N. T. Wright - *Jesus and the Victory of God: Christian Origins and the Question of God: v. 2* (London: SPCK Publishing, 1996), 130-131.

45   Acts 22:3.

invitation to become conformed to the lifestyle demonstrated by the rabbi. This was therefore understood as a deeply formative relationship involving a submission of the disciple's will. Kasdian therefore describes Jesus' call to us as one of learning "a lifestyle of making Jesus Lord."[46]

A different kind of Rabbi

Although the call to become a disciple would have been familiar in Jesus day, there were some significant differences between the way Jesus acted as a discipler and the methods of someone like Gamaliel. To begin with, far from calling the high-fliers, Jesus turns up and calls fishermen, tax collectors and other very ordinary men. He allows others to follow on the initiative of someone else! Nathanael had simply been observed resting under a fig tree, not debating skilfully with the Jewish Elders! Maybe this is why Jesus felt the need to remind them "You did not choose me. I chose you".[47] He may have been trying to lessen the pressure they felt to perform in the midst of a section of teaching on the ministry of the Holy Spirit. The implications of this are staggering.

To begin with it circumvents the fruitless discussions on predestination I recall having as a young Christian.[48] Jesus chose us (or allowed us to choose him) to be his disciples because he knows we can become like Him. This is not due to any innate ability in us but because he can live in and through us if we allow ourselves to be discipled. As with Israel, so with us: we are chosen, not merely to be saved, but to be instruments of God's blessing.

Let us remember that Jesus also allowed others to travel with him, some of whom weren't just ordinary but would have been considered a negative influence by other rabbis:

> After this, Jesus travelled about from one town and village to another, proclaiming the good news of the kingdom of God. The Twelve were with him, and also some women who had been cured of evil spirits and diseases: Mary (called Magdalene) from

....

46   The video Jewish Disciple can be found on www.higherpraisetube.com, www.sermoncentral.com and www.sermonspice.com.

47   John 15:16.

48   If you don't relate to this consider yourself blessed.

whom seven demons had come out; Joanna the wife of Chuza, the manager of Herod's household; Susanna; and many others. These women were helping to support them out of their own means.[49]

We are clearly meant to assume from Philip's conversation with Nathanael that Jesus has either explained more about himself or that the six men referred to in John 1 have been talking amongst themselves. They now have some understanding of who Jesus might be and, despite the enigmatic nature both of their call and of the one who has invited them, each of them sees Jesus as delivering an attractive opportunity.

So Jesus is willing to share his life with the kind of people other rabbis would not have touched with a barge pole. This is not, in itself, a commendation. Yet the reason I am writing this book is because of what those twelve became.[50] Something happened within a three-year timespan that turned this small group of simple men into world-changers. In fact, the truth is even more amazing than that. Something happened to twelve unpromising men that makes them able to pass on this transformative experience to many more new believers within a very short period of time. Ten of the twelve met an early death as the church expanded but the gospel spread was unhindered.

Jesus' discipling methods were also very different to a rabbi like Gamaliel. The degree of Jesus' uniqueness will unfold over the coming chapters but it is worth reminding ourselves at this early stage the core reason why onlookers were so amazed at his teaching. Many of the rabbis of Jesus' day were focused upon defining the minimum requirements of the law in order that individuals might stay safe and secure within its boundaries. Jesus was not interested in defining where such boundaries lay but in explaining the true intention of his Father's commands in order that God's people would be free to live as grace-filled priests of God.

By way of example, let us compare a ruling of Rabbi Hillel with a teaching of Jesus. Forty years before Jesus, Hillel famously taught "Whatever is hateful to you, do not do it to your fellow. This is the whole

---

49 Luke 8:1-3.

50 We will revisit Jesus' discipling methods in Chapter Nine.

Torah and the rest is commentary, go and learn it."[51] Compare this with Jesus' pithy summary of the whole law: "Love God and your neighbour as yourself". Jesus isn't concerned to define the bare minimum required to remain in God's good books but seeks to teach those who would follow him to learn to redirect their aim to a target beyond their own natural ability. Interestingly, this was an approach taken up by later rabbis who named this method *hasidut*, where the question to be asked by the *hasid*, or pious person is "what more can I do to please you?".[52]

My desire to study Jesus' discipling methods began as I read Acts 6 which records an upset about the way food was being shared. The Hebrew-speaking widows were getting more than the Greek speakers so the Apostles call a meeting at which it is agreed that something should be done. The Twelve didn't want to be distracted from prayer and preaching so they delegated:

"Choose seven men of good reputation," they instructed. "Let them sort it out." One of these was Stephen, who is described as "a man full of faith and of the Holy Spirit." Just a few verses later, almost in passing, it says "Stephen, full of grace and power, was doing great wonders and signs among the people".

"Quite a mundane task for someone so gifted," I thought. "Must've been a humble guy." Then I found myself asking a question: who discipled Stephen? Who taught him to do the wonders and signs? It wasn't Jesus, not directly anyway. Stephen wasn't one of the twelve. I guess he may have been part of the group of 72 in Luke 10 but it doesn't say. Clearly it didn't seem important – maybe because he wasn't the only one?.

I then jumped a few chapters to Acts 8. Philip was one of the table servers too. Here we find him sent to the main Gaza Road with little by way of explanation. When he gets there Philip receives the instructions he needs directly from the Holy Spirit and ends up evangelising an Ethiopian eunuch who has been to the Temple but not found God there. Not the living God anyway. Philip becomes the messenger he was looking for and then disappears.

....

51   Babylonian Talmud, Bava Metzia 59a.

52   Ann Spangler and Lois Tverberg – *Sitting at the Feet of Rabbi Jesus: How the Jewishness of Jesus can Transform your Faith* (Grand Rapids: Zondervan, 2009), 171-174.

Two examples don't make a pattern but I noted that here were two individuals who, in the days following the birth of the church, were already clear on the fundamental points of the gospel and were able to hear the voice of the Spirit and take great steps of faith as if it had become a normal part of everyday life. "Go into all the world, make disciples and teach them to do as I have taught you", commanded Jesus. It looks like at least a few people did.

I then noticed that the beginning of Acts 6 implies that the food issue arose because the believers were multiplying rapidly. When I think about church growth in Acts my mind is normally drawn to the coming of the Spirit at Pentecost. The Spirit comes and everyone hears the gospel in his own language. A big meeting with a great deal of power – who could fail to be impressed? The first Pentecost brought in 3000 new believers but only happened once, yet the church continued to grow. This led me to wonder whether Stephen and Philip weren't the only ones who hit the ground running. Perhaps Luke chose to write about Stephen because he was the first martyr and Philip because he was the first cross-cultural evangelist. Were there many more we don't know about? And are they the reason the church continued to grow hand over fist even after the Holy Spirit's most celebrated evangelistic turn?

I'm convinced that the missing ingredient within much of the Western church is that we don't know how to make disciples. Jesus does. The Twelve did, because he taught them. Stephen, Philip and countless others did because the Twelve showed them how to do what Jesus had taught them. But somewhere the knack was lost.

Open to being Led

Westerners like to consider themselves as logical, rational people. But if I affirm you as a logical individual I am only making a statement about the way you order the information you are presented with. Every day we are all bombarded with information in the form of facts, both sorted and unsorted, assumptions, intuitions, memories, feelings and perceptions. Each of these has to be interpreted and the frame of reference we use to do this often relies on previous interpretations we have made which may, or may not, have been tested for their validity. Things are further complicated when we realise that our personality types will suggest to us that certain kinds of information are more valid than others. An indicator such as Myers-

Briggs demonstrates the way one person is more naturally perceptive whilst another places more attention upon their feelings or their intuition. And someone's preference for blurting out their thoughts so they can sort them as they talk (extrovert) will also contrast significantly with the introvert who might retire to a quiet place for days before revealing what, to them at least, is the last word on the matter. All these people consider themselves logical.

Rationality adds another layer of complexity. To some, for example, it is rational to believe that the world is the product of random forces which happen to have come together in this instance to produce life which has evolved into the forms we see today. Others are being just as rational when they admit to the possibility of a super-rational being who possesses an intelligence far greater than their own. This sub-group of rational people may disagree on how this God (or god) created all that we see or how involved he is with his creation but each difference of opinion can still be equally rational according to the starting assumptions made within their chosen frame of reference.

Westerners also like to think of ourselves as 'civilised', and by this we mean that we are both logical and rational and have devised systems of society and government that we believe reflect these qualities better than more 'primitive' societies. Much of Western theology has become moulded into forms that are considered commendable for their balance. Our theology makes sense and rocks no boats. I have lived much of my life in such an environment and I've learned that, although it may succeed in producing true and lofty statements about God, these rarely change lives in the way Jesus did.

I submit that to be an open-system thinker who chooses to pursue a life that is open to stimuli from outside oneself is also rational, albeit in a different way. In recent years we have seen a rise of a militant kind of atheism whose high priests would have the rest of the world believe the world is a closed system with no God involved in it. I happen to believe that those of us who believe there is a God bear our share of responsibility for this atheistic backlash as we all too often call on ideas about God to do a task to which gracious actions would be better suited. In our frustration that we are not being heard much of our apologetics seems increasingly critical and defensive, in marked contrast to the way Jesus taught his disciples to follow the leading of the Spirit.

Writing over a century ago, William James took issue with those who called themselves *rationalists* and who argued that religious faith is irrational because it cannot be defined or explained in terms that do not involve an element of faith. James spots the weak point in their argument:

> If we look on a man's whole mental life as it exists, on the life of men that lies in them apart from their learning and science, and that they inwardly and privately follow, we have to confess that the part of it which rationalism can give an account is relatively superficial. It is the part that has the prestige undoubtedly, for it has the loquacity, it can challenge you for proofs, and chop logic, and put you down with words. But it will fail to convince or convert you all the same, if your dumb intuitions are opposed to its conclusions. If you have intuitions at all, they come from a deeper level of your nature than the loquacious level which rationalism inhabits... The truth is that in the metaphysical and religious sphere, articulate reasons are cogent for us only when our inarticulate feelings of reality have already been impressed in favour of the same conclusion... The unreasoned and immediate assurance is the deep thing in us, the reasoned argument is but a surface exhibition. Instinct leads, intelligence does but follow.[53]

Open-system thinkers who choose to follow the God of the bible have a choice. Westerners tend to think of life as a straight line with the past behind and the future ahead of them. Every attempt God makes to reveal himself to this world is fraught with immense difficulty since, however clear God makes himself to us in his terms, we can always choose whether or not we recognise what we are seeing.[54] To receive God is an act of faith, no matter how he chooses to reveal himself.

Philip Yancey also reflects on what it means for God to communicate to us:

> Unlike us, God has an all-encompassing point of view that takes in the world we see as well as other realms hidden to us. Moreover, God sees all our history at once, as a ball of yarn compared to the

53   William James – *The Varieties of Religious Experience* (New York: Penguin, 1985),73, 4.

54   I commend the following presentation if you want to explore this further: Rob Bell – *Everything is Spiritual* (DVD produced by Zondervan).

short, consecutive scraps of thread we experience. Unconstrained by a body, God exists in every place at once. The same barrier that keeps us from God keeps God from us, though in an entirely different way. Every time God chooses to manifest himself in our world, he must accept limitations. He "con-descends" (literally, descends to be with) to our point of view. Moses saw a burning bush that bedazzled him, changing the course of his life and of history. Out of flames of fire he heard the voice of God speaking. Yet God experienced that same burning bush as a limitation. To impinge on our world, God must subject himself to the rules of time and space. God had little choice, to put it crudely, if he wished to communicate in a way humans could understand. An analogy: conceivably we humans may one day master whale language, so that we can lower an underwater transmitter and communicate through squeaks and clicks in a way that whales understand. In doing so, we will interpret ourselves downwards, in a self-limiting way comprehensible to whales. They will not receive the full essence of what it means to be a human being; we can only "talk" together about fish and plankton and oceans, not about laptop computers and skyscrapers and football. That analogy gives a small picture of what it must be like for an all-powerful, all-knowing God to communicate with human beings.[55]

This means that your image of God is just that: your image. And mine is unique to me. But to both of us God promises to communicate. I said above that open-system thinkers who choose to follow the God of the bible are exercising a rational choice to follow a call they believe comes from God. True disciples, if we are to accept the definition of discipleship given above, have chosen to submit their need for proof to the call of faith, according to certain safeguards. We will see that Jesus goes on to teach His disciples to live in a far more open-system than they believed existed before they met him but for now it is enough that they leave the past behind in order to to follow Jesus. Just as he was with Abram, God was already pleased with the Twelve for seeing something in Jesus' call that made them willing to be led by him into the unknown.

The six disciples introduced to us by John find themselves presented with an opportunity which they choose to grasp. We often find ourselves

---

55   Philip Yancey – *Reaching for the Invisible God* (Grand Rapids: Zondervan, 2000), 115.

in similar situations but whether or not we recognise them is influenced by what we believe a disciple to be. Before we spend a great deal of time exploring the activities in which Jesus expected his disciples to become proficient I want to clear the ground as I debunk a few myths about what a disciple actually is.

What a Disciple is Not

The writers of the New Testament provide us with a great deal more than an account of the birth, death and resurrection of Jesus. Yet, if we use the historic creeds as our source of what is most important, we could be forgiven for thinking that the manner in which Jesus lived his life was not very significant. The writers of the creeds were understandably intent on demonstrating the divinity of Christ but their formulations only present part of the story. Like Michael Frost, I

> wonder which came first: the impulse to sanitize and tame Jesus by encasing him in abstract theology, thereby removing our motivation for discipleship, or our natural repulsion toward discipleship that forced us to domesticate Jesus to let us off the hook. Either way, when Jesus is just true light from true light, ethereal and otherworldly, we are only ever called to adore him. But when he is true human, one who loved and healed, who served and taught, who suffered and died and rose again, he becomes one we can follow.[56]

There are a number of ways of avoiding an issue. The most obvious is to try and ignore it and hope it goes away. If it refuses to do so it becomes necessary to research the problem at length and maybe put it on a mental 'to do' list so it feels like something is underway. People who are experts at putting things off also know the value of redefining the issue at hand in a way that removes its sting. This, it seems to me, is what we have done with the question of discipleship. We can all recall reading books or having conversations with people who use the words 'Christian' and 'disciple' so loosely that almost anyone who attends a Sunday service fairly frequently automatically becomes a disciple. Flattery will not cause anyone to follow Christ.

Christians are divided over whether the Emperor Constantine's

....

56 Michael Frost – *Exiles*, op cit, 32.

conversion to Christianity was a genuine work of God or whether it was an act of political statesmanship. There are also fundamental disagreements as to whether his patronage of the Church, resulting in the preferment of Christianity as the religion of the state, and the elevation of bishops and clergy to positions of influence which in turn brought great wealth and prestige, was good for the long-term health of the church.[57] My own sympathies tend towards the argument that the resulting idea of 'Christendom', in which a society based on Christian values can apparently be formed and upheld by institutions suffused with Christian doctrines and ideals, is inherently flawed. Maybe it is easier to criticise the Christendom concept in our current context in which we inhabit a society that is increasingly suspicious of institutions and authority figures – but the critique I am adopting is nothing new.[58]

Within such a mindset 'church' becomes conflated with 'Kingdom' to the detriment of the latter and the mission of God becomes what Ramsey MacMullen has called 'flattery and battery'. Flattery: everyone is supposedly Christian because they are born into a society that holds a certain set of morals and habits to be the accepted norm. Battery: anyone who steps out of line may face discrimination or, in the worst cases, persecution or death. Thus, in ages past, many were severely persecuted for pointing out that applying a respectable 'Christian' veneer over well-intentioned structures and institutions, and counting everyone in the nation as a 'Christian' as a way of encouraging them to conform to a certain moral framework, does not produce the kind of changed lives Christ intended. In fact history shows that religions formed on such a premise frequently become bulwarks against change:

> if you ask most people how they view religion, they'll answer that it is supposed to be a protector of the tradition. This is why, for so much of our history, we have made such good bedfellows with kings, queens, dictators and oppressive regimes. Just ask the French, the English, the Spanish, the Germans, the Austrians, the Russians, almost all Latin Americans, and Protestant North Americans. We have constantly been on the side of our particular

57   See Nigel G Wright - *Disavowing Constantine: Mission, Church and the Social Order in the Theologies of John Howard Yoder and Jurgen Moltmann* (Carlisle: Paternoster, 2000).

58   See Stuart Murray Williams - *Post Christendom: Church and Mission in a Strange New World* (Carlisle: Authentic Media, 2004).

ancien régime instead of the transnational kingdom of God, ever since Constantine invited us into his palaces in A.D. 313.[59]

Thus, whilst every reading of UK culture would call our population irreligious, ignorant of most of the basic tenets of the Christian faith, 71% of the UK population default to calling themselves "Christian".[60] There is not a little humour attached to this self-designation since recent polls suggest that only 35-40% of the population believe in a God of any sort and only 6-10% of the population attend a place of public worship at least once a month.[61] In ages past it seems that it was possible to maintain the illusion that we were a Christian country since people were more deferential and social disapprobation against nonconformity was strong. To my eyes, as someone who was born in the 1960s, it also seems as if any consensus there may have been as to what behaviours went into making a decent society have also been lost, meaning that fewer people aspire to become 'Christian' in the moral sense of the word. The most humorous example I have encountered of this designation was sitting in a public meeting and hearing one Jew commend another Jew for performing a 'Christian' act.

My reading of the state we now find ourselves in is that those who are middle-aged and older have grown up being told they were 'Christians' whilst never encountering the Christian God from whom the gospel message comes and whose Spirit produces the inner desire necessary to please God and the resources through which we may do so. The result of this is that the 'gospel' was never set free to do its work and thus never became the good news it could have been if a genuine change of heart and mind had been involved. We are thus presented with a state where millions of our fellow citizens are shedding the label 'Christian', thus effectively inoculating

....

59   Richard Rohr – *The Naked Now* (New York: Crossroad Publishing, 2009), 90. I have included this quotation partly because it comes from the pen of a Roman Catholic and also because it lifts our eyes from the UK context.

60   An example is data revealed in a Mori poll in August 2003 where only 55% of the English population could name one of the four Christian gospels whereas 60% could identify the Koran as the sacred book used by Muslims. From report found at http://www.vexen.co.uk/UK/religion.html#Ignorance.

61   See http://www.vexen.co.uk/UK/religion.html#God, http://www.vexen.co.uk/UK/religion.html# Sunday Attendance and The Christian Research English Church Census 2005, accessed online in 2008.

themselves against the Christian story for which familiarity has bred a sort of quiet contempt, whilst the church continues to offer a quasi-chaplaincy that is only demanded within a worldview that has all but disappeared.[62]

The saddest part of the state we now find ourselves in is that those parts of the Christian church which are desperately hanging on to the Christendom model because it represents to them a gospel legacy, now have a very shaky basis upon which to build a model of Christian discipleship that is anything close to the model Jesus suggests. If we are happy to follow the dictum that it is not what I say I believe that should be taken seriously but it is what I actually do that indicates what I truly believe, I have to conclude that the implicit message communicated by all too many churches of various kinds is that disciples are apparently formed by a mixture of the following factors:

1. Regular – or not so regular – attendance at church

There is no doubt in my mind that any understanding of what it means to be a disciple of Jesus is often compromised by poor evangelistic preaching. Too many people come to Christ in response to a call to have their sins paid for and receive a ticket to heaven that seems to require 90 minutes church attendance a week... or maybe a month... to keep it valid.

> Jesus clearly says the kingdom of heaven is among us (Luke 17:21) or "at hand" Matthew 3:2; 4:17). One wonders why we made it into a reward system for later, or as Brian McLaren calls it, "an evacuation plan for the next world." Maybe it was easier to obey laws and practice rituals for later than to actually **be transformed now**. [63]

Such a mindset is typified in the phrase 'going to church' and is reinforced by our temple-style worship services led either by ordained clergy or suitably trained professionals and 'consumed' by passive onlookers. It is probably a fairly harmless habit to talk about 'going to church' in such a

....

62   For an insightful and very funny indication of the truth of this observation read Kate Fox – *Watching the English* (London: Hodder and Stoughton, 2005), 353-4.

63   Richard Rohr – *Preparing for Christmas with Richard Rohr* (Cincinnati: Saint Anthony Messenger Press, 2008), 15.

way that implies that our main focus is either the building or the prescribed worship 'service', but I am a pedant and it frustrates me deeply. When Paul talks of church it is the people that are his main focus of attention. "Give my greetings to Priscilla and Aquila. ... Greet the church that meets in their home" Paul says to the Romans and such a greeting is typical.[64]

Christian disciples know they are the church because they are brothers and sisters with God as their Father. We are a mutually supporting body, a living temple, a holy priesthood designed for, and belonging to, God. These are all dynamic images which illustrate our new nature, giving us a basis of established fact from which to relate to each other and the world.

2. Theological and/or Doctrinal purity

The primary aim of the sermon or homily is apparently to help the laity become clearer about what they believe. Frost and Hirsch describe this in terms of a concrete/historical model of teaching versus a speculative/ theoretical approach. They point to the creeds in which

> nothing is said about the life of Christ, discipleship, ethics, life and mission. Their primary focus is a speculative kind of theology – taking basic phrases and ideas found in scripture and working them into a statement that is philosophically consistent and essentially closed. These are deduced from scripture rather than read from scripture... we can thus grow up being blind to the historic and practical implications of the faith.[65]

There was, they say, a point in Christian history when "orthopraxy gave way to orthodoxy' - when right acting was displaced by right thinking. They contrast this with Hebrew thought in which "right living provides the context for us to embrace right thinking". This is also the reason cited by James McClendon who feels the need to explain why his three-part systematic theology opens with a volume on Ethics:

> The first volume (Ethics) appeared... declaring how the church must live if the church was to be the church. Now the new volume addresses a question integral to the first - what must the church

....

64   Romans 16:5, 23; 1 Corinthians 16:19; Colossians 4:15; Philemon 1:2.

65   Michael Frost and Alan Hirsch - *The Shaping of Things to Come: Innovation and Mission for the 21st Century Church* (Peabody: Hendrickson, 2006), 120.

teach in order to live in this way? (So those who say I have "founded theology on ethics" are doubly wrong; wrong since ethics is already theology, wrong since this volume is not based on the previous one, but explores more deeply the one matter already opened there.)...Without Christian life, the doctrine is dead; without Christian doctrine, the life is formless.[66]

Yet, in all too many churches the drive for theological purity (or a particular definition of purity – this is what *we* believe) seems to be the primary motivation for preaching. Just recently a friend told me of a church she attends every now and then whose teaching seems restricted merely to repeated explanation of its denominationally distinctive doctrines. Christian disciples know that something cannot be said to have been learned until it is put into practise and they seek to preach and demonstrate Christ in ways that rely on the power of God rather than the wisdom of man.[67]

3. Endless activity

Every temperament or personality test I have done has me marked as a perfectionist, a problem-solver able to analyse a situation effectively and not afraid to ask difficult questions. I am an innovator, good at finding new and more effective solutions, even willing to test ideas that go against prevailing opinion. The downside to this temperament (my polar opposite will find it hard to see that there is even an upside!) is that my natural inclination is to feel driven to move on to the next thing before the last innovation I introduced has become embedded.

In the church I used to lead I became aware that some members believed that my restlessness was due to some lack in them and they believed I was seeking to drive them to give more or try harder. I was deeply distressed that I was creating this impression because it is such a dangerous belief that impacts our concept of God and our inner life. Christian disciples, we will discover, learn to do the right thing at the right time and live lives of balance where whatever activity they engage in is from

....

66   James McClendon – *Doctrine: Systematic Theology volume 2* (Nashville: Abingdon Press, 1994), quoted from the Preface. It is an embarrassing admission that on first discovering this set of volumes arranged in order on a library bookshelf I immediately selected the second volume on Doctrine as my first taste of McClendon.

67   1 Corinthians 2:1-5.

a position of rest.

4. Progression through planes of ever greater spiritual experience

Christian history suggests that our walk with Christ will include times of closeness with him and the occasional life-changing encounter. Christian biographies tell of profound experiences that have precipitated radical transformations within people who have gone on to give themselves completely to Christ for the rest of their lives. The New Testament also teaches us to expect that many trials will come our way and logic suggests that it is during trials that we are given the opportunities to choose the truths by which we will live. If the New Testament is in any way normative I suggest that Christians acting missionally will also stir up various forms of misunderstanding and persecution. Certainly many of our forefathers did not deny Christ in the face of acute persecution and intense opposition and some of them even faced martyrdom.

There have been many critics of charismatic expressions of Christianity who latch onto both the shallowness of some of its theology and the way in which some revivalists seem to resemble thrill seekers so caught up in their consumerist sub-culture that they rush from one meeting to another searching for the latest high. More thoughtful critics suggest this is due to an over-realised eschatology which cannot find a place for the 'not yet'. We will attempt to unpick what may be happening in some of these gatherings in a future chapter but for now I'll simply note that this kind of activity has great risks to it if the search for experience is allowed to go unchallenged without being balanced against the reality of spiritual conflict and human opposition. Christian disciples know that, in Christ, they already possess all they need for godly living,[68] whilst they also remain continually open to the renewing and empowering presence of the Spirit.[69]

5. Confusing conforming to Christian subculture with growth

It is very easy to think you are a good Christian if you have substituted all the nasty elements of popular culture for Christianised versions of the

68   2 Peter 1:3.

69   Ephesians 5:18.

same thing. I know someone who visited the home of a new Christian and, without invitation, plastered her walls with tacky 'Christian' posters of sunsets and kittens linked to motivational texts. The new convert was distressed to find that saying 'yes' to Christ also meant having your décor decided by someone who confused a Christianised sub-culture with the real thing.

Jesus taught about the need to subvert a dominant culture wherever it abused its power and he told us to remind ourselves that we are not 'of the world' even when it is benign. Acts gives us cameos of a counter-cultural church that demonstrates to onlookers how good it is to be ruled by God's standards and his indwelling presence. Christian disciples are focused upon putting the many 'one-anothers' into practice, knowing that it is these acts that will begin to define an enduring and attractive counter-culture.

6. Becoming a nicer person

When Paul taught that God has called each of us to a life of good works which he has prepared in advance for us to do,[70] the context of the passage in which this statement is found clearly suggests that the 'good works' flow from his grace toward us. Yet I have lost count of the number of times I have been told that someone would 'like to think of themselves as a good Christian' on account of their behaviour, as if being 'nice' is how we win God's favour. I have been heard to ask such a person whether they think God considers them a good Christian or whether they would use the word 'good' to refer to Jesus but it rarely sinks in. The point hardly needs to be made – the epithets 'nice' or 'good' rarely say much more about a person than the way the editor of the Hitch-hikers Guide to the Galaxy described the inhabitants of the Earth: 'mostly harmless'.

I recall the shock I received when I woke up to the fact that most Christians I knew were not actually a great deal nicer than their pagan neighbours. And neither was I. When Jesus talked about the testimony of good works he used the image of light – one he also used of himself – and indicates that there should be a quality and depth to our good deeds that instantly mark us out as godly.[71] Clearly he is talking about a great deal more than being nice, probably including a pure motive in his definition,

....

70   Ephesians 2:10.

71   Matthew 5:16.

and Christian disciples know that the only godly thing about them is the indwelling presence of Christ which is propelling them toward holiness.

7. Developing more spiritual gifts

I well recall the first Spiritual Gifts identification course I attended. At one level it was hugely helpful and affirming to discover that other people saw things in me that I could not see in myself. The problem came when I discovered that the definition of 'spiritual gift' in that church was restricted to things I could do for the church and mainly on Sundays. There also seemed to be little awareness that many of the gifts listed in the New Testament fell outside of the neat definitions or categories dreamed up by the course author. It looked to me like the only reason the church ran the course was so that it could sign up more people for more programs.

The other side of the spiritual gifts coin is where one quickly gets the suspicion that a group of Christians act as if there are two distinct classes of gift – and the wackier ones are those that are either ignored or sought after most! I embarrass myself when I think of the times I have coveted a gift or a ministry in order to impress others or have used a gift in a way that elevates my own sense of self-importance. Paul puts the 13th chapter of 1 Corinthians where it is for a very good reason and, just as not seeking a gift can be seen as a lack of love for others,[72] so seeking one and flaunting it has everything to do with 'me' and is hardly about Jesus at all. Christian disciples are desperate for the gifts of God, knowing that without them we will have nothing of enduring value to give away.

The Adventure Begins

"Can anything good come from Nazareth" asked Nathanael who was clearly expressing some sort of personal prejudice against the town. "Come and see for yourself" was Philip's wise response. As we have seen, the disciples chosen by Jesus will have had some experience of seeing rabbis with their followers but they will have had no real awareness of the all-consuming journey that was awaiting them. The final words of John's opening chapter belong to Jesus. The way they recall the life of Jacob the

....

72   My logic goes as follows: A gift is given me by God but it is not for me but for you. If I fail to acknowledge my gift, hone it or use it, it is you who is short-changed. Denying I have a gift or playing a gift down is therefore an excuse to be lazy or please myself. I will explore this further in Chapter Ten.

schemer may seem strange until we recall that Jacob's ladder was a symbol of God making himself present on earth through the activity of another. I like Tom Wright's comment where he suggests Jesus is saying:

> Don't think that all you will see is one or two remarkable acts of insight, such as you witnessed when I showed you that I knew about you before you even appeared. What you'll see from now on is the reality towards which Jacob's ladder, and even the Temple itself, was pointing like a signpost. If you follow me you'll be watching what it looks like when heaven and earth are open to each other.[73]

Who chose whom?

The best definition of discipleship was coined by Jesus when he told the Twelve to teach the next generation of his followers to do all the things he had taught them to do. Simple. Except that it isn't because he left no manual. Which is actually a good thing because you can't do discipleship by the book. Following Jesus is more like a values-driven exercise led by an invisible guide.

The first thing we need to be clear about is whether this is a journey we are prepared to take. I suggested above that Jesus seemed content that Andrew call his brother and Philip invite his friend because he knows that none of us can rely on any personal qualities that will make us any better at following Jesus than our friends. Truly anyone can be a disciple of Jesus and sometimes a theology degree makes it much more difficult. It is truly staggering that Jesus' call to follow him can be passed on from one person to another in such everyday scenarios. And Jesus accepts all who will follow, no matter who they are or where they are from. Do you find it reassuring that Jesus affirms Simon and Nathanael despite the fact that they seem to have muscled in to the party themselves? How did Jesus call you and how has he affirmed that call since those very first days? Are you up for the challenge of discovering how Jesus makes disciples?

---

73   Tom Wright – *John for Everyone Part 1* (London: SPCK, 2003), 18.

CHAPTER 3
The First Miracle

Carol Dweck explains the significance of developing a growth-minded mindset if we are to become mature human beings.[74] In her comparison of growth-minded and fixed-minded teachers she says:

> How can growth-minded teachers be so selfless, devoting untold hours to the worst students? Are they just saints?... The answer is that they're not entirely selfless. They love to learn. And teaching is a wonderful way to learn. About people and how they tick. About what you teach. About yourself. And about life. Fixed-minded teachers often think of themselves as finished products. Their role is simply to impart their knowledge. But doesn't that get boring year after year? Standing before yet another crowd of faces and imparting. Now that's hard.[75]

I find this challenging on so many levels. First, it clearly describes the difference in mindset between Jesus and his contemporaries. Second, it

74   Carol Dweck – *Mindset: The New Psychology of Success* (New York: Ballantine Books, 2008).

75   Ibid, 201.

calls into question what we mean by teaching and learning. Third, it implies that we can create our own learning experiences and don't have to wait for them to be delivered to us on a plate.

Opportunity Knocks

Matthew's Gospel suggests that the first event the Twelve encounter after they begin following Jesus is a sermon on a hillside. Mark has them witnessing an exorcism and several healings. Luke records some miracles followed by a slightly different version of the sermon recorded by Matthew. If the intention of any of these writers had been to recount a full and accurate chronological record of Jesus' teaching they'd have written their gospels much sooner than they did and the texts would have been more alike, and probably significantly longer.[76] John, who (according to Eusebius) makes a deliberate attempt to fill in more detail of Jesus' ministry prior to the imprisonment of John the Baptist,[77] has the disciples tagging along with Jesus on a family outing with his mother. What an inauspicious start!

After the grand opening of the first chapter we might have expected John to have placed Jesus in the Temple courts debating theology with the learned as Luke chose to do.[78] Instead, he chooses to begin the narrative section of his gospel by placing Jesus in the low-key setting of a village wedding. "How typical of Jesus", might be our reaction today, but that is because we possess the benefit of hindsight. We understand how Jesus' embodiment of holiness refused to label everyday events as profane. In this, he was so different to the Pharisees who seemed terrified at the thought of contaminating themselves with the activities and concerns of normal people.

This wedding seems to have been nothing special until the most catastrophic of events happens. To us, running out of wine might not seem like a big deal. We have the choice, either to send the caterers or the Best Man to buy some more or allow the guests to take it as their cue to make their way home. In a setting where the father of the bride will have been laying down a few barrels from each year's crop in preparation for this great day, buying more wasn't an option. Weddings in Jesus' day would have lasted many days and the lack of wine would therefore have been the source

---

76   John 20:30.

77   William Barclay – *The Gospel of John*, 3.

78   Luke 2:49.

of deep social embarrassment. Jesus mother took this as her cue to blow his cover:

> Mary to Jesus: "They have no more wine."

> Jesus to Mary: "So? Mum, don't interfere, my time hasn't come yet."

> Mary to the servants: "Do what he tells you."

Processing the Kairos Moment

For some time now I have been using a model which was taught me by friends who have now become my colleagues. They call it the Learning Circle and it is the first of a number of shapes I'll introduce in the course of this book.[79] In the previous chapter I mentioned the excellent DVD by Rob Bell in which he describes the problem God has in communicating to humans. Bell develops his talk from a book by Edwin Abbott in which an inhabitant of a two-dimensional world known as Flatland has all manner of difficulty making himself and his world comprehensible to an inhabitant of Lineland – a one-dimensional reality. Both, however, are united in their inability to conceive the possibility of a third dimension.

Abbott, who was both a mathematician and priest, reveals his reason for writing when the frustrated Lineland inhabitant finds himself reflecting after an argument with his precocious, but far more growth-minded grandson:

> I exclaimed aloud, "The boy is a fool." Straightway I became conscious of a Presence in the room, and a chilling breath thrilled through my very being. "He is no such thing," cried my Wife, "and you are breaking the Commandments in thus dishonouring your own Grandson." But I took no notice of her. Looking round in every direction I could see nothing; yet I still **felt** a Presence, and shivered as the cold whisper came again. I started up. "What is the matter?" said my Wife, "There is no draught; what are you looking for? There is nothing." There was nothing and I resumed my seat, again exclaiming "The boy is a fool, I say; 3^3 can have no meaning in Geometry." At once there came a distinctly audible reply, "The boy is not a fool; and 3^3 has an obvious Geometrical

---

79   Mike Breen and Steve Cockram – *Building a Discipling Culture* (Pawley's Island: 3DM, 2009). See chapter 5.

meaning."[80]

If there are just three dimensions we can perceive, assumed Abbott in 1884 (many years before quantum mechanics began postulating the possibility of ten, eleven or even an infinite number of dimensions), there may also be realms we cannot yet discern and will remain invisible to us unless and until we relax our fixed categories of thought. What better way to illustrate this conundrum, and the range of fixed mindsets arrayed against any and all radical shifts in world-view, than to imagine a fictional dispute between the inhabitants of a world that disagree about the three dimensions that are known and accepted by all his readers? His intention, of course, which Rob Bell exploits brilliantly, is to blur the thick lines closed-minded thinkers place between spirit and matter as a means of excluding the possibility of a spiritual realm because it is not accessible to humans through faculties that can be measured and verified.

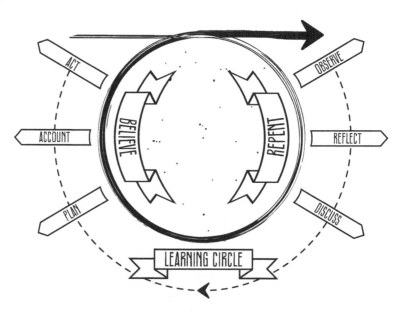

The Learning Circle assumes there are hidden opportunities open to us and lessons to learn as we travel our straight-line kind of life and that we need our attention to be jogged if we are to recognise them. In the diagram, his is represented as the point at the top of the circle - which is also the beginning of the circle. A Kairos moment may be an event that could initially

....

80   Edwin A. Abbott – *Flatland: A Romance of Many Dimensions* (New York: Dover Publications, 1992), 53-54.

be perceived by us as a distraction from our plans and meet with resistance. More positively, it can also be viewed as an opportunity to take new facts or ideas on board which may ultimately cause us to move in a more fruitful direction. We call these Kairos opportunities – Kairos, after all, means "just at the right time" and such a concept is only possible if, by faith, we accept that we have been born again into a Kingdom that is more real than the reality we are used to despite the fact that we are often oblivious to it.[81]

> *The circle represents our journey into the kingdom of God. To enter the kingdom, however, we must go through a process of repentance and belief. The process can be difficult and challenging and, more often than not, painful. It is through this process we learn how to lay down our lives and pick up the cross.*[82]

We enter the circle in the same way we enter the Kingdom – through repentance. What I love about using this word here is that it reflects Paul's use of it in Romans 2:4: it is God's kindness that leads us to repentance, not his frustration and anger at our inability to stay on the right path. A kind God desires good things for us even if this makes certain stages of the journey tough. For the Christian disciple an ongoing spirit of repentance simply means living with the fact that there may be more fruitful opportunities open to us than we can see with our limited mindsets. Repentance is being willing to think, not as we normally do, but as Jesus would.

Returning to the circle, observation leads to reflection: what might this unforeseen event mean? We are then encouraged to let someone else in to our lives and discuss it with them. The scriptures are full of invitations to do such things for one another and Christians need desperately to recover the many communal dimensions of our faith.

The second half of the circle develops our call to 'believe' – recognising that belief that does not lead to action is of no value at all.[83] It is all very well making a plan but, if you are like me, I tend to rush to a new plan too quickly and then forget all about it unless I've taken steps to make myself accountable for my actions. This is the second opportunity to involve others in the process and helps ensure that the action I decide to take is as fruitful

---

81   Mark 1:15.

82   Breen and Cockram, op. cit, 29.

83   James 2:26.

as it can be.

Cultivating an alertness to the voice of God was nothing new to a devout Jew in Jesus' day. Some of the Old Testament commands may seem strange to modern sensibilities, such as the instruction that faithful followers were to attach blue tassels to the corners of their garments.[84] The purpose of them, however, was to act as a frequent reminder to recall, and figure out how to obey, the commands of God in each new scenario. We see Jesus taking his disciples through a similar process in the teaching Matthew selects as his first discipling scenario.[85] Here in John, Jesus is modelling the circle even if he's not explaining each stage to the disciples. It is as if Jesus is thinking: "my mother is not going to back down so might this be an opportunity I hadn't seen coming but my Father intends to use to make himself known?"

An Earthy Miracle

Cana, just a few miles from Nazareth,[86] was the last place anyone hunting for a messianic figure would look.[87] The region of Galilee had been isolated from the rest of Jewish Palestine for generations, surrounded as it was by a host of gentile nations and thus open to Hellenising forces. A century and a half before, during the two Maccabean revolts, faithful Jews had been withdrawn to the safety and religious purity of the south. That Jesus is present at a simple wedding in such humble surroundings is surprise enough but, of all the events he could have chosen, John selects this one as one of seven highlights of his Gospel. What is he up to?

A literal translation of Jesus' reply to his mother is "Woman, what is that to you and me? My hour has not yet come." Calling your mother "woman" may seem rude to us but it was a normal figure of speech in that culture. John uses the word 'hour' six times in his gospel and each time he is referring to the moment of Jesus' death, the denouement of his account. I am guessing Jesus adds a wink to Mary at this point, or at least

---

84   Numbers 15:38-39.

85   This is described in Breen and Cockram, op. cit, p 35-37.

86   The exact location of Cana is not certain but there are three likely candidates all within ten kilometres of Nazareth.

87   John 7:50-52.

has a twinkle in his eye – certainly Mary can see that he has put the pieces together in such a way that he can see a Kairos opportunity unfolding before him. His hour may not have come but his Father wishes to hallow this unique moment in time.

The miracle itself is undramatic; so much so that the bridegroom, master of the banquet and most of the guests may not have discovered the source of the wine until their hangover had worn off the following day. Jesus tells the servants to fill six stone water jars, normally used for washing profane things in order to make them holy, with water and take it to the master of the banquet with no hint of further explanation. We are to assume that the vessel used to draw the wine from the jar was normally used for this purpose. Certainly the master expects to find wine in it and asks no questions of the servants. The only surprise is its quality. As he tastes it he knows instantly that this is of a vintage that only those who have drunk plenty of wine over their lifetime can verify.

At first it seems as if the only beneficiaries of Jesus' first miracle were party guests who have already drunk enough but are given an opportunity to enjoy wine of a quality they otherwise may not have been able to afford. Over the next few days the Disciples would have reflected on what they had seen and recognised a quality to the events that John describes as 'glory'. What was it they saw?

A simple comparison to the other six miracles John chooses, and the many others recorded in the other gospels, may suggest that the trick with the wine is somehow less worthy. It was hardly necessary was it? But maybe this is precisely the point. I agree with Michael Frost:

> The miracle is a perfect one to begin with, really. It shatters the age-old partition between the sacred and the profane. It sacrilizes the everyday wonder of being part of a community that celebrates and eats and drinks together. It includes hardworking, nonreligious "sinners" in the circle of God's care and protection.[88]

We should therefore see this miracle as a straightforward sign of outrageous grace – Jesus giving more than was asked for, or was even necessary, simply because he wished to bless simple people under the approving eye of His Father. John tells us that this is the first of seven signs

88   Michael Frost – *Exiles*, 45.

around which he is going to construct his gospel. Each sign will tell us some timeless truth about God. Surely this one indicates to us that Jesus intends to be fully present in every situation, thus dignifying the ordinary events of life. He is prepared to use the humblest of servants as his co-conspirators and has no need to draw attention to himself as he does so. Even if, in a party of hundreds of people, only a few recognised the meaning of his intervention, the act is enough. This is the sort of thing we should expect when Word becomes flesh in an everyday world.[89]

C. S. Lewis suggests that the ordinariness of this miracle should cause us to reflect on the presence of God in those events we think of as common or everyday:

> *God creates the vine and teaches it to draw up water by its roots and, with the aid of the sun, to turn that water into juice which will ferment and take on certain qualities. Thus every year, from Noah's time till ours, God turns water into wine. That, men fail to see. Either like the Pagans they refer the process to some finite spirit, Bacchus or Dionysus: or else, like the moderns, they attribute real and ultimate causality to the chemical and other material phenomena which are all that our senses can discover in it. But when Christ at Cana makes water into wine, the mask is off. The miracle has only half its effect if it only convinces us that Christ is God: it will have its full effect whenever we see a vineyard or drink a glass of wine we remember that here works He who sat at the wedding party in Cana.[90]*

Blurring the boundaries between sacred and secular

The tendency to segment ideas and practices into sacred and secular compartments has been practiced and reinforced over many centuries. In previous generations, Christians would take a stand against social evils such as widespread alcohol abuse by limiting their own freedom for the sake of 'the weaker brother' and thus creating a safe space from which to provide care and support. Within certain Christian sub-cultures it would

89   John 1:14.

90   C. S. Lewis – *God in the Dock: Essays on Theology and Ethics* (Glasgow: Fount, 1989), 16.

then become a commonly accepted assumption that Christians would not consume alcohol for the sake of the mission imperative. In an age when personal freedom is deemed so important it may be difficult to imagine a mainstream Christian grouping taking such a stand, especially if it leads to a "Jesus plus..." gospel (in this case Jesus + temperance) and reinforces a mission-by-intervention mindset.

Whilst mission-by-intervention often results in good work, and lives are changed as result, we cannot lose sight of the fact that Jesus practised and taught mission by incarnation. And incarnation is not just a theological statement applicable only within a sacred realm. By joining the wedding celebration at Cana Jesus was blurring the cultural boundaries that had become confused with religious strictures in his age – although the point of debate was not the consumption of alcohol but the company he kept. I believe this is important to note because false sacred-secular distinctions invariably close down mission opportunities where we are prevented from seeing the Spirit at work in places where he 'should not' be.

Although I have spent a good deal of effort tearing down the false mental partitions between sacred and secular in my own mind I still find myself shocked at how easily they re-establish themselves. Maybe the most profound lesson the disciple needs to learn from the story of Jesus turning water into wine is that God is already present and wants to be fully recognised in every event of life. He invites us to recognise him but he is not going to surround each appearance with fanfares and lights. Unless we accept this is the way in which God most frequently works within our world we are going to find it very difficult to recognise his presence and engage with him in those places where he is already present, thus making common things sacred.

For this reason the Learning Circle, although a simple tool, becomes a gateway into a profound discipleship journey. These are themes we return to numerous times but for now it may be helpful simply to invite God to help you become aware of the daily miracles he sends your way and use the Learning Circle to dignify the first one he shows you.[91]

---

91   I commend Michael Frost - *Seeing God in the Ordinary: A Theology of the Everyday* (Peabody: Hendrickson, 2000).

BOOKMAKER 1.43

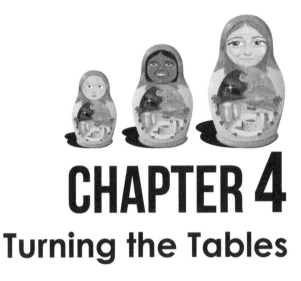

CHAPTER 4
Turning the Tables

To those with eyes to see, the use of "water-jars, used for Jewish purification rites, [was] a sign that God [was] doing a new thing from within the old Jewish system, bringing purification to Israel and the world in a whole new way."[92] The wine produced by Jesus had been a reminder of the blessings of God, secured for Israel by their faithfulness to God's covenant. For the sake of those who were blind to this reality, Jesus was about to make this message a great deal more explicit. After continuing his journey north to Capernaum, Jesus again heads south to Jerusalem just as the Passover feast was drawing near.

In total contrast to the village of Cana, "the Temple was the beating heart of Judaism... the centre of worship and music, of politics and society, of national celebration and mourning... the focal point of the nation and of the national way of life."[93] As the crowds are gathering for this important annual commemoration of God's deliverance of his people Jesus decides that this is to be the moment for his first run-in with the religious authorities.

....

92   Tom Wright – *John for Everyone... Part 1,* 22.

93   Ibid, p25.

But before we get to the main event, we have a conundrum to resolve.

The other gospel writers record an event that is similar to this temple-clearing but place it at the end of their accounts rather than at the beginning. Scholars proffer a number of reasons for this apparent disparity. The other gospels locate Jesus in Jerusalem twice, once as a child and the second time just before his death, and it has been suggested that including the temple-clearing at this later point in his ministry helps to explain the tension that is soon to end at the cross. John has Jesus travelling backward and forward throughout the gospel and maybe this seems to him as good a time as any to insert this story, especially since he has just introduced Jesus as the Lamb of God, an image that alludes to the Temple. Or maybe such an event happened more than once? Whatever the reason, it fits well here since it illustrates Jesus' understanding of his mission so perfectly.

The Question of Authority

To the vast majority of the inhabitants of Jerusalem and the towns and villages of Galilee, Jesus would have seemed like any other Rabbi – until he began embodying his teaching in ways that provoked both speculation and opposition. At the end of the parable of the wise and foolish builders Matthew tells us:

> When Jesus had finished saying these things, the crowds were amazed at his teaching, because he taught as one who had authority, and not as their teachers of the law.[94]

A few chapters later Matthew gives further insight into what it must have felt like to have been caught up in the tumult caused by this new teacher when, after he heals a mat-bound man, we read

> When the crowd saw this, they were filled with awe; and they praised God, who had given such authority to man.[95]

The story of Jesus turning over the tables in the Temple is found in all four gospels but the events are described more fully by Mark in chapter 11 of his gospel. We read there how Jesus selected a colt and entered the city surrounded by jubilant crowds. To my mind there is something that jars

94   Matthew 7:28-29.

95   Matthew 9:8.

about the shift from verses 10 to 11: one minute Jesus is surrounded by an adoring throng and the next he is able to enter the temple with no one paying him any attention despite the inevitable presence of a significant military show of strength in the run up to such a prestigious festival. Mark records that Jesus entered the temple, "looked around at everything, but since it was already late, he went out to Bethany with the Twelve."[96] We get the distinct feeling that he has a plan in his mind but decides to wait until the morning to enact it.

The Fig Tree and The Temple

The next morning Jesus and his disciples return to Jerusalem. Both Matthew and Mark mention, seemingly in passing, that the route into Jerusalem took Jesus past a fig tree which, apparently apropos to nothing, he curses for having no fruit. Both writers also tell us that it was not the fruit-bearing season and this story is left hanging, making little sense until we link it with what is about to happen. Jesus enters the Temple and is distressed to see that a vast service industry has grown up in the outer courts and he allows his anger to draw another crowd to whom he explains his outburst:

> And as he taught them, he said, 'Is it not written: "My house will be called a house of prayer **for all nations**"? But you have made it "a den of robbers". The chief priests and the teachers of the law heard this and began looking for a way to kill him, for they feared him, because the whole crowd was amazed at his teaching.[97]

This is clearly one of the best choreographed acts of Jesus ministry, and yet we easily miss the point if the allusions aren't made clear. We saw in the first chapter that the reason God brought the nation of Israel into being from the loins of an old man with a barren wife was in order to create for himself a people who would be well-positioned to know him and obey him, thus mirroring him to the surrounding nations. The promise given to Abram in Genesis 12 demonstrates this clearly: "I will bless you and make your descendants into a great nation. You will become famous and be a blessing to others."[98]

....

96   Mark 11:11.

97   Mark 11:17-18.

98   Genesis 12:2.

God's intention in choosing a people for himself was to engineer a grand object lesson, the purpose of which was to indicate to the surrounding nations what had been lost by choosing autonomy instead of fellowship with their creator. Even the design of the Temple makes it clear that God intended this centrepiece of worship to be the ideal place for enquirers and worshippers from all nations to gather once Israel had learned to love and walk humbly with her God. God's desire, remember, was to bless a people who had learned to receive that blessing and pass it on. Christopher Wright puts it well:

> Knowing God is a responsibility. If God blesses you, it is so you can bless others. If God redeems you, it is so you can demonstrate redemptive grace to others. If God loves you, feeds and clothes you, then you should go and do likewise for others. If God brings you into the light of salvation, it is so you can shine with a light that attracts others to the same place. If you enjoy God's forgiveness, then make sure you forgive others.[99]

The Court of the Gentiles was by far the largest open space in the whole temple complex. But, Jesus opined, instead of acting as a magnet for people of other nations loved by God, God's chosen people had become as blind and hard-hearted as their godless neighbours. The Court of the Gentiles was designed to house a huge throng of worshippers and was thus intended to be the place where people from all nations could gather to join God's people at worship. But this vast space was empty and had now become the place where money changers gathered to make a living from the offerings of worshippers who were seemingly blind to the irony each time they exchanged their money for acceptable sacrifices or temple currency.

This is the point at which the disciples would have understood what the cursing of the fig tree meant, since figs were a popular symbol of Israel's fruitfulness. As he entered Jerusalem, Jesus knew he was about to expose the sham of a people who rejoiced in their identity as the chosen people of God but, whilst parading their outward obedience, had entirely failed in their calling. This is the point at which Matthew uses the word 'authority' again:

....

99   Christopher Wright - *The Mission of the People of God: A Biblical Theology of the Church's Mission.* {Grand Rapids: Zondervan, 2010), 151

Jesus entered the temple courts, and, while he was teaching, the chief priests and the elders of the people came to him. 'By what authority are you doing these things?' they asked. 'And who gave you this authority?'[100]

The Authorities Test Jesus' Claims

The writers of the synoptic gospels suggest that opposition to Jesus' teaching from the religious authorities was incremental. So, this is the first time in Mark's Gospel that the teachers of the law ask Jesus a direct question. This is significant. In the inter-testimental period the Jewish people had agreed upon a means of testing any claims to Messiah-ship which may arise in the future. We know that there were many popular figures who made messianic claims around the time of Jesus and the question still arises within certain branches of Judaism to this day. It was decided that, if and when someone either claimed or was proposed by others to be the Messiah, a team of religious teachers would follow that person and watch their actions – but they were not allowed to ask questions. If, after this first examination, the question of Messiah-ship was still a live issue, the teachers were allowed to begin asking questions and weighing up the response.

What becomes immediately clear is that, despite never making an outright claim to be the Messiah, Jesus' life and teaching were being monitored all through the gospels. His Messiah-ship was therefore suspected and being tested by the Jewish authorities. In the early chapters of Mark we note that Jewish teachers are frequently present when Jesus teaches publicly and that they never address him. Jesus reads their thoughts,[101] the teachers question the disciples[102] and question Jesus about the disciples[103] but it is only after Jesus' table-turning act in the Temple courtyard that they begin questioning him. Jesus had clearly passed the first test and, despite the growing hatred felt by some towards him, we must remember that the Jews considered open, and sometimes heated, debate to be the way religious scholars tested their ideas and learned from each other. We should therefore be wary about reading too much into these early

....

100   Matthew 21:23.

101   Mark 2:8.

102   Mark 2:16.

103   Mark 2:23 + 7:5.

exchanges.[104]

Something else it is easy for those who are not familiar with First Century Judaism to miss is the way Jesus was toying with his observers throughout this period of examination.[105] The first example is revealed by the question relating to the authority Jesus was claiming for himself. Both the question and his refusal to answer are very revealing. Within Judaism different people had differing levels of authorisation to expound the Torah: Scribes could comment on it but not make binding rulings whereas Rabbis and Torah teachers had greater freedom. The authority possessed by each Rabbi would normally be made clear in their pronouncements which would begin with something like: "I say to you in the name of Rabbi X...". An alternative method of authentication would be "you have heard it said", followed by a section of Torah and a statement by the Rabbi that would contradict or supplement a previous ruling made by an earlier Rabbi.

Within first century Judaism the authority to teach Torah was therefore a derived authority and many examples of such are found in the Talmud. When Jesus made no attempt to derive his authority from a reputable Rabbi, this refusal to follow established practice effectively made him the originator of the ruling. The point would not have been lost on his hearers, especially when Jesus refused to enter into debate on the matter.[106]

A second difference between Jesus' teaching and the established practice of his day was in the way Jesus distinguished Torah from Oral Torah. We have already seen how the mode of rabbinic Judaism that Jesus' hearers were familiar with had set great store by their practice of establishing 'hedge laws' or 'Oral Torah' around God's holiest statements. The logic of Oral Torah was that the establishment of laws and teachings around the Torah would act as a brake to prevent the unwary from transgressing the sacred Torah itself. It is these rulings of Oral Torah recorded in the Talmud that Jesus felt free to challenge when he began a

104   See Ann Spangler and Lois Tverberg – *Sitting at the Feet of Rabbi Jesus*, Chapter 2.

105   The following two examples are taken from Rabbi Andrew Sheldrake – *Contours of Messianic Judaism* (Norwich: Adat Yeshua, 2007).

106   John is clearer that Jesus claims to speak directly from God but one suspects that passages like John 12:49-50 and 14:10 owe their existence either to later private conversations between Jesus and his disciples and/or to John's own piecing together of the evidence.

teaching with the phrase "You have heard it said…" and goes on to dispute those statements in the Oral Torah that departed from the spirit of (written) Torah.

By the time of Jesus, Jewish tradition alleged that Oral Torah had been given directly to Moses by God on Mt Sinai as a kind of commentary on Torah, yet Jesus was clearly unhappy at the weight being given to such 'traditions of men' and he challenged them frequently.[107] Thus, despite the fact that the Targum of Isaiah 12:3 makes the fascinating prediction that Messiah would bring a renewed and revitalised Torah,[108] those who were in the best place to judge in which direction Jesus words and actions pointed lagged far behind popular opinion.

What is very clear from the Gospels is that the crowd that followed Jesus were amazed both at what he taught and the manner of his teaching. The fact that they frequently missed the point he was making, often because he chose to use teaching methods that obscured the main thrust from those without 'ears to hear', didn't seem to diminish his acclaim. It seems to have been the coherence of Jesus' words and actions that amazed them, together with the fact that his actions illustrated something far deeper than rhetoric ever could. The fact that he was also bold and fearless in his exposure of a religious system which seemed only to serve the religious elite and alienate the common people would also have played to his advantage.

John also recalls that this event elicited a challenge to Jesus' 'authority'. The teachers of the law try to tempt Jesus into performing another miracle but we've already seen that John intends to mete these out sparingly in his account. Instead John inserts an enigmatic statement made by Jesus about his body as a temple which would be torn down and rebuilt but he is speaking to a spiritually deaf audience. Instead it is the common people who believe in Jesus and become the witnesses of unspecified signs as a reward for their faith.

There is no doubt that, by placing the account of Jesus in the Temple at this point in his gospel, John intends to make it a major turning point. This is because it asks such a fundamental question. The Temple was the hub

....

107   Matthew 16:2, 3 + 6 demonstrates three examples of this in a single discourse.

108   David Daube - *The New Testament and Rabbinic Judaism* (Peabody: Hendrickson, 1994).

of Jewish religious life and was designed to be the centre of worship for all nations. The empty gentile court told its own story. Jesus simply needed to point it out.

Jesus' Purpose in Being Abstruse

It is generally agreed that Jesus chose to engage in forms of dialogue that were designed to make his listeners ask deeper questions, thus prompting them to engage more honestly with what was going on under the surface of their lives. The fact that this left his blindest, and harshest, critics high and dry seems not to have concerned him. The sub-text of Jesus' various parables and stories were questions like:

➤ Are the promises you are living by really satisfying you?

➤ Do you have a deep hunger/thirst that other people can't see?

➤ What is it that makes you do the things you do?

➤ Will you allow me to heal that which is masking your awareness of your true value?

➤ Are you really the person you are pretending to be?

➤ If you were to describe yourself as a fruit tree what kind of fruit do you bear?

On every occasion these questions were uniquely tailored to each specific situation in which Jesus found himself, even where his audience was a single individual. Sometimes he gave his stories a sharp point – mainly where he encountered pomposity in the lives of those who were blind to their arrogance or when he detected hardness of heart in people who believed their own self-righteous rhetoric. Always the undertone was:

Are you ready to leave all this and join me on a grand adventure of great loss and eternal gain?

Despite all we have said about Jesus' willingness to let anyone follow him, discipleship always is on his terms not theirs. This is what John means when he says that "Jesus would not entrust himself to them, for he knew all men. He did not need man's testimony about man, for he knew what was in a man".[109] In Jewish understanding, the only being who truly knows what is in a person's heart is God and Jesus makes it clear that he knew all there was to know on this matter.[110] Like the other Gospel writers, John also presents Jesus as fully human and thus able to understand our struggle with weak flesh. In this context, Jesus was wary of letting those who believed in him on the basis of miracles performed by him dictate his agenda. We will reflect more on the double-edged blessing of miracles in a later chapter but at this point it seems that John is provoking us to ask the question: What was it they believed in?

John tells us that "while he was in Jerusalem at the Passover Festival, many people saw the signs he was performing and believed in his name". The compilers of the text are unclear whether or not John wrote 'believed in his name' or 'believed in him'. Some suggest that believing in someone's name has a touch of derived authority to it since, in Hebrew thought, 'name' implies some intrinsic awareness of their nature. It is clear to me that Jesus is wary of allowing himself to become the hostage of someone else's vision. He knew the necessity of spending three years with twelve individuals if they were to have any hope of catching his agenda and learning to live as he did. He also understood the fickleness of human promises to follow him and just how attached we are to maintaining our egos which Richard Rohr calls "the unobserved self" or "just another word for blindness".[111]

Rohr believes that "most Christians are good theists who happen to have named their god Jesus."[112] A theist would have us understand God to be a remote being who sometimes intervenes. Such a view is not open to seeing any true humanity in Jesus or to expecting that God may be willing to relate to humans in any meaningful way. The inevitable result of this biblical picture of God is to make god in our own limited image, not realising what St Augustine meant when he said "If you understand it, then it is *not* God."[113] Jesus was simply recognising this human tendency

---

109   John 2:24-25.

110   C. K. Barrett – *The Gospel According to St John* (London: SPCK, 1956), 169.

111   Richard Rohr – *The Naked Now*, 90.

112   Ibid, 69.

113   Ibid, 75.

to attempt to follow with our still unredeemed understanding. Such an endeavour is

> *not easily achieved, and never without authentic conversion first. Mature religion involves changing ourselves and letting ourselves be changed by a mysterious encounter with grace, mercy and forgiveness. This is the truth that will set us free (John 8:32). Yet much of our history has involved trying to change **other** people – with **our** ideas. This has gotten us almost nowhere, and it allows us to remain untransformed and unconverted ourselves.*[114]

> *The ego is not evil but it can lead us to do evil without realising it... It leaves you blind to your own illusions and convinced that you see perfectly... Many people have not been offered a different mind, only different behaviors, beliefs and belonging systems. They do not necessarily nourish us, much less transform us. But they invariably secure us and validate us where we already are... This is at the heart of the problem of conversion and the very nature of spiritual transformation.*[115]

Any engagement with Jesus' discipling methods must take note of the fact that he had (and still has) a profound understanding of what it means to be human and how we change. Our tendency is to prefer a religion that serves us in the ways Rohr describes. Jesus' methodology involved a profound and on-going interaction with his disciples as he led them on a journey that turned everything they thought they knew about themselves, the world and God upside-down. Discipleship is not a journey for the faint-hearted.

Seeing as Jesus Saw

In coming chapters we are going to reflect in some depth on how Jesus saw what he did. Richard Rohr believes it is essential that we learn to see reality in non-dual terms if we are to stand any chance of ministering to an unholy and imperfect world. By 'non-dual' he means resisting the tendency to see everything in relation to ourselves and describing what we encounter in mutually exclusive (black or white, good or bad, right or wrong) terms. In

---

114   Ibid, 88.

115   Ibid, 91.

matters of faith,

> non-dual seers are the only experts. Sinners, saints, lovers and
> poets, and all those who have swum in this ocean of mercy can
> hold contrary evidence together because they have allowed God
> to first of all do it in them – over and over again.[116]

I have found this a tough exercise. To accept that someone who is very
different to me can have something to teach me about myself or about
God was something I struggled with, especially if by 'different' I meant
of a different faith background or a from non-western culture. It may be
that some of you are struggling with my use of the writings of a Catholic
Franciscan! We'll see later that practising what Rohr calls 'non-dual' thinking
is a delightfully Jewish way of looking at the world but for now you might
want to reflect on the following question:

> The way you and I live our lives makes some kind of sense to us.
> How would assuming this is true of others help you to see them
> as they really are?

We have also seen that, in choosing Peter, Jesus had the ability to see
potential in him, seemingly by receiving information directly from his Father.
Revelations like these encourage me to remind myself to thank God that he
also knows me far more intimately than I know myself and accepts parts of
me I do not fully understand. As I do this I find myself wanting to expand the
limited categories I put God in, in order that I can see more of him. I have
discovered that the God who kept giving himself new names in scripture
loves to play these games.

So, although God is forced to restrict himself in order that he may
appear to me in ways that my limited imagination can comprehend, it
becomes possible to see more of him if I accept each new revelation by
faith and resist the urge to fully understand it. In the beginning stages, I had
to take myself to task and ask myself time and again whether a god who
is little bigger than the culturally-determined box I have put him in is really
worthy of my worship. This is a humbling question but is the place for a
Christian disciple to begin if we are to learn to mirror the way God engages
with people he loves and who are not yet as we may wish them to be.

---

116   Ibid, 83.

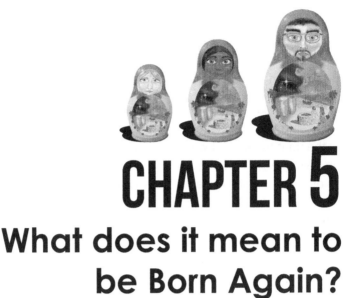

CHAPTER 5
What does it mean to be Born Again?

Are you Born Again? The question has become a cliché. It has also led to a great deal of unhelpful stereotyping and not a bit of humour. I recall, for example, speaking to a regular attender at our local Parish Church who, thinking that the phrase referred to a preference for happy-clappy worship, declared to me that she most certainly did not want to become born again! It should also make us hang our collective heads that the pejorative use of the phrase has caused some followers of Jesus to think that they are a better class of Christian than others and that so many outside the faith see the term as a brand name for a distinct set of personal preferences.

When Nicodemus came to Jesus at night, presumably "to avoid giving the impression that he intended to become a committed disciple",[117] he had, at least, come to the conclusion that Jesus was 'a teacher who has come from God'. This was on the basis of the miracles Jesus performed which, for this Pharisee at least, were all the proof he needed to reach such a conclusion. But Nicodemus' expression of belief was not accepted by Jesus as a profession of faith and he replies: "I tell you the truth, no-one can see

---

117   R. Tasker – *John, Tyndale New Testament Commentary* (Leicester: IVP, 1983), 66.

the Kingdom of God unless he is born again."[118] Such an answer would have been received as highly provocative by any Pharisee who, by definition, prided himself in longing for the Kingdom with greater fervour than most, and considered himself more righteous before God than the motley crowd who called Jesus their Rabbi. The very idea that a Pharisee might not see the Kingdom he longed for would have been abhorrent to Nicodemus.

The message we should draw from this is that correct beliefs about Jesus aren't all that is required if we are to be his followers. Nicodemus was on the right track but it was not enough. Jesus was inviting him to process the Kairos event that began with the miracles Nicodemus had seen with his own eyes. Much of Jesus' activity was an overflow into the present of a realm he called the Kingdom of God. This is why he was alert to signals others couldn't see and was able to heal the sick and even raise the dead. The Kingdom of God exists on a parallel plane to our own and what is normal within the Kingdom of God can be experienced on earth 'as it is in heaven'. The Kingdom Jesus speaks of and demonstrates is ruled by a King (his Father) who has ultimate authority which he is prepared to delegate to his Son.

In order to live and move within this Kingdom it was necessary that Jesus possessed a soft heart which was in touch with the compassion of his Father, ears which were open to hear from him, a second pair of 'spiritual' eyes through which he was able to see things which may not be visible to others but were real nevertheless, and a new way of thinking which was able to appreciate a deeper kind of supra-rational reality. In the conversation recorded in John 3 Jesus was trying to help Nicodemus understand that the miracles he was witness to were a sign that the boundaries between the two realms can be blurred by faith. All he is doing, insists Jesus, is using those faculties which must be received by faith and can be nurtured by repeated use. In order to participate in bringing the rule of the Father into the present Jesus is explaining to Nicodemus that it will feel as if he is receiving and learning to use an entirely new body – eyes, ears, heart, mind, intuition, hands and feet. But, unlike our flesh, the different components of this new body must be delivered to him by the Spirit.

The key teaching on discipleship that can be distilled from this encounter is that the way to please and follow God, according to Jesus, was not simply to believe facts that are true but "to enter the Kingdom of

118   John 3:3.

God".[119] In the light of all that follows, it is clear that Jesus is trying to explain to Nicodemus that the whole point of *believing* was so that he might *see* and *participate*. As with Nicodemus, so with us. Our seeing must lead to us to participate in Kingdom reality, by which Jesus means the activity of God within creation.[120] This feels, says Jesus, like living according to the beat of a drum no one else can hear and the results can be entirely unpredictable according to human logic.[121] At this point in their conversation poor old Nicodemus' questions reveal to Jesus that, despite his willingness to believe facts about him, this man who was revered as a teacher of religious truths knows nothing about God's ways or his Kingdom. It is therefore impossible for their conversation to progress any further since Nicodemus is not able to receive truth directly from God but is stuck within the confines of his mind and the traditions which govern what he is willing to believe. Thankfully, the two further references to Nicodemus in John's gospel suggest that he eventually joins the band of Jesus' followers but I'm sure it was not an easy journey.

Living Life in Three Dimensions

In chapter three I introduced you to the Learning Circle and explained that it was the first of a number of shapes I would be inserting into this book. The Triangle helps us envisage a life that has three dimensions. If we take Jesus as the pre-eminent example, the Up dimension describes Jesus' relationship with his Father. This is the element Nicodemus was unable to grasp because, despite his theoretical knowledge of a God who intervenes, walking with such a deity was outside both his expectation and experience. The In point of the triangle refers to the relationship Jesus had with his disciples and a few others. These were his close community with whom he shared himself and experienced the blessings of being in community. The Out represents everything Jesus did and taught to crowds and other individuals who encountered him in daily life.[122]

For Jesus, the Up was the source he drew on throughout his ministry.

119   John 3:5.

120   Note how similar this explanation is to James' comments on faith and deeds in James 2:14-26.

121   John 3:8.

122   Mike Breen and Steve Cockram – *Building a Discipling Culture*. See chapter 7.

In order to live life under the rule of his Father he knew it was necessary to make every effort to maintain contact with him using every one of the faculties he was trying to describe to Nicodemus. It was this that gave Jesus the resources he needed to mentor the twelve, his 'In-crowd'. Jesus shared life with this group, relaxing, eating and walking together and this was the relational base from which he ministered Outwards to people he encountered as a normal part of daily life and who often had deep and profound needs.

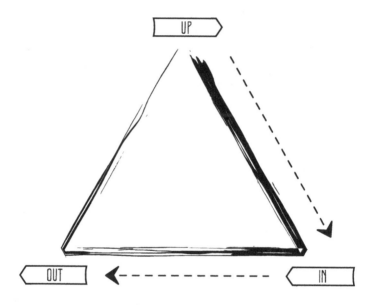

The Triangle is a hugely flexible concept. It could be used, for example, to illustrate Jesus' statement that he is the Way (Up: to the Father), the Truth (In: to be inwardly digested) and the Life (Out: to be lived).[123] It can also be used, as Breen and Cockram do, as a yardstick to define a healthy church. Frost and Hirsch suggest a similar three-sided framework using the terms communion (Up), community (In) and commission (Out).[124]

Mike Breen develops his own model by using the Triangle to describe the dynamic of living within a covenantal relationship with God:

> *The Covenant begins with the Father, who gives us our identity.*
> *Now we are able to obey because as children of God we are*

123   John 14:6. The Way, Truth and Life actually referred to the three gates of the Tabernacle which led, in order, to the Holy of Holies.

124   Michael Frost + Alan Hirsch – *The Shaping of Things to Come*, 76-81.

empowered to do so. At times, we may find ourselves seeking to approach God through obedience rather than in simple recognition of our identity. When we do this we fall into the trap of the Pharisees whom Jesus encountered. As we are God's children, he is already pleased with us, and this knowledge liberates us from the legalistic observance that so often leads to frustration and guilt.[125]

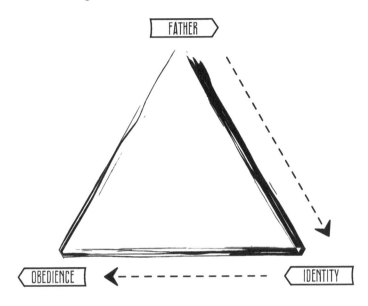

Nicodemus clearly didn't get this, but he could have done because all the ingredients he needed were found in his scriptures. He simply needed to focus upon identity before obedience. The shift that was way beyond him is described by using the Triangle as a descriptor of the Kingdom, as represented by the triangle on the following page.

> *The Kingdom begins with the King, who exercises authority through us as his representatives, and with that authority, he sends power for us to be able to do all that he wants us to do.*[126]

We will develop the question of Kingdom living as we progress. For now, I want to return to Jesus' conversation with Nicodemus.

....

125   Mike Breen – *Covenant and Kingdom: The DNA of the Bible* (Pawley's Island: 3DM, 2010), 227.

126   Ibid, p 229.

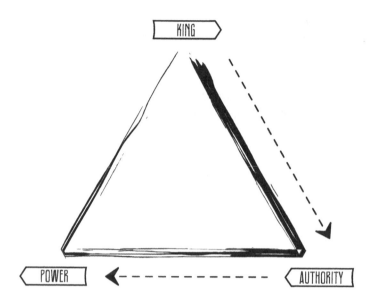

For God so loved...

Within the evangelical tradition John 3:16 has become the commonly accepted short-hand definition of the Gospel message: "For God so loved the world that he gave his one and only Son, that whoever believes in him shall not perish but have eternal life." Yet, as we have just seen, if we understand 'believe' to mean merely 'assent to', or 'believe facts about', we would be making the same mistake as Nicodemus. The context in which the meaning of the term is best understood has to be the recognition that Jesus chose twelve disciples who have left everything and are malleable in his hands in a way Nicodemus was not prepared to be.

I have lost count of the number of times I have heard an evangelist invite his hearers to insert their name in place of the word 'world' in this text. Whilst I am convinced that God loves me far more than I will ever understand whilst I inhabit my present body, we cannot overlook the fact that Jesus was speaking to an individual and yet chose to say 'world'. This has to be significant and the previous two chapters provide the reason: God's people had restricted the language of Covenant to themselves and thereby lost sight of the fact that God created the Jewish nation to be the gateway for the world to enter God's grace. In doing this, God's people had lost touch with the very God to whom they believed they were bound by an irrevocable covenant.

In the opening salvo to his Gospel John made it abundantly clear that Jesus was the true light sent for every person and in 3:16 he includes the whole non-human creation amongst the ultimate beneficiaries of his gift. And yet the message I responded to at the age of 14 told me that if I had been the only person on this earth Jesus would still have died for me. Once again, I do not doubt the truth of this assertion. But how we are limiting the scope of John's Gospel if we persist with this limited view of the mission of Jesus!

What I'm going to write next may shock you: when Jesus died on the cross it was not the end in itself but a means to the end. What I mean is this: when Jesus died sin already had a solution. God had promised that the blood of an unclean animal would wipe away all sin in the life of a person of faith. Yes, I know that we Christians see the Old Testament as the shadow of the more perfect sacrifice that was to come, but let us not forget that the reason it became a shadow of a better system was that Israel refused to be God's missionary people. Do we really think God called Abraham, led Moses, formed Joseph and put the prophets through such agonies when he knew it was all going to fail, allowing him to send his son and rescue everything like Bruce Willis at the end of a cheesy action movie?

When Paul spends so much time and effort explaining the theological significance of the life and death of Jesus and the writer to the Hebrews explains how, in every respect, Jesus' blood is better than the old Covenant they are right. Perfectly correct. But the only reason they needed to write these words was that Jews needed to fully understand the continuity between what Jesus achieved and the Old Testament revelation. Jesus is more of the same, only much better.

The mistake we often make is to begin with Paul's letters and to boil the Gospel down to just one thing: the death of Christ that paid for our sins. Jesus didn't die to offer us a free gift but to bring us life. A life that needs to be lived in faith that we don't need to worry any more about being fully accepted by and acceptable to God. A life that can only be lived when we are fully abandoned to this truth and completely available to God to live through us as Paul explains in Galatians 2:20.

For me, the fact that John places this encounter with Nicodemus immediately after the cleansing of the Temple is therefore equivalent to double-underlining the word 'world' in 3:16. Jesus continues to refer to a mission beyond rescuing the nation of Israel throughout the gospel. This is seen most notably in John 12:20-36 where John mentions a group of Greeks who are seeking Jesus. As far as John is concerned, Jesus clearly understood himself to be reinstating the global scope of his Father's mission and, in order to highlight this fact, John reintroduces the metaphors of 'light' and 'darkness' both here and in chapter 12.

Chapter 3 then continues with further testimony from John the Baptist who ends by assuring us that 'whoever' believes in the Son has eternal life. The third chapter of the gospel thus ends as the first began and in the next section of his gospel John will begin to demonstrate what this looks like in practice.

Living Three Dimensionally

If the Triangle is to be anything more than a clever teaching aid, the idea of living a balanced life must be more than an aspiration. The first challenge has to be to ensure that our understanding of the gospel is as comprehensive as Jesus intended. I have emphasised the fact that Jesus understands himself to be the perfect embodiment of his Father's missional intention first expressed in Genesis 12 for a very good reason. This is to emphasise that wherever and however Christians gather, we must be prepared to rethink the Out dimension of our life in much the same way that the Pharisees and others were being invited to do in Jesus' time.

When we think 'Out' we all too often do so from within a Covenant, rather than Kingdom, mindset. We want people to become like us and our evangelism reflects this in the methods we use. Whether it be through holiday clubs, seeker services, guest events or Alpha courses we are inviting people into our space at a time we choose in order to participate in an event we have control over. There may be a place for each of these but they are only going to reach people who are, at best, ambivalent to people who go to church. Jesus taught his disciples that his Father's Kingdom extended beyond the cultural, and literal, walls put up by people of the covenant. We face the same challenge they did as we learn to copy the way Jesus practised the Out dimension.

As soon as we begin taking the Triangle seriously it becomes clear that most of us live two-dimensional lives most of the time. It is adding that elusive third dimension that provides the challenge. And for each of us the dimension which goes AWOL most often will be different. Breen and Cockram discuss the issues involved in maintaining a three dimensional life far more fully than I have space to discuss here. The challenge I wish to leave you with at the close of this chapter is the one of living accountably.

I know all too well that more exercise will do me good but my preference for reading and writing means that I'm unlikely to get enough if I am left to my own devices. It is also my experience that I am far more likely to give in to temptations of all kinds if I rely merely upon my own willpower to resist. James urges us to confess our sins to one another and promises that we will experience healing as a result.[127] The final chapter of 1 Peter urges us to be submissive to one another, thus clothing ourselves with humility before God and other people. The reason, Peter warns, is because the devil prowls, seeking for someone (singular) to devour.[128]

If we read the bible in almost any language other than English it would be abundantly clear that most of God's promises are given to groups of people. The English language limits our appreciation of this fact simply because the word 'you' is ambiguous. Does he mean 'me' or 'us'? Well, most of the time the writers mean 'us' and yet we think we can inherit all the promises of God as isolated individuals.

I believe that, if churches are going to be successful in equipping disciples to live three-dimensional lives, it is essential that we understand the degree to which mutually accountable relationships are the bedrock of consistent living. They are also essential if any significant growth in faith and skill is going to happen on a wide-spread basis. Is this a challenge you are willing to rise to? If you are I recommend you begin by studying chapter 4 of Breen and Cockram's book, *Building a Discipling Culture*.

127   James 5:16.

128   1 Peter 5:8.

CHAPTER 6

The Rubber Hits the Road in Samaria

Nicodemus' attention had been grabbed by Jesus' miracles but he wasn't prepared to follow, despite his confidence that Jesus was sent by God. Others were impressed by the depth of Jesus' wisdom or the authority with which he taught. We have already commented on the way, as early as the second chapter of his gospel, Luke places the boy Jesus in the temple courts, amazing established teachers with his insight. A couple of chapters later we encounter Jesus using the Old Testament scriptures with great authority, and he reveals the clarity with which he understands his life's mission as he reads from the Isaiah scroll. There then follows an early demonstration of his power over the forces of evil and human sickness and a record of him teaching in synagogues throughout Galilee.

In Luke 5 we discover that Jesus is able to 'see' fish that career fishermen cannot spot and we note his authority over the socially isolating disease of leprosy along with his ability to discern hidden depths in someone from another group that had become an outcast within Jewish society – a tax collector. We have already reflected on Jesus' ability to see differently to others and noted that the essential starting point is that he is able to visualise people and events through his Father's eyes. In John 4 we are going to find what I believe is the key to Jesus' ability to apply the contents of this Kingdom toolbox.[129]

Breaking All the Rules

John tells us that Jesus and his disciples had been in Judea (in the south) where they also encountered opposition from the religious authorities who found themselves increasingly challenged by the fact that Jesus was becoming a focal point for popular acclaim. Jesus therefore leads his disciples on a trek north, back to their home territory of Galilee. The journey takes them through the town of Sychar in Samaria, previously known as Shechem, today called Nablus. The simple fact that Jesus chose to take the shortest route from Judea to Galilee would have set alarm bells ringing. Most Jews would have skirted around Samaria via the eastern shore of the River Jordan, preferring to walk three sides of a large square to avoid defilement. Jews and Samaritans had 'history'.

When the Assyrians attacked the Northern Kingdom of Israel in 722BC they had deported many of the inhabitants of the ten Jewish tribes who lived in the land and encouraged their own people to take their place. Many of these inter-married with the Jews, producing the race known as Samaritans. Both Samaritans and Jews looked to the God of the Pentateuch but the Samaritans had opposed the building of the Jerusalem Temple in Nehemiah's day and this still angered Jews many centuries later. In the past there had been a rival temple built on Mt Gerizim but it had been destroyed roughly two centuries before by a Jewish raiding party and had remained in ruins ever since. Despite this, Samaritans continued using the mountain as a place of worship. Samaritans still mocked the Jewish holy site and, a few years before Jesus was born, under cover of night, they sought to defile the Jerusalem temple by scattering the bones of the dead on the eve of Passover. Memories live long in religious disputes.

It is the middle of the day and Jesus and his disciples are hot and hungry so the Twelve go off to buy some food. Jesus sits down to rest next to a well which we later learn had been built by Jacob, the grandson of Abraham. The well was in the shadow of Mt Gerizim, overlooked by its sacred worship site. As Jesus was sitting, resting, a woman approaches.

....

129   Many of the cultural details in this chapter are taken from Kenneth Bailey – *Jesus Through Middle Eastern Eyes: Cultural Studies in the Gospels* (London: SPCK, 2008).

Most women in Jesus' day would have drawn water early in the morning and again in the evening because these were the coolest parts of the day. It would therefore have been unusual for a woman to visit the well alone at midday and this was a clear sign that she was considered something of a social outcast by the villagers. We later learn that the woman was living a promiscuous lifestyle which suggests she may have been a prostitute. The Mishnah suggests that Jesus should have withdrawn at least 20 feet and avoided making eye contact but he remains seated. Jesus then does something very surprising given the social customs and the power of taboo in this society - he engages the woman in conversation.

Jesus has already broken two Jewish prohibitions. Samaritans were sworn enemies, a fact that has already been illustrated by the history of the rival temples. This entrenched animosity features heavily in the story Jesus told that we now call the Parable of the Good Samaritan. In fact, the parable makes little sense until we appreciate the embedded hatred - to a Jew there was no such thing as a 'good' Samaritan who were popularly referred to as 'dogs'. What is more, it is Jesus who asks the woman for a drink. This request throws the woman completely because she knew that Jews thought Samaritans were unclean and her water jar would also have been contaminated.

The second apparent *faux-pas* made by Jesus was the fact that he was talking, apparently in a friendly manner, to a woman who almost certainly had a bad reputation. Ancient accounts show that even asking water of a woman could be interpreted as flirting with her, especially if she had come without a chaperone.

The Woman's Journey of Discovery

Let us approach this encounter from the woman's perspective. She has come to Jacob's Well in the middle of the day to avoid the attention of others, almost certainly because of her reputation and in order to avoid attention. She has learned the pecking order and is trying to respect it. She then encounters a man, a Jewish man, who breaks all the conventions and seems to have no ulterior motives – unlike many of the men of her own race of which, we later discover, she has had plenty of experience. Her stereotypes are becoming totally confused. We read:

"You are a Jew, and I am a Samaritan woman. How can you ask

me for a drink of water when Jews and Samaritans won't have anything to do with each other?" Jesus answered, "You don't know what God wants to give you, and you don't know who is asking you for a drink. If you did, you would ask me for the water that gives life." "Sir," the woman said, "you don't even have a bucket, and the well is deep. Where are you going to get this life-giving water? Our ancestor Jacob dug this well for us, and his family and animals got water from it. Are you greater than Jacob?" Jesus answered, "Everyone who drinks this water will get thirsty again. But no one who drinks the water I give will ever be thirsty again. The water I give is like a flowing fountain that gives eternal life." The woman replied, "Sir, please give me a drink of that water! Then I won't get thirsty and have to come to this well again."[130]

The interchange between them is fascinating since it begins with Jesus asking her for a drink – she has the bucket and can meet his need. It quickly leads on to a conversation in which he offers *her* something that sounds much more refreshing than the water he asked her for and in the meantime he seems to have forgotten he's thirsty, unless the story misses out the detail that Jesus defiles himself by drinking some water. The heart of the encounter is exposed when Jesus makes what seems a simple request of the woman – something that may seem to be an attempt to legitimise their social contact:

Jesus told her, "Go and bring your husband." The woman answered, "I don't have a husband." "That's right," Jesus replied, "you're telling the truth. You don't have a husband. You have already been married five times, and the man you are now living with isn't your husband."[131]

When teaching on this passage this is the point at which I usually play a video clip entitled 'Spoken Word: Woman at the Well'.[132] The video is a powerful monologue from the woman's perspective and goes like this:

I am a woman of no distinction
Of no importance

---

130   John 4:9-15 (CEV).

131   John 4:16-17 (CEV).

132   www.studentlife.com.

I am a woman of no reputation save that which is bad
You whisper as I pass by
And cast judgement or glances
Though you don't really take the time to look at me or even to
get to know me
To be known is to be loved and to be loved is to be known...

I want to be known
I want someone to look at my face
And not just see two eyes, a nose, a mouth and two ears
But to see all that I am and could be
All my hopes, loves and fears
That's too much to hope for, to wish for or pray for
So I don't
Not any more.

Now I keep to myself
And by that I mean the pain that keeps me in my own private jail
The pain that's brought me here at midday
To this well.

To ask for a drink is no big request
But to ask it of me
A woman, unclean and ashamed
Used and abused, an outcast, a failure
A disappointment, a sinner
No drink passing from these hands to your lips could ever be
refreshing, only condemning
As I'm sure you condemn me now
But you don't.

You're a man of no distinction though of the utmost importance
A man with little reputation, at least so far
You whisper and tell me to my face what all those glances have
been about
And you take the time to really look at me.

But don't need to get to know me
For to be known is to be loved and to be loved is to be known

And you know me
You actually know me
All of me and everything about me
Every thought inside and hair on top of my head
Every hurt stored up, every hope, every dread
My past and my future
All I am and could be
You tell me everything
You tell me about me.

And that which was spoken by another would bring hate and
condemnation
Coming from you brings love, grace, mercy, hope and salvation
I've heard of one to come who would save a wretch like me
And here in my presence you say 'I am he'.

To be known is to be loved and to be loved is to be known
And I just met you but I love you
I don't know you but I want to get to
Let me run back to town
This is way too much for just me
There are others
Brothers, sisters
Lovers, haters
The good and the bad
Sinners and saints
Who should hear what you've told me
Who should see what you've shown me
Who should taste what you gave me
Who should feel how you forgave me.

For to be known is to be loved and to be loved is to be known
And they all need this too
We all do, need it for our own.

Truth can Set People Free

I recall reflecting on this passage the first time I saw this monologue
performed and it occurred to me that if I had experienced life as this woman

had done, and in a society with such strict standards, the last person I would want to meet would have been a prophet. Prophets see hidden things and they are strict on sin. John records her response as almost matter-of-fact: "I see you are a prophet, sir", but it becomes clear that deep inside her something profound is happening.

➤ "You knew all this about me and yet you risked your reputation to speak with me."

➤ "You knew all this about me and you treated me with the utmost kindness and respect."

➤ "You knew all this about me and you haven't jumped to the usual conclusions."

➤ "You are a prophet who sees the whole truth – but as you tell me about my life, the shame that has accompanied me for so long no longer stings."

At no point does Jesus condone, but neither does he feel the need to condemn. In this meeting with Jesus this woman is brought face to face with truth yet in a way that leaves her no longer feeling the need to hide. In this one encounter she has moved from what she sees with her eyes to a far deeper understanding of who Jesus is:

➤ You are an unusual man (4:7)

➤ You are a Jew (4:9)

➤ You are a Prophet (4:19)

This is the point in the account at which the disciples return from their shopping trip. Instantly we see that they are confused but not one of them asks why Jesus is talking to the woman. She is clearly of no significance to them. The woman, however, is profoundly moved and her badge of shame no longer prevents her from engaging with everyday people. The text says:

> The woman left her water jar and ran back into town. She said to the people, "Come and see a man who told me everything I have ever done! Could he be the Messiah?" Everyone in town went out to see Jesus.[133]

---

133   John 4:28-30 (CEV).

And a few verses later we read:

A lot of Samaritans in that town put their faith in Jesus because the woman had said, "This man told me everything I have ever done." They came and asked him to stay in their town, and he stayed on for two days. Many more Samaritans put their faith in Jesus because of what they heard him say. They told the woman, "We no longer have faith in Jesus just because of what you told us. We have heard him ourselves, and we are certain that he is the Saviour of the world!"[134]

Surely the woman arrives at the conclusion that Jesus is the Messiah not because he could see facts about her that others couldn't but because of the manner in which he told the truth to her. John has already told us that Jesus was "full of grace and truth"[135] and now we see how what it looks like when God combines those two features in human form.

Until I allowed myself to encounter this passage in some depth I always saw truth as rather abstract. The idea of truth being embodied in a person whose primary motive was grace thrilled me. It reminded me of a story recounted by George D. Aldrich which appeared in The Washington Post on 16th June 1901:

I heard Dr Conan Doyle tell a good story during a trip I made to London last winter. He said that at a dinner party he had attended the guests began discussing the daily discoveries made to the detriment of people occupying high stations in life and enjoying the confidence of the business world. Dr. Doyle said that it had always been his opinion that there was a skeleton in the closet of every man who had reached the age of forty. This led to a lot of discussion, some of the guests resenting the idea that there was no one who had not in his past something that were better concealed. As a result of the controversy, Dr. Doyle said, it was suggested that his views as to family skeletons be put to the test. The diners selected a man of their acquaintance whom all knew only as an upright Christian gentleman, whose word was accepted as quickly as his bond and who stood with the highest

----

134   John 4:39-42 (CEV).

135   John 1:14.

in every respect. We wrote a telegram saying 'All is discovered;
flee at once' to this pillar of society, said Dr. Doyle, and sent it. He
disappeared the next day and has never been heard from since.

This woman had been hiding from polite society simply because the truth about herself had been too much for her to bear. When her truth was viewed with eyes tinted by grace and applied by the Son of God, the woman was released from her prison. At this point I found myself asking questions of Jesus and, as I began exploring this encounter even more deeply, the thing that struck me most forcibly was the fact that Jesus refused to stand in judgement and seems not to have been at all concerned about how this made him look to others.

There must have been villagers observing them: "why is that man talking to 'that' woman?" And the disciples: "what is our rabbi doing *now*?!" Yet Jesus wasn't prepared to let fears about his own reputation stop him from affirming and restoring the dignity of a woman who had been destroyed by the bad reputation she had earned herself. Jesus, the prophet, knew the truth and yet, as the writer of the monologue reveals so beautifully, her experience of being fully known was one of knowing herself completely loved.

Jesus Refuses to Make Judgements

We are faced with the simple fact that Jesus, the only sinless man who ever lived and therefore the one most entitled to make a judgement on someone else's behaviour, refused to do so. If we read the New Testament carefully we see that this refusal to stand in judgement over others was no accident. In the last chapter we featured John 3:16 heavily but I omitted any reference to verse 17. When I am speaking in public I ask if anyone can quote it, and rarely do I find more than one or two people who recall that it says; "For God did not send his Son into the world to be its judge, but to be its saviour."

So God sent Jesus because a planet full of humans created to know themselves accepted and loved by him had no worthy revelation of their creator. Generations of self-centred and self-serving individuals have built cultures that are resistant to God and have engaged in countless acts, large and small, hidden and notorious, that have caused untold suffering. Even those who try and live God's way seem incapable of getting it right. And yet... Jesus refuses to stand in judgement of all but those from whom more is expected: the religious establishment. Jesus explains why later in the Gospel:

> Jesus said, "I tell you the truth: the Son can do nothing on his own; he does only what he sees his Father doing. What the Father does, the Son also does... Nor does the Father himself judge anyone. He has given his Son the full right to judge.[136]

So Jesus has the right to make judgements and yet...

> If people hear my message and do not obey it, I will not judge them. I came, not to judge the world, but to save it.[137]

Of course, this doesn't mean there is no judgement:

> Those who reject me and do not accept my message have one who will judge them. The words I have spoken will be their judge on the last day![138]

It seems to me that Jesus sees acting as the world's judge and its saviour to be mutually exclusive. He knows he can't be both at the same time and thankfully has no need to try. Final judgement is waiting in the wings but is reserved until his return in glory. In the meantime, Jesus' teaching and example stands as the standard by which those of us who seek to follow his Father can judge our progress.[139]

Yet Jesus ministered in a world where judgement was rife. This woman was reduced to coming into the marketplace at midday because of judgements that had been made about her which had their origins in the religious rules and traditions of her day. Her critics must have felt so self-righteous because of the good company they kept. One of the things I find it helpful to recall is the degree to which Jesus felt the heat from these critics wherever he went.

---

136   John 5:19-22.

137   John 12:47.

138   John 12:48.

139   John 9:39.

Jesus under Pressure

In the 400 year period between the Testaments the Jewish authorities were engaged in a long-running discussion amongst themselves about how they would recognise the Messiah when he came.[140] The authorities had decided upon a two-stage plan by which they would assess the teaching and behaviour of anyone who claimed, or was suspected of being, this long-awaited saviour of the nation. The first stage was to send a team of teachers of the law to listen and observe for a period of time. They were allowed to ask questions but not enter into any debate. If the individual passed this first test, the second phase would begin during which the assessors were allowed to challenge and comment.

If you open and read Mark's gospel (probably the most chronologically accurate gospel) with this in mind it becomes clear that in the early chapters a group of religious professionals are frequently present as Jesus teaches but they are silent. We read of them 'talking amongst themselves'[141] or asking questions of his disciples.[142] In order to confront them Jesus is forced either to read their minds[143] or overhear their discussions.[144] There is no hint of direct confrontation. As the gospel progresses we see a distinct shift, suggesting that the test has moved into the second phase. I think it is helpful to remind ourselves that, throughout his ministry, Jesus would have been acutely aware that within his audience there were critics, probably provocatively dressed in their religious garb, just waiting to pounce when the time was right.

My experience is that all human societies are similar in this respect. Consider the way an ugly rumour spreads and mud sticks, even in some churches. I am shocked by the number of people who really do want to know the latest celebrity gossip and am reminded of the fact every time I see those trivial magazines all lined up near the till at the supermarket

....

140   The following detail comes from Beresford Job – *Biblical Church* (Epping: Bethany Publishing, 2007), 31-35.

141   Mark 2:6.

142   Mark 2:16.

143   Mark 2:8.

144   Mark 2:17.

with their bold headlines designed to tempt me into indulging myself in the most pathetic and sordid stories. The *News of the World* may have got its comeuppance for the way it gathered its exclusive material but it hasn't stopped the feeding frenzy that follows every tabloid revelation or tell-all confession in other sections of the media.

What feeds this is the deep need we all have to feel better about ourselves. If we cannot derive a healthy sense of our own worth from God, our conscience and our friends, one of the easiest ways of bolstering our own egos is by revelling in the worst facts about others. And, sadly, religious people often have the worst reputation for being small-minded and judgemental. So many people I meet expect me to be harsh and critical despite the fact that my Lord was not. I believe it is our responsibility to introduce them to the real Jesus.

How not to live like Jesus

As I grappled further with this question my mind was drawn to the Officer's Mess at an RAF station I once served as a civilian chaplain. The highlight of my short stint came as the full-time chaplain was posted to Basra and I was asked to attend a 'dining in' evening in order to deliver the grace. Dining In events happen at RAF stations every so often as a way of welcoming new postings to the station and saying goodbye to any who may be moving on. They are formal events, sometimes with VIP guests, and uniforms are everywhere.

I am not from a military background and, if I'm honest, I found the whole culture to be rather strange and confusing. As the evening drew near I began to receive a flurry of emails, most of which I didn't understand. I recall being informed that the dress code was "number 5s" which I knew I didn't possess. I was told this part of the dress code didn't apply to chaplains but I wasn't completely reassured. All I had was a borrowed clerical shirt. I also picked up snatches of RAF folklore such as the fact that the port had to be passed a certain way around the table and must remain in the air at all times. To fall foul of this or any other tradition of which I was still unclear would incur a forfeit of some kind. And then there was the question of the grace. No one could tell me what was expected of me and I had no way of finding out.

By the time the evening arrived I really wasn't sure I wanted to be there at all. As I walked into the mess I recall reassuring myself that, since I was only there because it was expected of me, I would leave as soon as I could. As I entered the lounge I was self-conscious and very aware that it really wasn't my scene. As an introvert I find these occasions unreal at the best of times and this was not the best of times! I recall being introduced to a small group of guests on arrival and that this made social contact far easier than I'd feared but I still felt edgy, on the alert, trying to remember my rehearsed lines for the endless new conversations I knew would be expected of me.

It was only as I looked back at the event that I became aware of the number of mental defences I had built up to distance me from the occasion. My guard was up, presumably to prevent me from being embarrassed by my discomfort. It looked to me as if everyone else was far more comfortable than I was and, as a way of excusing my fears, I began to entertain judgemental ideas that everyone apart from me was there to enhance their reputation, get promotion or build up contacts. All that was achieved by these thoughts was that my fears were being massaged by a rather pompous brand of cynicism.

There are so many ways of classifying people so as to put distance between them and us. Consider a social occasion such as the one I have described. My eyes may scan the room and I recognise a few faces in the crowd, some of whom come with judgements attached:

> Mr football-obsessed – I don't like the game so I classify him as "boring"

> Ms life and soul - she seems so confident – I'm overawed

> Miss socialite – too shallow – she's not worthy of my company

> Mr successful – everything he does succeeds – I feel jealousy dressed up as scorn

> Mrs Posh Jag – she flaunts her wealth – I feel plain

> Mr handsome/ Miss stunning – I'm tongue tied for fear of making a stupid comment

At the heart of thoughts like these is the fear that I won't fit in. The result is that, even before I step into the room, my attention is upon me and my fears. Self-consciousness is an uncomfortable state so I feel the pressure to justify that state to myself and the most convenient way to do that is to make judgements about others. This has the happy result of making my discomfort someone else's fault.

To return to my RAF evening, I was in a room of fascinating people but my attention was mostly upon myself. In order to justify my fears, I'd made judgements. Those judgements had categorised people and prevented me from getting to know them as individuals. The result was that this room full of amazing and fascinating people were never given the opportunity to prove me wrong.

The reality was that the event wasn't as bad as I'd feared, mainly because the RAF are so good at arranging such gatherings. The whole evening was well choreographed and even the grace went well. I had decided not to come with it written down in advance because I wanted to lead the assembled service women and men in a thanksgiving which came from the heart. This no doubt added to my advance fears but I was told by many that it was one of the most moving prayers they had heard. Yet, looking back, I was acutely aware that, throughout the whole evening, my attention had been upon myself. Any thought that I was wearing a clerical collar, and was therefore a visible representative of Christ, was the last thing on my mind.

Jesus the Party Animal

Contrastingly, when Jesus attended a society do, even one in which he became the centre of attention in the most embarrassing of ways, he still found himself free to act with composure and integrity and do the work of his Father. I'm now thinking of the occasion when Jesus finds himself as a guest of honour in the house of Simon the Pharisee.[145] Simon was just the kind of man any other religious teacher who wanted to gain a hearing would have done his best to impress. On this occasion, however, another woman who had lived an immoral life heard that Jesus was having dinner with Simon and, in her desperation to see him, gate-crashed the meal. Luke tells the story in such embarrassing detail - she enters the room in floods of tears and runs straight to where Jesus is sitting, pours expensive perfume on his feet and then wipes off the excess with her hair.

This is *scandalous* behaviour! The text calls her "a woman in that town

---

145   Luke 7:36-50.

who lived a sinful life" so we are left to assume she could only have earned the money to buy such perfume in the most immoral of ways yet, not only does Jesus seem to be unconcerned about her past, he actually allows her to touch him, drawing him into the pollution of her world. What is most shocking is that Jesus doesn't seem to be overawed or embarrassed by this sudden turn of events. In fact he makes things worse for himself by drawing Simon's attention to the contrast between the poor level of courtesy he, as host, has shown him as an invited guest and the lack of inhibition demonstrated by this sinner. He then crowns the evening by telling a story which suggests that God might be more pleased with her than with this definer of impeccable doctrine.

As the host, Simon's attention is upon himself and his desire to be seen at his beneficent best. The guests are no doubt embarrassed for Simon whilst also intent on catching every juicy detail. Jesus' attention is on the one person who matters most in this scenario: a woman whom he has clearly met previously and who feels the need to thank him for the most precious gift she has ever received. Jesus practises a quality Timothy Keller calls 'gospel-humility' - "not needing to connect things with [him]self"[146] which causes him to see this woman differently to most other men. I think there are at least four keys we can discern and learn from:

> Jesus knows and is assured of his true identity and therefore has no need to impress others or prove himself.

> It is Jesus' deepest desire that all come to the Father and are not turned away.

> Jesus knows that true love covers over others' sins as an act of gratuitous kindness.

> Jesus has filled himself with grace and truth and chooses to live from those reserves – truth sets others free and grace empowers them to live differently.

These are the reasons Jesus is able to make this woman his number one priority and these are the factors Jesus was referring to when he said: "Stop judging by mere appearances, but instead judge correctly."[147]

....

146   Timothy Keller - The Freedom of Self-Forgetfulness (Leyland: 10Publshing, 2012), 32.

147   John 7:24. See also John 8:15.

Surrendering the Right to Judge

We have discovered Jesus' position on judging others and, it seems, if he refuses to be our judge, we're walking a dangerous path if we feel the need to take his place:

> For the mouth speaks what the heart is full of. A good man brings good things out of the good stored up in him, and an evil man brings evil things out of the evil stored up in him. But I tell you that everyone will have to give account on the day of judgment for every empty word they have spoken. For by your words you will be acquitted, and by your words you will be condemned.'[148]

> 'Do not judge, or you too will be judged. For in the same way as you judge others, you will be judged, and with the measure you use, it will be measured to you.[149]

> He also said to them, "Pay attention to what you hear! The same rules you use to judge others will be used by God to judge you - but with even greater severity.[150]

> Be merciful, just as your Father is merciful. 'Do not judge, and you will not be judged. Do not condemn, and you will not be condemned. Forgive, and you will be forgiven.[151]

Right now I can anticipate an objection: "What about sin – surely Jesus has told us to love the sinner but condemn the sin." Has He? Is it in the Bible? I've heard this phrase repeated so many times over the years that you'd have thought it should be there somewhere. But it isn't. Sure, we must make a judgement about sin but only so that we can apply that judgement to ourselves.

Conviction of sin, which is an essential part of the gospel message, is a task that rightly belongs to the Spirit.[152] My experience is that whenever

148   Matthew 12:34-37.

149   Matthew 7:1-2.

150   Mark 4:24 (CEV).

151   Luke 6:36-37.

152   John 16:8.

I have tried to do his work for him without being given permission I get it wrong and I exhibit condemnation rather than conviction. Jesus, on the other hand, refuses to condemn either of the women we've encountered in this chapter but they go away with their sin brought into the light, disarmed and totally forgiven.

Jesus commands that we love others but, when we are full of judgement that is rooted in our own needs and insecurities, it is impossible for us to lift our attention to engage those he fully accepts and welcomes. I am convinced that dealing with this deeply destructive judgemental spirit is a crucial foundation of all Christ-like living.

Slaying the Judgement Monster

As the woman approached the well, Jesus saw exactly the same person as her neighbours and the disciples as they returned from buying food. He saw a woman. They saw a woman. Yet Jesus also saw a whole lot more, primarily because he allowed himself to, He chose to resist the fear of what others would think as they saw him initiating a conversation with someone who had a tarnished reputation and allowed the Father to put him in a position to minister grace and acceptance.

In my student days I lived very near the red-light district in Nottingham and, on days when lectures ran late, I can recall the mixture of fear and fascination as I ran the gauntlet of invitations to 'have a good time'. I can also remember watching other men approach these scantily dressed ladies with only one intention on their minds. My biggest fear was being caught in conversation and then being seen by my friends and, as a result, I would walk quickly with my head down, pretending to be deep in thought. Even after reading these gospel stories I find it hard to imagine how I could have heard God's voice in this heightened state, but if being a disciple of Jesus means doing as he did I clearly have lessons to learn.

Let me be clear, I am not suggesting that we should make no judgements of any kind. This would be ridiculous and highly irresponsible. Yet, most of us have become so used to hearing our own judgements that we are probably unaware of what an unholy mixture of thoughts pass through our minds. My point is that we need to test our judgements about other people and re-frame them whenever they are unkind, unfair or unfounded.

The first step is to work hard on assuring ourselves who we are in Christ. This may seem a strange place to begin but I have discovered that, if I have no need to prove myself to myself or to others, I am less likely to make unkind judgements. The truth is that we are already fully accepted by God and nothing we do can make us any more or less acceptable in his eyes. It is also true that Jesus can only live through you to the degree that you know this fact to be true. If you feel that you need to work on this may I recommend the Discipleship Course produced by Freedom in Christ.[153]

The second thing we can work on is our attitude. This begins with logging our first impressions and also includes reflecting upon the way our opinions of other people are formed. For example, how significant is the clothing other people wear, their skin colour, accent or fashion sense as you form your first impressions of them? Once we have taken an honest account of these things it is necessary to make a deliberate choice to suspend our judgements. This begins with pulling ourselves up short or asking ourselves questions about the person rather than rushing to an opinion.

We can also ask questions of God. Try asking him "What would 'grace' see in this person?" As you sense his response it is vital that you act on what God shows you because it is when you pray for them, cross the room to talk, or plan to do some kind act for them that your heart becomes engaged. It then becomes possible to hear God's voice more clearly.

That this is a missional issue is clear from the story in John 4. We read that the woman re-engaged with her community, they welcomed Jesus amongst them and enjoyed his presence for two days.

> They said to the woman, "We no longer believe just because of what you said; now we have heard for ourselves, and we know that this man really is the Saviour of the world."[154]

---

153   www.ficm.org.uk.

154   John 4:42.

PART 2

Themes from John's Gospel

CHAPTER 7
Jesus Engages the Forces of Religion

I have always loved John's gospel. Whilst it surrenders some of the immediacy of the other gospels, John more than makes up for this by offering us a rich reflection upon the meaning of the life of his Lord. He achieves this by constructing his account around seven sayings of Jesus, some of which are illustrated by a sign that makes the claim impossible to overlook:

➤ John 6:48 – I am the Bread of life

➤ John 8:12 - I am the Light of the World

➤ John 10:9 - I am the Gate

➤ John 10:11 - I am the Good Shepherd

➤ John 11:25 - I am the Resurrection and the Life

➤ John 14:6 - I am the Way, the Truth and the Life

➤ John 15:1 - I am the True Vine

element in the Temple ...?

Each statement has been carefully inserted into the narrative much as a jeweller might design a brooch in order to display the best facets of a particularly striking diamond. The statement referring to himself as Bread followed an occasion in which he had fed more than 5000 people and was delivered in public at the synagogue in Capernaum. The reaction, even from his *own* disciples, was ""This is a hard teaching. Who can accept it?"[155] Jesus' insistence that he was the Light of the World was made in the Temple courts with Pharisees present and his claims to be the Gate and the Good Shepherd followed Jesus' insistence that the Pharisees were spiritually blind and therefore useless guides to God. Jesus' assertion that he was the Resurrection and the Life is reported to the Pharisees by witnesses who had seen Lazarus raised from the dead and led to a specially convened meeting of the Sanhedrin. As a result, the first plot to kill Jesus was hatched and a public statement was issued that he be arrested as soon as possible.

If Jesus' multiple claims are true, further conclusions are inevitable. Even in his use of the phrase "I am" Jesus is borrowing a Hebraism reserved for statements about God and he is therefore issuing a serious challenge. If Jesus represents God, the Pharisees and other religious leaders have got their theology spectacularly wrong. Jesus is uncompromising in his denunciation: the Pharisees may be students of the law and the scriptures but they fail to practise what they say they believe.[156] Their religion is therefore of human origin,[157] is isolating them from true knowledge of God[158] and is of no redeeming value.[159] Jesus is making it abundantly clear that his opponents may come dressed in religious garb but are politically motivated schemers with no connection to God and his plans.[160]

The Pharisees' charges against Jesus and the schemes they dream up make sense only within their own system. Jesus is a law-breaker but the hedge laws he sees fit to break are only those that hamper the will of

....

155   John 6:60.

156   John 5:39; 7:19-24; 9:39-41.

157   John 5:44; 9:28-29.

158   John 5:38-47; 8:19, 31-47, 55; 10:1-6.

159   John 8:24.

160   John 11:45-57; 19:7-15.

God because they are founded upon human wisdom.[161] The traps they lay for Jesus are carefully planned but warped in the extreme,[162] their growing paranoia entrenches them in their self-righteousness[163] and sows nothing but confusion amongst the people they believed themselves to be serving.[164] Serious talk of murder can only make sense to minds that have completely lost their bearings but the Pharisees are so enraged that they are closed to any possibility of self-correction.[165]

We have already seen that Jesus took no delight in opposing the keepers of false religion but did so because of the way God's larger mission was being thwarted. I have charted the downward trajectory of Israel as God's people of promise. Israel was intended to be an object lesson to the nations but are living instead under religious and political oppression whilst being led by myopic guides. Jesus' miraculous provision of top-quality wine and his cursing of the fig tree were prophetic signs that a radical revision was on its way. Nicodemus' inability to discern spiritual truth and the level of unbelief that was evident within the people brought about Jesus' actions in the Court of the Gentiles. The Father loves the world so much that he is compelled to send his only Son to re-establish his missional purposes upon the earth.

Jesus, John makes it patently clear, knew himself to be about his father's business.[166] This fact was evidenced by the numerous signs and wonders,[167] the quality and authenticity of his teaching[168] and the transformational results of his forgiveness.[169] The festivals had been

....

161   John 5:10, 18; 7:20-23; 9:13-16.

162   John 8:1-11.

163   John 7:11; 11:56-57.

164   John 7:13, 25-26, 32, 45-49; 9:22.

165   John 5:18; 8:59; 10:31, 39; 11:53; 12:10; 16:1-4.

166   John 5:17-30, 37, 43; 6:37-40; 7:16-18, 28-29; 8:14-19, 27-30, 38, 49-59; 9:14-18; 10:25-38; 14:6-31; 15:9-10, 22-24, 26; 16:5-15, 25-33; 17.

167   John 5:36; 7:31; 9:16, 32-33; 10:21, 24-25, 38.

168   John 7:14-32; 8:1-11; 10:34-38.

169   John 4:28-30, 39-42; 6:53-58; 8:1-11.

designed and instituted by God to act as visual reminders of his covenantal faithfulness and yet, whenever Jesus made himself present he felt compelled to provide an additional commentary.[170] If I might carry over an image from chapter 5, God's people had become so entrenched in covenant thinking that they had rendered themselves entirely unable to make the shift to the Kingdom triangle. They were children of Abraham in name but not in nature.

I have already demonstrated how Jesus' conversation with the Samaritan woman at Jacob's Well illustrates, not just that he saw more deeply into situations than his fellow teachers, but also that he interpreted what he saw differently. Jesus demonstrated a deep compassion for individuals which he displayed freely, even in situations where they were trapped in lifestyles the Torah denounced. Jesus also ascribed every gracious act to his Father, insisting that his intimate relationship with Yahweh led him to act as he did. Before we consider our own relationship with religion and society I want to examine two particular encounters in more detail.

Jesus and the Blind Man

> As Jesus walked along, he saw a man who had been blind since birth. Jesus' disciples asked, "Teacher, why was this man born blind? Was it because he or his parents sinned?"[171]

Every time we view a human body our minds recognise it as such because, for all the years of our conscious existence, we have viewed countless thousands of bodies and have laid down a mental pattern of what one normally looks like. It takes a millisecond to match the body we see with the embedded pattern stored in our brains and the whole process is completely subconscious. When we scan a crowd or meet someone for the first time, we subconsciously match our store of embedded images to search for features we recognise. This is the point at which people who look different is experienced by us as a shock to the system.[172]

---

170   John 5:1; 7:2, 10; 10:22; 12:12ff. These are the only specific references in the Gospel.

171   John 9:1 (CEV).

172   See Malcolm Gladwell – *Blink: The Power of Thinking Without Thinking* (London: Penguin Books, 2005) for further explanation and application written in a popular style.

Human disability therefore creates a tension. We will all tend to stare at a bodily form we've not seen before simply because something that is usually a subconscious act (viewing a body and recognising it as such) is being drawn to our conscious awareness and we are thus forced to deal with the unusual visual data that is before us.

As a physically disabled person I am very aware that, when I am walking in a public place, my very presence is disturbing to everyone I come into contact with, sometimes profoundly so. My arms were damaged by the thalidomide drug prior to my birth and they look different. So people who notice me are forced to make an instant decision about which they have not been forewarned. Many stare, others look away, some do a double-take, children ask questions of their parents, and occasionally people ask me why I am different.[173]

The disciples noticed a man with glassy eyes, or maybe with no eyeballs at all, and, fascinatingly, the very first question that entered their minds was a theological one: "why was this man born blind? Was it because he or his parents sinned?"

In the culture of Jesus' day, the disabled, the diseased and the afflicted were more visible than they are within the society in which many of us live. This is because they were forced onto the streets by economic necessity.

In traditional Middle Eastern society beggars are a recognised part of the community and are understood to be offering 'services' to it. Every pious person is expected to give to the poor. But if the poor are not readily available to receive alms, how can this particular duty be fulfilled? The traditional beggar does not say "excuse me, mister, do you have a few coins for a crust of bread?" Instead, he sits in a public place and challenges the passer-by with "Give to God!" He is really saying: "My needs are beside the point. I am offering you a golden opportunity to fulfil your obligations to God. Furthermore, this is a public place and if you give to me here, you will gain a reputation as an honourable, compassionate, pious person. When a beggar receives money, he usually stands up and in a loud voice proclaims the giver to be the most noble person he has ever met and invokes God's grace and blessing on the giver,

---

173   The most humorous example was a teenage American boy who encountered me in a restaurant in San Francisco and asked, in all seriousness, "sir, are you an alien?".

his family, his friends and associates, his going out and coming in, and many other good things. Such public praise is surely worth the small sum given to the beggar.[174]

The problem created by such a tradition is that the beggar is forced to expose the part of himself that sets him apart from others in order to make a living. In doing so, he is in great danger of being defined in his own eyes by his limitations rather than his abilities. He also has no opportunity to receive genuine grace from others within such an arrangement since he becomes the net receiver of money in exchange for honour. Which of these, money or honour, is more important to our sense of dignity?

Returning to the encounter with the blind man, the question posed by the disciples reveals something about the way they were re-processing the world as a result of their journey with Jesus. Within their theological system there were two options: the sin that caused the disability was either located with the parents or the man himself. They were about to discover that there was at least one more option they'd not thought of but, before we get to that, I want to touch on the issue of the way we do our theology when faced with difficult questions.

Disability is only a theological question for those of us who believe in both a good and sovereign God. Yet, in my experience, most people tend to avoid this sort of hard question, maybe out of fear that the map they use to make sense of the world might not be up to the job. The disciples ask the very question I wanted answers to throughout the whole of my early years as a Christian. Yet, for me, this was a high stakes question for at least four reasons:

➤ It risks upsetting the relative harmony of the present moment

➤ It risks putting the other person in an embarrassing situation

➤ It risks creating a scenario where 'any answer' will be dragged in as a stop-gap

➤ It risks unmasking the possibility that no satisfying answer exists

174   Kenneth Bailey – *Jesus through Middle Eastern Eyes*, 173-4. I am relying on Bailey for many of the cultural details underlying the encounters with the blind man and the adulterous woman.

I have encountered numerous painful comments and actions from Christians who, on meeting me, clearly sensed the need to restore balance to their view of God and his relationship with the world as quickly as possible. These range from a worshipper who was overheard asking exactly the same 'sin' question the disciples asked as I led a service in her church, to Christians who jump straight to the insistence that I should be 'healed' (i.e. made to look like them) even before they have got to know me.

The lesson I learned from numerous encounters like these in my younger years is that I was an embarrassment to some and that it was therefore unsafe to explore questions that would make people feel even more uneasy. Later in that story we discover that the Jewish leaders had already bolstered their theology against any breach, a fact that is revealed by their response to the recipient of Jesus' grace: "You Mamzer" they shout, a term used for person entirely born in sin and therefore beyond redemption. Neat and tidy theology is not only invariably wrong. It also has little place for any degree of compassion.

Jesus, as we might expect, saw things differently. Once again, he refuses to begin with the question of sin. He sees the individual through the lens of the Kingdom of God and seems also to be aware of the opportunity to re-calibrate the grace equation:

> "Neither this man nor his parents sinned," said Jesus, "but this happened so that the works of God might be displayed in him. As long as it is day, we must do the works of him who sent me. Night is coming, when no one can work. While I am in the world, I am the light of the world."[175]

Such a question may be received as a threat by a religious teacher who saw it as his task to leave no loose ends within his theology but the disciples seemed to have known they could be honest with their Rabbi and were confident Jesus wouldn't fudge the issue. Jesus' response thereby shifted the question from the realm of academic theology and created a *kairos* opportunity for the blind man. Theoretical theology thereby became practical action in the same blink of time others would have used either to stare, turn away, do the double-take or ask the kind of question posed by the disciples.

Healing the Blind Man

....

175   John 9:3-5.

"Shame," Brené Brown reminds us, "is real pain". She points to a recent study which reveals that "as far as the brain is concerned, physical pain and intense experiences of social rejection hurt in the same way... Shame is particularly hard because it hates having words wrapped around it. It hates being spoken," and thus remains hidden where it lurks as a constant source of humiliation and embarrassment.[176]

In Jesus' day and today, beggars would make a living by using the one currency they possessed: the ability to manufacture feelings of remorse, thus reinforcing the reality of their own social isolation. Emotions of passers-by are engaged simply because they are stored in the subconscious memory along with our patterns of what is 'normal'. People can't avoid noticing a disabled person in the street and therefore can't do a great deal to influence their initial reaction which will invariably be accompanied by a feeling. They do, however, have a choice to make about what their actions are going to be. Most avoid the choice altogether out of fear or indecision. I'd like to think the disciples threw a few coins as they turned their discomfort into a theological question. Jesus acted, and every detail of his response is significant.

There are thirty nine things that cannot be done on the Sabbath according to the Mishnah. In this story it is probable that, even before he healed the man, Jesus broke two laws contained in the oral Torah: building (mixing clay which is counted as a building material) and kneading/mixing (adding water was permissible but not mixing it in). He then put the mud on the man's eyes which, if it was done with the intention of healing, broke a further law. We have already noted that, although Jesus didn't consider himself bound by oral Torah, he wasn't an intentional law-breaker either. He could have simply touched the man and restored his sight but chooses to make himself more culpable in the eyes of his critics by involving spit and mud. Why are the details important and what do they signify?

I suggest Jesus has at least three things in mind. John tells how Jesus chooses to create a scenario whereby the man is forced to wash himself in order that he may test his eyesight. In doing this, Jesus was giving the man a part to play in his own healing, thus dignifying him. By sending him away he was also presenting the man with an opportunity to receive without feeling the obligation to honour his healer to the hilt. Jesus clearly desired to heal the person in addition to restoring his sight. Finally, in sending the man

---

176   Brené Brown – *Daring Greatly* (London: Portfolio Penguin, 2012), 71.

away and melting into the background as he went, Jesus was protecting the man from the religious authorities who had already made up their minds against him and would therefore persecute the previously blind man once they found out he had encountered the trouble-maker they were determined to kill.[177] The religion of Jesus' day seemed to have no discernible mission beyond protecting itself from difficult questions and preserving the *status quo*.

Jesus and the Adulterous Woman

Our second story unfolds during Succoth, the Feast of Booths. On each day of the festival, a priest would carry water from the Pool of Siloam in a gold jug and pour it into a basin underneath the altar. On the last day of the festival the Priest would read from Isaiah 12:3: "With joy you shall draw from the wells of salvation." The reading would be accompanied by blasts from golden trumpets and chanting from the Hallel: "Lord, please save us… blessed is he who comes in the name of the Lord".

> *On the last and greatest day of the festival, Jesus stood and said in a loud voice, 'Let anyone who is thirsty come to me and drink. 38 Whoever believes in me, as Scripture has said, rivers of living water will flow from within them.'*[178]

Jesus' invitation is thus perfectly aligned with the theme of the festival and is also a clear allusion to what God says about himself in Isaiah 55:1-3 (CEV):

> *If you are thirsty, come and drink water! If you don't have any money, come, eat what you want! Drink wine and milk without paying a penny. Why waste your money on what really isn't food? Why work hard for something that doesn't satisfy? Listen carefully to me, and you will enjoy the very best foods. Pay close attention! Come to me and live. I will promise you the eternal love and loyalty that I promised David.*

A generation earlier Rabbi Hillel had taken language about God and applied it to himself but, by the time of Jesus, Jewish tradition had decided, somewhat expediently, that Hillel had not intended that his 'claim' should be

---

177   John 9:22.

178   John 7:37-38.

taken seriously. The religious authorities were still nervous, especially around festival time when the Roman guard would have been placed on special alert, preparing themselves for any attempt at an insurrection.

This is the context in which John places one of Jesus' most controversial encounters – this time with an adulterous woman. The first question to clear up is whether or not this is an authentic account since most bibles include a textual comment warning us that John 7:53 – 8:11 is missing from many early Greek manuscripts. Other early editors included the story as part of Luke or in the margins.

Some textual commentators suggest this portion is an *agrapha* – an oral story that was so popular that it was finally recorded in the margins and was later included in the text. A further possibility is that it was excluded from privately-financed copies of scripture because in such a culturally conservative culture the honour of a family was attached to the sexual behaviour of its women and the story was simply regarded as too dangerous.[179] The question remains whether or not it is a historically accurate account of Jesus and his teaching and most commentators believe it to be so. Whether or not the account was written by John and was intended for inclusion at this point in his gospel, my feeling is that it illustrates 7:51 and 8:15 so well that it must be taken seriously as an authentic act of Jesus witnessed by John.

The Pharisees have their minds made up and can see that the crowd is divided. So comes an astute game intended as a trap before numerous witnesses. According to Jewish law the day following the feast was to be observed as a Sabbath. Jesus entered the temple area and sat down to teach, itself a sign of rabbinic authority. As he does so a group of teachers and Pharisees lead a woman to the front of the crowd and make her the subject of their own real-life drama:

> *Teacher, this woman was caught sleeping with a man who isn't her husband. The Law of Moses teaches that a woman like this*

---

179   Dr David Instone-Brewer deals with this question in *Christianity Magazine* (CCP, London: Feb 2012) p 62-3. At the time of writing the article is available in the magazine archives at www.christianitymagazine.co.uk. He also summarises it briefly in *The Jesus Scandals* (Oxford: Monarch, 2012), 115.

should be stoned to death! What do you say?[180]

They seem to have Jesus well and truly snookered with three equally unplayable options.

The first is to agree with the Pharisees. She is guilty and should be stoned. This would have led to an immediate commotion since it was a challenge to the right of Rome to trump Jewish law with its own. It is the same dilemma found in John 18:29-31 (CEV):

> *Pilate came out to them and asked, "What charges are you bringing against this man?" They answered, "He is a criminal! That's why we brought him to you." Pilate told them, "Take him and judge him by your own laws." The crowd replied, "We are not allowed to put anyone to death.*

Herod the Great had built a fort and connected it to the north end of the Temple court. Josephus tells us that during feast days armed Roman soldiers would patrol the whole area because they had learned that unrest was more likely to occur at such times. To cause any kind of commotion would have led to Jesus' arrest and trial for sedition.

Jesus' second option was to fudge the issue, thereby ducking the challenge in the name of political expediency. The religious teachers would then have been able to discredit him as a coward and his following would have waned as a result. The third alternative, which would surely have been the one Jesus' opponents were expecting and hoping for, was that he would rule in favour of the woman, thus breaking not just an oral ruling but the Torah itself.

The authorities were taking a gamble since, if Jesus were to be arrested, it may have increased his short-term popularity. But it would also have taken him out of the public eye and possibly led to a trial which they may have been confident they could manipulate to their own advantage. However, -

> *Jesus bent down and started to write on the ground with his finger... they kept on questioning him.*[181]

Remember, the eighth day of the festival was treated as a Sabbath so

....

180   John 8:4 (CEV).

181   John 8:6-7.

the Sabbath day laws were in full force. The primary requirement was to do no work and writing was one of these prohibited activities. But Jesus knew the law in detail and Mishnah Sabbat 12:5 states that writing in dust or sand is permissible because such writing made no permanent mark.[182] Jesus is calmly demonstrating a high degree of shrewdness in this simple action.

I never pondered on the words Jesus may have written until I encountered Kenneth Bailey's opinion: "I am convinced that he wrote 'death' or 'stone her'. Certainly his following words presuppose that he decreed the death penalty."[183]

> Finally, he stood up and said, "If any of you have never sinned, then go ahead and throw the first stone at her!" Once again he bent over and began writing on the ground.[184]

Keeping the law is all very well, but it cannot be enforced if there is no individual willing to take the responsibility to report her. Jesus' answer "puts a name and a face upon everyone in the crowd".[185] If the stoning had gone ahead everyone knew that two people would be arrested: the instigator and the perpetrator:

> With this challenge Jesus says to his opponents, 'Gentlemen, you clearly want **me** to go to jail for the law of Moses. I am willing to do so. I have ordered that she be killed. But I want to know which one of **you** is willing to accompany me into that cell.[186]

Bailey also suggests that, in the shame-based culture of his day, Jesus would have been confident that none of the woman's detractors would risk claiming themselves to be sinless. They would have been acutely aware of two key texts – "All we like sheep have gone astray"[187] and "Surely there is

---

182   The Mishnah was not recorded as a book until AD 200 but it is known to be the best source available to us describing Jewish life and practice in Jesus' day. The detail here seems to suggest that this 'oral interpretation of Torah' was in force in Jesus' day.

183   Kenneth Bailey, op cit, 235.

184   John 8:7-8 (CEV).

185   Kenneth Bailey, op cit, 235.

186   Ibid.

187   Isaiah 53:6 (CEV).

not a righteous man on earth who does good and never sins".[188]

In that culture the people would turn naturally to the eldest amongst them, and the woman discovers that the one who has lived longest also has the most of which to be ashamed. Jesus turns his face once more to the ground, displaying no desire to gloat on the humiliation his opponents have suffered, but in doing so he takes the anger that had been directed towards the woman onto himself, thus turning his toughest test into another unexpected demonstration of costly love.

The Law cannot bring Life

Both these accounts have demonstrated the truth of Jesus assertions about the Pharisees. There are unanswered questions such as how religious professionals catch a woman in the act of adultery or what they had done with the offending man (the law said both should be stoned). And whilst there is certainly a line in the law that states stoning to be an appropriate punishment for adultery this was not the first and last word on the subject. Uncovering the whole truth is always a far more nuanced affair than is demonstrated here.

Bailey sees the whole scenario to be about justice. He turns us to Isaiah 42:3 (CEV):

Here is my servant! I have made him strong. He is my chosen one; I am pleased with him. I have given him my Spirit, and he will bring justice to the nations. He won't shout or yell or call out in the streets. He won't break off a bent reed or put out a dying flame, but he will make sure that justice is done. He won't quit or give up until he brings justice everywhere on earth, and people in foreign nations long for his teaching.

The Pharisees demanded strict interpretation of the law for reasons that seemed commendable. In their zeal to see the promised Messiah they had concluded that the people needed to clean up their act in order to force God's hand.

The law matters, people do not. The woman is used as a pawn in a power play to discredit Jesus and reaffirm their authority. For the accusers in the story turf is more important than truth, justice

---

188   Ecclesiastes 7:20.

or people.[189]

Jesus had different reflexes. He sees the bruised reed and a dimly burning wick and is equally concerned about establishing the Kingdom rule of God. Jesus knows that the law the Pharisees are seeking to uphold was given within a Covenant relationship and was thus a privilege to live by, not just a list of requirements. To his eyes, these Pharisees are too quick to reduce the law simply to a sentence pronounced on any who are found guilty. Jesus knows the context and feels for the powerless individuals who were being ground down by the religious machine.

Yet, if I'm honest, I find some sympathy within me for those Pharisees. I wonder if this is because I know I could so easily become one, as do all of us whenever we are tempted to rest on our own virtues. I am sad to say that find myself defaulting to their position so naturally. It feels so good to live in a black and white world and to be such a vociferous supporter of God's high standards.

I cannot think of a single occasion when I've heard this text expounded and the teacher has not felt the need to give greater attention to Jesus' parting words to the woman: "You may go now, but don't sin any more" than to the story itself. We know all too well that the woman's adultery was a sin against God, against her spouse and against her body and yet we feel the need to underline it despite the fact that it has nothing to do with the main thrust of the story. Why is this?

I can't help wondering whether the reason the legalist in us rises up as we read such an account may be because we detect in ourselves the same potential weaknesses and can thus identify with the woman and are ashamed of a fact we do not wish to face. We know that, given certain circumstances, each of us could have been that woman and we are so ashamed of the revelation that we try to hide the truth from ourselves. But why should we be so alarmed? Surely this is exactly what Jesus was trying to engender in the crowd and is therefore the reason it is permanently recorded in scripture. Why is it such a shock to us that, like her accusers, we still default towards fleshly desires?

The religious authorities are trying to use the woman as a scapegoat, like so many others who have fallen foul of one law or another, and this is

---

189   Kenneth Bailey, op. cit, 236.

why she is given no opportunity to tell her side of the story or explain what had happened. She had simply been caught in the act and was now at the mercy of her accusers who saw her as easy prey. We must remember that her testimony wouldn't have been worth as much as the man she was found in bed with. John clearly intends the story to be a commentary upon Nicodemus' question: "Is it legal to convict a man before he is given a hearing?"[190] And yet this is something all humans do much of the time. In need of an illustration I turned to one of the numerous web sites which allow people to make confessions as a way of receiving therapeutic relief. In early 2011 I read the following confession which received the following response:

> **Confession**: *I had sex inside a church with my ex-boyfriend, I felt really guilty afterwards and things have gone wrong ever since, my mum is now dying of cancer, is this my fault am I being punished?*

> **Reply**: *The real punishment is after death, this is just a foretaste. Repent and you can avoid it all though.*

How sad it is that, having felt the need to confess an act about which she felt guilty, the religious respondent thought nothing about helping her receive the forgiveness that God longs her to experience. In her desire to find relief from her mental torture this poor woman is given an added burden of future judgement by a vengeful God and no pointers as to how she can unburden herself before God or learn about the delightful holiness of sex in its right context.

Jesus recognises that the woman standing before him has sinned against God and society by her unfaithfulness but he is far more interested in giving her reason to keep the law in future than punish her for an event that is now in the past. And this same Jesus says that he only ever does what he sees the Father doing, which means this really is what God is like.

Jesus the Psychologist

Let's cast our minds forward to Jesus' final words for just a minute: "Forgive them Father. They don't know what they are doing." Just as on this occasion, a bunch of powerful individuals had agreed on a course of action that they are convinced was the will of God. They feel they are defending God's name, his standards, his honour. They are united in a common bond

---

190   John 7:51.

that binds them in their certainty. They are in the right and have never been more convinced of the fact that crucifixion is the punishment Jesus deserves. Yet Jesus recognises their need for forgiveness along with the fact that they are blind to their true motivations. The Father knows, Jesus knows, but the individuals who are driving the story along are bereft of such self-awareness. Even whilst on the receiving end of their hateful punishment Jesus cannot help but remind his Father of their inability to see things as they truly are.

Back to John 8. The woman knows what she has done but maybe not why. The religious crowd aren't interested in her, just her guilt. Is Jesus saying: "Forgive her Father. She doesn't know what she is doing... but I think I do"? I honestly believe he is. I'm not suggesting that he's a mind reader who knows every detail but Jesus knows what it is to be human, understands the futility of judging every wrong turn humans make and is concerned, above all else, to help her change.

Everyone who truly understands how people change knows that unless we are led to examine the way our past has shaped us we remain prisoners to it. Likewise, unless we choose to question the presuppositions we grew up believing, together with the assumptions we subsequently chose to adopt as our own, they are likely to remain in place throughout our lives. By focusing on what they saw with their eyes, whilst remaining blind to their own drives and motives, the Pharisees and teachers had become experts in deceiving themselves. Jesus sees what is going on, both within the woman and her accusers, and manages to address both issues with the single response.

Just as with the woman at the well, Jesus' main concern is to treat those in need with the compassion, dignity and respect that are denied them by others. It may be an unusual way of approaching the story to view this woman as someone in need but I am convinced that Jesus knew by instinct many of the insights modern psychology has unearthed for us in more recent times. He knew that humans are driven by a certain set of basic needs and that, when these go unmet our psyche can become damaged and we may find ourselves driven to try and meet them in ways that seem warped or illogical to someone not familiar with our life-story.

Jesus may also have been alert to a fact we have only recently identified which indicates the degree to which those who have already been abused are statistically far more likely to attract further abuse or lead aberrant lives. It is as if there is some kind of hidden signal they emit which suggests to a potential abuser that this damaged person remains unable to differentiate between unhealthy attention and wholesome love.

I recall finding myself dwelling on these issues when someone close to me began questioning their sexual identity. To the person in question the issue they were grappling with was whether or not they were heterosexual or homosexual in orientation. From my vantage point it was clear that there were far deeper questions under the surface. I knew, for example, that my friend's drive to determine his sexual orientation was driven by a need to love and be loved that was being frustrated by his fear of women which had sabotaged a series of relationships. Learning more about my friend's background helped me to see that growing up with no father figure had robbed him of the male role model his female partners were expectant he should adopt, whilst his struggle with an abusive mother had contributed to his deeply ingrained fear of the women he also found himself attracted to. Experimentation with male partners was simply a way of providing my friend with the love he needed without the tensions and confusion that often makes relationships with the opposite sex so colourful. He needed predictability and he needed love.

As I prayed for my friend I began to become aware of an inner voice which told me to suspend my judgement and be there for him, thus repressing the maxim to 'love the sinner and hate the sin' which I had been taught to apply to such situations. The reason the phrase isn't in the Bible is because it is not what Jesus practised, for reasons I have already explored in the previous chapter. Whenever I have attempted to do both at once I have found that hatred of sin overwhelms my love because I'm such an expert in standing in judgement upon others.

Jesus' approach in John 8 was simply to treat the woman with grace and compassion, trusting that the Spirit who is present in every encounter was also bringing inner conviction of sin.[191] No one needs to be told by others they are doing wrong when the Spirit is convicting them and their lives are full of pain and guilt because of their poor choices. What people need is a safe place to examine their drives and the direction their choices are taking them. My friend eventually discovered by himself that his sexual orientation was not at the heart of his dilemma, but I fear this would not

---

191   Jesus, after all, knew this was the Spirit's task: John 16:8.

have been the case if I had made it a defining issue and he had then felt it necessary to defend his wrong belief.

I think I found myself able to sympathise because, like the crowd in John 8, I am aware of my own inconsistencies that sometimes tempt me to act, or feel like acting, in sinful ways. If I had begun with the demands of the law as these Pharisees did, responding in judgement as a way of making me feel better about my own failings, my presence may have been rejected and I would also have reinforced my own buttress against the Spirit who brings true revelation that leads to *my* ongoing repentance. What we all need at times like this are others who are honest enough about their own struggles whilst being living signposts to a more wholesome life. These are the people we will want to let close and are thus best placed to become trustworthy confidants. Jesus was both of these and calls us to allow ourselves to become the same.

Those who would Point the Finger...

Jesus is clearly using this encounter to do something just as loving for the crowd who were so quick to gather in judgement. Once again, Jesus saw the situation as it was and knew that the best gift he could offer those standing in judgement was a dose of humility and self-awareness. It is not difficult to see how the woman's life may have been impacted and how she may also have been bolstered to begin looking for love and acceptance in more wholesome ways. If we stop here, however, we miss the fact that in this story there was more than one person who went away from the encounter with something to think about. If sin is best defined as a consistent refusal to change,[192] and I am kept humble enough to understand that there will always be change that is required of me, the most important truth about my life is not the sin I am currently battling with but the direction my journey of obedience is taking me.

This is well illustrated in a true story told me by a friend. A few years ago the church he then led was applying for significant funding for a community project and came into contact with a woman whose job it was to help community-based organisations write applications to grant making trusts. In the course of a number of conversations the woman in question became interested in the project she was helping to secure funding for and began to attend the church. At the end of a morning service the woman came to

192   This is something I will develop in chapter 11.

my friend with a question: "I have just heard a voice in my head telling me that I needn't spend so much money on clothes and make up because I am already beautiful. The voice told me to give some of that money away. Do you think this may be God?" My friend asked her what she thought and the woman did as she was bidden.

Over the next few weeks her life began to change as she examined her attitudes and priorities and my friend could see that the Spirit of God was at work. Not long after the woman had made several more significant life-choices in the right direction my friend got a distress call. In the course of her job the woman had met another church leader and had begun telling him that she was beginning to journey with God. Somehow the church leader knew or found out that the woman was still living with her partner whilst unmarried and he instantly jumped in with both feet and sought to apply the letter of the law, thus throwing her into turmoil.

As we mused together on the story over a pub lunch a group of leaders with whom I met regularly reflected that if the God who can never forget or excuse the many transgressions against him can treat us as though we had not sinned (a fantastic definition of mercy) whilst showering us with blessings we do not deserve (an even better definition of grace), the only thing that is important in our dealings with others is that we do not get in the way of the next thing he is trying to say to those who are seeking to be his disciples. After all, was the Spirit of God delighted at the progress she was making as he revealed the next steps she should take or was he the bearer of a check-list that currently scored her 1 out of 10 because she had such a long way to go? Our call is to follow Jesus, who seemed to know exactly the right thing to do and say on each occasion precisely because his primary concern was to aid the Holy Spirit in his task of leading people to fullness of life.

For those who have truly sown the principle of journeying with God into the foundation of their lives the only things that become important is the direction our feet are heading and the next step we are about to take. It seems to me that it is as we muse on images like this that it becomes possible to see 'repentance' in the way Paul does when he chooses to call it a gracious gift from the hands of a kind God.[193] Paul is only able to use such an image because of recorded encounters such as the one between Jesus and this adulterous woman.

193   Romans 2:4.

Making Repentance Good News

Compare the verse to which I have just referred with the images that are conjured up in the minds of believers and unbelievers alike if the word 'repent' is used in everyday conversation today. The first images that come to my mind are either a hell-fire and damnation preaching evangelist, expertly tutored in the use of manipulation through guilt or a dour clergyman known more for the practices he prohibits than the fullness of life promised by Jesus. Have I made the distinctions between the Pharisees and Jesus clear enough?

To summarise, I have come to the understanding that everything I do, good and bad, wise and foolish, is done for reasons that make (or once made) some kind of sense to me. Some of my actions are rooted in past habits or experiences. Others are well-tested ways of shielding myself from past events or, more accurately, the messages delivered to me by those events. There are a huge number of memories, events and assumptions that influence the way I respond to people and situations and Jesus is interested in every one of them. His physical encounters with flesh and blood humans indicate to me that Jesus is as concerned to straighten the tangled mess that is under the surface of my life as he is with the misdemeanours that are the fruit.

Dealing with sin remains important since, until we learn to overcome the power of our sinful flesh, we find ourselves shaped by forces other than the gospel even after entering the Christian life. Discipleship must therefore be understood as a process of personal formation through which we are led to examine the hidden roots and foundations that have made us what we are so that we can then be taught to test everything under the watchful eye of the Spirit, finding healing where we need it whilst learning to embrace everything that will play its part in forming us into more Christ-like disciples.[194]

Loving God more than Religion

Over the last month I have spent time marking a set of essays on spiritual development. One of the models being analysed was the following

---

194   Galatians 4:19.

four-stage journey to maturity suggested by Scott Peck.[195]

1. Chaotic/Anti-social – people with absent spirituality and are totally unprincipled.

2. Formal/Institutional – people dependant on an institution for their governance and who rely on 'form' as their liberation.

3. Sceptic/Individual – truth seekers, deeply involved in society but not necessarily religious.

4. Mystical/Communal – people who see interconnectedness and also speak in terms of paradox. They are resigned to not being able to solve every mystery and are comfortable with the fact.

After having read dozens of essays I had a revelation: those students who struggled most with the insights of Peck and others like him were invariably those who were, themselves, at stage two. They seemed bound by the assumption that unless a model could be shown to be 'Christian' it could not in any sense be true. Their definition of 'Christian', however, was that a bible text needed to be found to support every minor insight.

The Pharisees were also stuck at this stage. For them, their version of religion defined all aspects of reality. People who dared to go beyond the boundaries of doctrinal safety were therefore beyond the pale. When people followed Jesus without being able to verify every detail about their Rabbi (stage three) they were mocked for their foolishness. When the Rabbi chose to answer straight questions with woolly answers we call parables (stage four) he had to be exposed as a fraud and done away with using whatever means were necessary.

In his excellent book *Addiction and Grace*, Gerald May asserts his belief that the love of God

draws us toward itself by means of our own deepest desires...
Working against it is the powerful force of addiction.
*Psychologically, addiction **uses up** desire...We succumb because*
the energy of our desire becomes attached, nailed, to specific
*behaviours, objects, or people. **Attachment**, then, is the process*

....

195   M. Scott Peck - *Further Along the Road Less Traveled: The Unending Journey*
toward Spiritual Growth (New York: Touchstone, 1993), 105-109.

that enslaves desire.[196]

When Jesus calls us to love God and each other as we do ourselves he is calling us away from religions that encourage attachments to themselves. Instead we are invited to journey towards a God who is the one those desires were created for. Bernard of Clairvaux wisely reminds us that even a journey towards divine love has stages, each one more mature than the last. Initially each of us love ourselves for our own sake and therefore love God merely for our own good. As such love matures we begin to love God for God's sake, eventually loving ourselves for the sake of God.[197]

I am going to develop some of these themes in the next chapter but at this point I wonder if it may be helpful to reflect upon whether religious certainty, whether it be doctrinal or institutional, can ever lead us into the kind of truth Jesus describes. In recent years I have begun to wonder whether truth is as much about an experience as about believing facts. If Jesus *is* the truth, I am never going to live in the truth until I am living fully in him. I think this may be the reason Paul loved to use the phrase '*In Christ*' to describe the present state in which Christ-followers exist. If the kind of religion Jesus opposed happens when humans feel the need to defend truths they are not experiencing, the call on all who would follow Christ is surely to love God and others with as much honesty and humility as we can muster, in faith that this will be the means by which we know more of the truth that sets us free. Bring it on.

....

196   Gerald G. May - *Addiction and Grace: Love and Spirituality in the Healing of Addictions* (New York: HarperCollins, 1991), 12-13.

197   See G. R. Evans trans, *Bernard of Clairvaux: Selected Works, The Classics of Western Spirituality* (Mahwah, NJ: Paulist Press, 1987).

CHAPTER 8
Disciplehip and Mission in a Post-Christian Context

The final 36 hours of 2011 felt hugely significant to me. I had completed the first draft of the previous chapter just before Christmas and was content to relax with the family and read a few books. Over that relatively short period I read or heard the following five snippets:

➤ **Rival Clerics In Brawl At Jesus' Birthplace**
A fight has broken out at the church built on the spot where Jesus is said to have been born. Palestinian police stormed the basilica of the Nativity in Bethlehem after rival groups of Orthodox and Armenian clerics clashed in a row over the boundaries of their respective ancient jurisdictions inside the church.

Armed with brooms, around 100 priests and monks came to blows during the cleaning of the church in preparation for Orthodox Christmas celebrations. The former Palestinian minister of tourism and head of the Palestinian forces in Bethlehem were slightly injured. Administration of the church is shared by Catholic, Orthodox, and Armenian Apostolic clerics. The relationship between these groups has often been difficult, and there have been similar scuffles in previous years over jurisdiction.[198]

> It's important to understand some of the differences between the faith groups, because a lot of them are profound and serious. An obvious one, with special relevance if you live in Northern Ireland, would be Protestants versus Catholics. Protestants and Catholics believe very different things. Different entirely; their whole approach is world apart and diametrically opposed. Hence the 'troubles'. Protestants believe that God sent his only son, our lord Jesus Christ, down to earth to die for our sins and that the only way to the Father is through the Son. Whereas Catholics believe something very different. They believe that God sent his only son, our lord Jesus Christ, down to earth to die for our sins. And that the only way to the Father is through the Son **via a man in a hat**.... You see, different entirely. There's no way these two groups could ever share an understanding and so even the most committed pacifist observers can see how it would become important for them to spend decades killing each other and destroying other people's lives in the interim...

If you want to know whose God is best – follow the money. If you want to know who will fight hardest for their God – follow the money. If you want to understand how religion has taken hold to such an extent and with such a merciless grip on so many of us – follow the money. If you want to know which religion does the most for the poor and needy – follow the money. Religion is big business. A lot is at stake. Ever so much more than the souls of the faithful, which are by comparison easy to account for. It's roughly one each and they divide into two sorting trays. Inbox for Heaven, Outbox for Hell. Stick a few quid in the collection plate and you're in the inbox. Easy.[199]

> I have problems with a religion which says that faith in itself is enough for a ticket to heaven. In other words, that the ideal is your ability to manipulate your own common sense to accept something your intellect rejects. It's the same model of intellectual submission that dictatorships have used throughout time, the

---

198   Viewed on the Sky News web site on 30th December 2011.

199   Marcus Brigstocke – *God Collar* (London: Bantam Press, 2011), 178, 180.

concept of a higher reasoning without any obligation to discharge the burden of proof.[200]

> *I think the thousands of women burnt at the stake or hung or drowned being falsely accused of witchcraft in the name of Christ would vehemently disagree that "Christianity .....was actually deeply reverential towards women". And in more modern times the thousands of babies taken from their mother's [sic] (and who, up until the 1950's [sic]) could be incarcerated in institutions for the 'sin' of having children out of marriage. just 2 examples - of many - where Christianity have [sic] oppressed women.[201]*

> *My name's Alan Moore, and I make a living by making up stories about things that have never actually happened. When it comes to my spiritual beliefs that's perhaps why I worship a second-century human-headed snake god called Glycon who was exposed as a ventriloquist's dummy almost two thousand years ago. Famed throughout the Roman Empire, Glycon was the creation of an entrepreneur known as Alexander the False Prophet, which is a terrible name to go into business under. A live, tame, boa constrictor provided the puppet's body, while its artificial head had heavy lidded eyes and long blond hair. In many ways Glycon looked a bit like Paris Hilton but perhaps more likeable and more biologically credible.*

> *Looks aside, I'm interested in the snake god purely as a symbol. Indeed, one of humanities' oldest symbols, which can stand for wisdom, for healing, or, according to ethno-botanist Jeremy Narby, for our spiralling and snake-like DNA itself. But I am also interested in having a god who is demonstrably a ventriloquist dummy. After all, isn't this the way we use most of our deities? We can look through various of our sacred books and, by choosing one ambiguous passage or one interpretation over another we can pretty much get our gods to justify our own current agendas. We can make them say what we want them to say. The big advantage of worshipping an actual glove puppet of course is that, if things*

---

200   Jo Nesbo – *The Redeemer* (London: Vintage, 2009), 156.

201   Part of a discussion within an 87-member 'secret' group on Facebook, 30th December 2011.

start to get unruly or out of hand, you can always put them gack in the gox. And you know, it doesn't matter if they don't want to go gack in the gox, they have to go gack in the gox.[202]

OK, so I was consuming more media than usual during that 36 hour period but, apart from Brigstocke's book, I wasn't seeking out critics of religion. In the case of the *Facebook* conversation I was the moderating voice. A normally quiet site where thalidomide survivors occasionally post questions relating to their disability came alive with 81 posts in a single day as soon as the topic of religion reared its head.

This juxtaposition of critiques felt significant in the light of all I had just written on Jesus and religion. So much so that this entire chapter would not have been written without them. Everything we have studied so far demonstrates that God's primary concern is that people of faith live and act in ways that cause others to ask questions about the *positive* quality of their lives,[203] yet each of the snippets seem to indicate that many of those who label themselves 'Christian' are doing more harm than good. Sure, the last four contain the odd fact or interpretation that is somewhat open to debate, but do any of them appear completely wide of the mark?

They are also symptomatic of dozens of conversations I have had with people who are sick and tired of the religion they have encountered in a wide variety of churches and yet remain open to persuasion because they are also discontented with the direction of their lives. Such people will often talk about Jesus at length. They know there is more and they are often seeking something that will help them to change but they don't encounter people in churches who are living any differently to themselves.

Brian McLaren is correct in his observation:

> *The Christian religion is very often part of the problem instead of part of the solution in our world. Its as if the message that Jesus intended as a revolutionary message to change the world gets domesticated and just becomes a kind of religious chaplaincy*

---

202   Broadcast on the Today Programme, BBC Radio 4, 31st December 2011. Guest editor Stewart Lee wasn't keen to suggest a guest for the Thought for the Day slot but instead asked Alan Moore to provide an alternative.

203   John 17:20-21; 1 Peter 3:1, 15.

that keeps the world going as it is.[204]

In fact, it is often worse than that. Just as in Jesus day, there are a variety of reasons why many in our world often consider it "a moral decision to be an atheist rather than believe in that kind of God"[205]

I have a feeling that all the commentators above would agree with Wendell Berry:

> *Especially among Christians in positions of wealth and power, the idea of reading the Gospels and keeping Jesus' commandments as stated therein has been replaced by a curious process of logic. According to this process, people first declare themselves to be followers of Christ, and then they assume that whatever they say or do merits the adjective "Christian".*[206]

People are looking for something to believe in that will transform the way they live but all too often find an interloper has taken the place of the new life Jesus taught his followers to live.

An Oak Tree

I need to explain what I mean by the last sentence and will do so by making reference to a clever art installation I recently viewed at Tate Britain. *An Oak Tree* consists of an ordinary glass of water placed on a small glass shelf of the type normally found in a bathroom. The shelf is attached to the wall about 10 feet from the ground. Michael Craig-Martin composed the following series of questions and answers to accompany the objects and displayed them in a picture frame hung on the wall below and to the left of the shelf and glass:

> **Q. To begin with, could you describe this work?**
> *A. Yes, of course. What I've done is change a glass of water into a full-grown oak tree without altering the accidents of the glass of water.*

204   Brian McLaren - Video clip entitled "Domesticated Jesus".

205   Brian McLaren – Video clip entitled "Atheist".

206   Wendell Berry – *Blessed are the Peacemakers: Christ's Teachings of Love, Compassion and Forgiveness* (Washington: Counterpoint, 2005).

Q. The accidents?
A. Yes. The colour, feel, weight, size ...

Q. Do you mean that the glass of water is a symbol of an oak tree?
A. No. It's not a symbol. I've changed the physical substance of the glass of water into that of an oak tree.

Q. It looks like a glass of water.
A. Of course it does. I didn't change its appearance. But it's not a glass of water, it's an oak tree.

Q. Can you prove what you've claimed to have done?
A. Well, yes and no. I claim to have maintained the physical form of the glass of water and, as you can see, I have. However, as one normally looks for evidence of physical change in terms of altered form, no such proof exists.

Q. Haven't you simply called this glass of water an oak tree?
A. Absolutely not. It is not a glass of water anymore. I have changed its actual substance. It would no longer be accurate to call it a glass of water. One could call it anything one wished but that would not alter the fact that it is an oak tree.

Q. Isn't this just a case of the emperor's new clothes?
A. No. With the emperor's new clothes people claimed to see something that wasn't there because they felt they should. I would be very surprised if anyone told me they saw an oak tree.

Q. Was it difficult to effect the change?
A. No effort at all. But it took me years of work before I realised I could do it.

Q. When precisely did the glass of water become an oak tree?
A. When I put the water in the glass.

Q. Does this happen every time you fill a glass with water?

A. No, of course not. Only when I intend to change it into an oak tree.

Q. Then intention causes the change?
A. I would say it precipitates the change.

Q. You don't know how you do it?
A. It contradicts what I feel I know about cause and effect.

Q. It seems to me that you are claiming to have worked a miracle. Isn't that the case?
A. I'm flattered that you think so.

Q. But aren't you the only person who can do something like this?
A. How could I know?

Q. Could you teach others to do it?
A. No, it's not something one can teach.

Q. Do you consider that changing the glass of water into an oak tree constitutes an art work?
A. Yes.

Q. What precisely is the art work? The glass of water?
A. There is no glass of water anymore.

Q. The process of change?
A. There is no process involved in the change.

Q. The oak tree?
A. Yes. The oak tree.

Q. But the oak tree only exists in the mind.
A. No. The actual oak tree is physically present but in the form of the glass of water. As the glass of water was a particular glass of water, the oak tree is also a particular oak tree. To conceive the category 'oak tree' or to picture a particular oak tree is not to understand and experience what appears to be a glass of water

as an oak tree. Just as it is imperceivable it also inconceivable.

Q. Did the particular oak tree exist somewhere else before it took the form of a glass of water?
A. No. This particular oak tree did not exist previously. I should also point out that it does not and will not ever have any other form than that of a glass of water.

Q. How long will it continue to be an oak tree?
A. Until I change it.[207]

It did not take me long to realise that *An Oak Tree* was unusually and unexpectedly profound. As I stood and reflected on the installation it began to feel that I was viewing a perfect illustration of the church in the UK as seen by a sympathetic but unconvinced onlooker. Christians may make bold claims about God's ability to produce kinder people, but there is sometimes little discernible evidence. Add to this a raft of theological statements that are believed implicitly by Christians but don't seem to make much difference to the way they live their lives. To an outsider, that which seems ethereal and cannot be verified except by faith is next to useless unless it makes some kind of discernible difference.

On returning home I found the Tate web site and was not surprised to discover that *An Oak Tree* is based on the concept of transubstantiation which is described thus:

> *the notion central to the Catholic faith in which it is believed that bread and wine are converted into the body and blood of Christ while retaining their appearances of bread and wine. The ability to believe that an object is something other than its physical appearance indicates requires a transformative vision. This type of seeing (and knowing) is at the heart of conceptual thinking processes, by which intellectual and emotional values are conferred on images and objects.*[208]

John tells of Jesus coming to his people but they could not recognise him. The religion of Israel had long ceased to concern itself with the larger

---

207   www.mat.upm.es/~jcm/craig-martin--an-oak-tree.html

208   www.tate.org.uk.

purposes of God and had become a self-maintaining institution. The Jews were convinced of their status as People of the Covenant but had wrongly assumed that God's covenant with them was the whole story. Their own faithfulness to the letter of the law had become their sole preoccupation and Jesus was attempting to show *them* that this approach inevitably undermined its spirit and thus frustrated its purpose. Tragically, God's covenant people opposed him to such a degree that the author of the law and the covenant found himself nailed to a cross.

It is my view that the church has largely done the same thing with the gospel. After allowing itself to be re-defined over centuries of Christendom, the established church has become viewed by wider society as a socialising force by which people become passive, conservative and nice and the Christian church in general is seen as a refuge for the weak-minded. Many churches persist with forms and structures that are oriented around Temple-style models which ordain religious professionals to deliver a range of spiritual services to largely passive consumers. The most common response to our attempts to persuade others of the truth of the gospel therefore begins "that's great if it works for you...", demonstrating that the vast majority view our beliefs simply as a life-style choice they do not wish to adopt. In a recent article on the 2012 budget, John Rentoul described the decision to cut the top tax band from 50 to 45 pence as "a matter of almost theological belief. It is not well supported by the evidence".[209] Rentoul's readers know what he means because most of them also associate theology with abstraction and irrelevance. Only in such a closed system can 'faith' be defined as willingness to believe superfluous doctrines like transubstantiation in preference over a willingness to follow the person of Jesus. The verb 'faith' has thus, sadly, become a worthless noun in the understanding of the British population.

Such churches may succeed in winning converts to their beliefs but are not well-placed to make disciples; and disciples are what are necessary if we are to persuade confused and spiritually hungry people that life can be a great deal more real if it is lived as a follower of Christ. The church will always have a problem whenever we begin by trying to convince others of the correctness of our doctrines because the theology of God being

---

209   John Rentoul - *"What on earth was Osborne thinking?"* in The Independent on Sunday. 25th March 2012, p 42.

crucified on a cross is not, in itself, an attractive proposition.[210] It is, however, an inescapable and glorious conclusion where there is persuasive evidence of the character of Christ being formed in the lives of his followers and this requires us to shift our thinking from producing converts to making disciples.

Convert or Disciple?

In my early years as a Christian I recall feeling distinctly short-changed by the fact that I didn't possess a dramatic conversion experience. Dramatic and powerful testimonies are indeed things to be welcomed and marvelled at but we also need to take great care not to place too great an emphasis upon them. As Derren Brown has recently demonstrated, it is relatively easy to provoke emotions that may also accompany a true conversion experience without any encounter with God having occurred.[211]

> *Revivalism has always assumed that only its own type of religious experience can be perfect; you must first be nailed to the cross of natural despair and agony, and then in the twinkling of an eye be miraculously released... Candidates for conversion at revivals are,... when tested by hypnotism, proved to belong to a subclass which [may be called] 'spontaneous,' that is, fertile in self-suggestions, as distinguished from a passive subclass, to which most of the subjects of striking transformation belong.[212]*

James insists that this observation does nothing to diminish the significance of sudden conversions. We simply need to be aware that certain personalities will be more prone to them and, as I have witnessed myself, will be liable to slide back with equal force unless supported and discipled. For people with different temperaments

---

210   For example: 1 Corinthians 2:6-10.

211   See Derren Brown - The Specials: Fear and Faith, Available on 4OD, courtesy of Channel 4 Television. Brown induces a powerful 'conversion' experience in the life of Natalie, an avowed atheist with no intention of adopting any kind of religious faith. In an earlier programme entitled "Messiah" Brown reproduced phenomena associated with certain charismatic gatherings, demonstrating how it is possible to manipulate suggestible individuals to experience powerful feelings that replicate some of the features of revivalist meetings. We will consider these issues further in Chapter Ten.

212   William James – *The Varieties of Religious Experience*, 240-1.

conversion must be gradual if it occur, and must resemble any simple growth into new habits... The real witness of the spirit to the second birth is found only in the disposition of the genuine child of God, the permanently patient heart, the love of self eradicated.[213]

All true conversions which lead to a transformed lifestyle are the result of a work of the Holy Spirit.[214] We must be clear, however, that Christians are not being born anew into a different camp or tribe (a static image) but into the distinctly new "lifestyle of making Jesus Lord" we met in chapter two. Every convert is called to a lifetime of following Jesus and this involves looking ahead in faith, not backwards in shock or amazement at what they used to be.

Many Christians with the mindset of a convert will tend to develop a negative, even hostile, opinion of the society that tolerated their previous lifestyle, especially if the circumstances of their conversion were dramatic. Their view of evangelism will look more like a 'rescue and retreat' raiding party and they will often find it difficult to engage in any form of long-term social outreach. The 'lost' will tend to view these converts as narrow-minded, fearful and judgemental even if, as in the abortion clinic news story quoted below, their motivations are loving and well-intentioned.

Christians who have the attitude of a disciple may find themselves struggling to see how God is already present within the communities they came from but, as their spiritual eyes adjust to the variety of shades of grey all around them, they learn to discern his presence. Not-yet-Christians will view them as strange beings with nonsensical, upside-down values but they will find themselves attracted to the kind of community that these disciples create. Some of them may even ask questions about what makes these disciples of Jesus think and act as they do.

Covenant or Kingdom, or both?

Surely the real reason for the frustration felt by many Christians is that a lot of the time we ourselves wonder whether the gospel is as efficacious as we claim to believe. Those who see Jesus' message simply as a call to

....

213   Ibid. p 242, 238.

214   John 16:8.

believe in him so they can go to heaven when they die will not experience such angst since their hopes and expectations are largely placed in events that are still to come. It is those of us who believe the Kingdom of God can and should be experienced now who suffer the deepest yearnings and struggles. I can recall times when I felt that the church I led was growing on the basis of promises I was not confident we could deliver and fed by second-hand stories of breakthroughs in other places which we did not know how to replicate. As I sought to unravel the source of my dis-ease I found the Covenant – Kingdom distinction we have already described very helpful.[215]

It felt as if the church I led was content, in much the same way as the teachers and Pharisees of Jesus' day, to live within in a safe theology of the covenant whilst I wanted us to experience the challenge of living in the tension between the Covenant and Kingdom triangles. We sang songs which declared our belief in a full range of Kingdom-related manifestations of the gospel but were experiencing few of them. Every word I sang seemed to mock me. I was teaching a distinctly Kingdom-focused theology which was attracting new converts but I knew we were not prepared to make the radical shifts required to inhabit both triangles and I therefore felt my own words to be empty.

I believe this is a common problem in churches where the majority of the congregation see themselves as converts and combine this with a clergy-laity or professional-pew filler mental divide. Yet, since the truth can only be known when it is lived, every Christian must be taught to embody that truth in daily life if their claim to believe it is to be viewed as authentic. Without a shift into the Kingdom triangle, groups of Christians will forever feel the need of a kind and loving pastor to feed the milk of the gospel to them week by week in order to help them maintain their largely passive faith. Such churches may console themselves with testimonies of converts won but have little understanding of how to follow Jesus by way of the Spirit.

When Judaism and Christianity became more concerned about covenant-keeping than covenant-living they both began placing the majority of their attention upon themselves rather than the unbelievers they were called to save. In the case of Israel, on returning from their captivity in Babylon the Jews were rightfully and understandably concerned that they would never again find themselves punished for their unfaithfulness to the

215   See chapter 5.

Torah. In addition to reading the scriptures in public places, Ezra began the school of the *Sopherim* (the Scribes) whose function it was to explain the 613 laws of Moses in order to help the people both understand and obey them. After Ezra's death it was a later generation of *Sopherim* who devised the fence laws or oral Torah we have already encountered. This was known as *Pilpul* logic (*pilpul* means pepper, pepper being stimulating to the taste). Let us consider an example of the way man-made traditions invariably distort the law of Moses.

At the time the Torah was given there existed a Canaanite fertility ritual during which a kid was boiled in its mother's milk which was then sprinkled on the fields. This explains the Mosaic command that God's people should not defile themselves by adopting similar worship rituals.[216] With the passage of time *Pilpul* logic lost sight of the context in which the law was given and the reason God was so determined to bless his people. The *Sopherim* reasoned that, since there is always the possibility that a cup of goat's milk could be from the mother of the goat whose meat you have just eaten, meat and milk could conceivably mix and be heated in the stomach thus breaking the Mosaic law. Therefore, Jews who wanted to be certain they were keeping the law were required not to eat meat and dairy produce at the same meal. Humans being what they are, this logic was further extended to not eating meat and dairy foods from the same plate or even at the same table. This explains an anti-religion story my atheist father loves to tell about his time in the airlines when waiters at the Tel Aviv hotel that served *British Airways* staff would rudely insist that a whole table of diners be moved to a new table in the middle of the meal, without any kind of explanation, if both dairy products and meat had been ordered together.[217] [218]

Incredibly, to one Sabbath commandment were added some

------

216   Exodus 23:19.

217   All the details above can be found in the Tractate Shabbat.

218   Just the other day I was reminded that this kind of thinking is still prevalent within some branches of Judaism as I ate a meal in one of those gastro-pubs that decorates its walls with bookshelves. Next to me was a volume entitled *Shabbat and the Modern Kitchen* by Rabbi L. Halpern. In it were chapters debating whether hot metal should be considered as 'fire' and whether gas and electric were 'fire-related heat', all with the intention of advising the 20th century chef how to avoid breaking Jewish law on the Sabbath.

*1500 fence laws... Later developments took a rather different, and sinister, turn. The **Sopherim** kept it very clear in their minds that these fence laws were man-made and not in any way inspired by God... But a later generation of rabbis came along called the **Tannaim** who felt that the hedge erected by the **Sopherim** had too many holes in it. They [also] changed the underlying principle of operation... The first set of fence laws... came to be considered as being as binding and authoritative as the Law of Moses itself. In AD200 Rabbi Judah Hanasi compiled the existing fence laws and teachings into a document called the **Mishna**. A commentary on the **Mishna** called the **Gemara** was eventually added with the entire compilation becoming known as the **Talmud**, every orthodox Jew's final authority.*[219]

I do not mean to ridicule righteous attempts to live lives that are pleasing to God, nor to suggest that there is not a place for straightforward obedience to the law. As A. J. Jacobs discovers in his brilliant, and very funny, book *The Year of Living Biblically*,[220] the willingness to submit to wisdom does deliver some surprising benefits. Jesus walked a similar tightrope when he opposed the Scribes and the Pharisees and looked to them as if he was relativising many of the cherished symbols of ethnic separation taught by his Father.[221] The reason he did so was that it was the *Sopherim*, Scribes and Pharisees who set in motion the processes which turned God's missionary people into an inward-looking religion which today struggles even to accept the possibility of converts from other cultures. The degree to which the church sees itself as synonymous with the Kingdom, and conforming to the norms of a Christendom-formed society to be an acceptable alternative to the transforming power of the Holy Spirit, is the degree to which the Gospel of Christ is equally compromised.

Those are harsh words that I wish I could soften. I can't do so because of the many good people I have met, and already referred to, who are looking for what Christ offers but are not finding life-changing practices taught in Christian churches. Instead they often encounter strange, world-excluding, communities of faith whose sub-cultures seem to be divorced

---

219   Beresford Job – *Biblical Church*, 23-25.

220   A. J. Jacobs - *The Year of Living Biblically* (London: Arrow Books, 2009).

221   N.T. Wright – *The Challenge of Jesus* (London: SPCK, 2000), 38.

from everyday reality.

Some of my friends comment that it seems to them that the only thing Christians are confident they can offer the world is frustrated critique, in much the same manner as the Pharisees did in Jesus' day. This is a symptom of the ghetto mentality described above. To my eyes, Michael Craig-Martin is parodying the way some Christians have become better known for blaming the world for being unable to see the truth than they are for living Christ-like lives within it:

> I considered that in **An Oak Tree** I had de-constructed the work of art in such a way as to reveal its single basic and essential element, belief that is the confident faith of the artist in his capacity to speak and the willing faith of the viewer in accepting what he has to say. In other words belief underlies our whole experience of art: it accounts for why some people are artists and others are not, why some people dismiss works of art others highly praise, and why something we know to be great does not always move us.[222]

Christians with a covenant-only mentality will tend to see society as persecuting them, often mocking their way of life. They will feel protective of their traditions and rights, maybe even crying 'foul' if their preference for wearing a cross around their neck or praying at work is challenged. They will insist that their voice is heard, will try and ensure their views on a range of moral issues are bolstered by the laws of the land and may join other Christians in pleading that God send Revival, since without it the mission of God seems to be doomed.

Christian disciples know that they are sojourners in a world that will never understand them until they too are 'born again'. They seek to uphold the rights of the poor and the marginalised, knowing that the Kingdom of God includes such as these. They too long for God to intervene, via Revival if he wishes, but know that in the meantime he is present in and through their daily acts of grace and mercy.

....

222   Dorothy Walker - *Michael Craig-Martin: Landscapes* (Dublin: Douglas Hyde Gallery, 2001), 20.

For or Against?

On the radio this morning there was a piece on *40 Days for Life*, a vigil during which a group of Christians are maintaining a presence outside abortion clinics in order to "provide a solution to the 'crisis' of abortion."[223] Declaring their intention "to show love", campaign members have been handing out leaflets and trying to dissuade women from visiting the clinic. The chief executive of the British Pregnancy Advisory Service was quoted as saying "they should think really carefully about whether what they are doing is really Christian".

I am not calling the motivation of the campaigners into doubt or commenting on the issue of abortion in today's society when I find myself wondering whether it is possible to 'show love' in such ways. Yet, as I have already said above, the church feels it is part of its duty to campaign on a number of moral issues, often taking the 'conservative' or 'traditionalist' position and campaigning against the behaviour and choices of people who are not as we'd wish them to be.

The Scribes and Pharisees were passionate in their desire for God to send the promised Messiah and rescue the nation. They had become convinced God would not keep his promise until Israel cleaned up her act, hence their uncompromising demand that everyone adhere to every article of the Law which, in turn, became the very reason they failed to recognise Jesus as the one they were waiting for.

David Instone-Brewer, Senior Research Fellow in Rabbinics and the New Testament at Cambridge University, explains how careful study of the Dead Sea scrolls reveals a great deal about practices that had become normal within Judaism at around the time of Jesus.[224] The manuals of the Qumran community indicate that they operated a strict policy of ejecting sinners from amongst them:

> *If a man sins against the law, and one person alone sees him, he should denounce and reproach him before the Inspector. The Inspector writes it down in case he commits that sin again in the presence of only one person who denounces him to the*

---

223   BBC Today Programme website. Accessed on 15th March 2012.

224   Dr Instone-Brewer was speaking at the Cambridge School of Theology on 16th October 2011.

Inspector. If he does repeat it and is spotted by one person alone, his judgement is complete, and he is excluded from sharing the pure food. However, when there are two separate people who witness different incidents, the man is only excluded if they are trustworthy, and they denounced him before the Inspector on the same day they saw him.[225]

One the face of it, this seems to be the same system Jesus taught his disciples.[226] But there are differences, and it is the differences that are important. The first is that Jesus refuses to accept condemnation from a single witness. The Old Testament instructed that discipline could only be applied if a sinful act was witnessed by two trustworthy witnesses. The problem with sin, of course, is that it tends to be committed in private. The likelihood of two witnesses being present was therefore small and sin was therefore going unpunished. The Qumran community demonstrated its keenness to spot sinners and exclude them by accepting corroborating testimony from two single witnesses on different occasions. To this end, an inspector was appointed to keep an up to date record of each persons' sins, thus making it possible to tie two 'sightings' together.

This demonstrates the degree to which Jesus preferred to keep sinners (like Judas) in the fold, in the hope that they may be reformed by sharing in the activities of the redeemed community. His desire is made explicit in the passage as Jesus declares "if they listen to you, you have won them over." Jesus is less concerned about maintaining purity through exclusion as with helping sinners to reform. Christian discipleship is therefore a higher priority to him than community discipline.

There has been a lot of talk in circles I frequent about the need to rethink the way we welcome and include non-Christians in our church communities. The tendency for newcomers to be allowed to feel they belong only if they already believe and behave has been called into question. A Jesus-style welcome must put the offer of a place of belonging before anything else. Godly behaviour, after all, is not possible without the indwelling Holy Spirit who comes to us as we believe. Believing rarely happens in a vacuum and is far more likely to be provoked by interaction with others who are putting their faith into practice.

225   *Damascus Document* 9.16-24.

226   Matthew 18:15-17.

The church I led took this one step further when we decided to open all our discernment and decision-making meetings to non-members. This meant that, theoretically at least, some of these may be non-believers. It was made clear that decisions would be made only be those who had expressed a commitment to Christ and were playing a full role in the life of the fellowship but we made a point of inviting everyone along in the expectation that it would help them become more aware of our values and the meaning of our faith.

We also changed our language and practice when it came to church membership. Out went the visits of a leader and a member to everyone who expressed an interest in membership and an acceptance vote at the following church members meeting. Instead we began to talk of partnership in God's mission and we adopted the practice of signing an annual covenant. Just after Easter each year everyone who was part of our worshipping community was invited to consider whether or not they were In Christ and wanted to follow him by playing their part in his mission through the church for the next year. In the early years we spent time in the previous months praying together about what our priorities for the coming year should be.

To my mind this change in emphasis played its part in stimulating some creative initiatives we called 'Grace Projects'. We began devising a series of random acts of kindness, each accompanied by a jargon-free reminder that God's love was unmerited and free. These helped us to open our hearts to the community around us and opened the door for others in the church who could envisage larger and more long-term projects. It is the experience of many missionally-minded churches that, as they focused their attention upon forming Kingdom-focused disciples, thus equipping them to love and serve the lost, they also found themselves tapping into a huge reserve of joy and adventure that is available to all who make plans to co-operate with Jesus.

As I confessed at the beginning of this chapter, the last 6000 words weren't part of my original plan. They just happened. It is true to say that this has been both the easiest and hardest chapter to write. Easiest in that it flowed from somewhere deep within me. Hardest because I have had to edit it so many times, weeding out the raw parts, softening my many disappointments about the way the religion supposedly founded by Jesus so often looks nothing like him - I say 'supposedly' because I really don't think Jesus came to found a new religion at all. He began by attempting to awake what we know of as Judaism but the Father still calls his 'chosen people'.

As I write this I am sitting in a small cafe in Madrid. After having ordered a glass of red house wine I have been brought half a bottle with a nod and a wink by the head waiter. The waitress who has served me my food has done so with such diligence and care that her attentiveness has made me feel special. Both the wine and the attention took me right back to Cana in Galilee and to Simon Peter's house. Earlier in the day I passed a Priest in the street whose face looked as if he was bearing the weight of the world on his shoulders. No judgement is intended here - we all have bad days - but I'm finding myself reflecting on how the pressures of running a church sometimes turned me into a grumpy workaholic.

How and why was Jesus so different and how can I learn from him? I am convinced that the key is that he only ever did what he saw his Father doing. There is such a difference between doing what you are told to and joining in with what someone else is already doing. The elder brother in the Parable of the Extravagant Father always did what he was told, and probably more besides, but there was no honour towards his father or joy in his service.

There's a maxim expressed fairly frequently by the folks I work with that, whereas Jesus invited his followers to live a life that was simple to understand but profound and costly in the living, we have invented a Christianity that is complex to understand and yet easy to live. We believe that when Jesus took on human flesh he did so, not just in order to identify with us or bear our sins (the theological answers), but to show us how life is best lived, even in what we might believe are minor details. I have tried to describe what I believe some of the keys to living a life that is less religious but more faithful might be and before we end this chapter I must explore one final LifeShape.

Everybody Involved

At its heart, much of the church knows that it is exhibiting to the world a pale shadow of what it could and should be. If churches are to recover their vitality I am convinced that they need to allow themselves to be reformed by the gospel they claim to believe. The news today has been full of talk about the tensions and divisions within the Anglican communion following the announcement of the resignation of Rowan Williams from the post of Archbishop of Canterbury. The popular view is that Williams' natural talents have been overshadowed by the need to hold the church together during a decade of wrangling over sexuality and women. My mind was drawn to the passage referred to earlier in this chapter:

> My prayer is not for [the Disciples] alone. I pray also for those who will believe in me through their message, that all of them may be one, Father, just as you are in me and I am in you. May they also be in us so that the world may believe that you have sent me. I have given them the glory that you gave me, that they may be one as we are one - I in them and you in me - so that they may be brought to complete unity. Then the world will know that you sent me and have loved them even as you have loved me.[227]

The assumption is often made that unity within the body of Christ will be achieved by Christians respecting each other's differing opinions on non-core doctrines and worship preferences. I do not doubt that some of these questions are important but we must never forget that Paul's letter to the Ephesians suggests that the key marker of already-bestowed unity is our ability to minister to the world alongside each other, and using the full range of gifts made available to the body.[228] Unity is the result of different individuals with differing gifts, abilities and outlooks combining their differences in order to serve those Christ loves but do not yet know it. "Then", says Paul, "we will no longer [act] like children... Instead, speaking the truth in love, we will grow to become in every respect the mature body of him who is the head, that is, Christ."

At first sight, the LifeShape known as The Pentagon seems nothing new. The subject of Ephesians 4 Ministries has spawned church networks, conferences and numerous books and articles. Its genius is its unusual starting premise:

> It has been a traditional teaching that the fivefold ministries in this passage are five roles for leaders in the church. But that is not what the verse says. "To each one" refers to every member of the church, not just leaders. What the bible says is that each one of us

....

227   John 17:20-23.

228   Ephesians 4:11-16.

has received a portion of grace in one of five roles. That grace has come to us in the form of a call to be one of five types of people.[229]

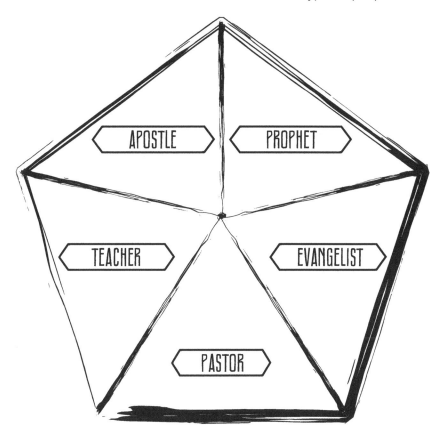

Everyone has been given a ministry gift that leads to a ministry role.[230] I've not got space here to define the ministry gifts or explain how Breen and Cockram differentiate between 'base' and 'phase' ministries or Pioneers and Settlers. I simply add my own testimony of the way groups of leaders I have worked with have been transformed in their thinking by engaging with this passage of scripture through the lens of the Pentagon. The recognition that Christians have no need to establish unity but are already one in Christ is also profound. Our call is to maintain our unity and this is best done as we serve the lost together. This is why Paul says that we are all intended

229   Mike Breen and Steve Cockram – *Building a Discipling Culture*, 98-99.

230   Breen and Cockram explain the differences between Spiritual Gifts and Ministry Gifts in chapter 9.

to grow to maturity by bringing our unique gifts and temperaments to teams that would be incomplete without them. The Pentagon is therefore an invaluable tool for converts who want to become missional disciples of Jesus.

This chapter has touched on some profound paradigm shifts that must be embraced if Christian disciples are to help turn the tide of anti-religious sentiment in our nation. I'm not sure that all leaders and churches will be able to make some of these profound changes on their own, which is why there are groups of coaches such as those I work with, who are offering a variety of services to Christian leaders who are beginning to embrace much needed change. 3DM is a community of leaders who have all played a role in building missional communities in the US, the UK and Europe.[231] I trust that as you follow the call of God to form people who are able to engage with his missional heart he will lead to connect with people who have been on the journey for a while and can help you see what next steps you need to take.

---

231   See www.3DMEurope.com and www.3dmeublog.com for more details.

CHAPTER 9
Doing Mission Jesus' Way

At the end of Matthew's Gospel we read:

> *Jesus came to them and said, 'All authority in heaven and on earth has been given to me. Therefore go and make disciples of all nations, baptising them in the name of the Father and of the Son and of the Holy Spirit, and teaching them to obey everything I have commanded you. And surely I am with you always, to the very end of the age.'*[232]

The history of my dealings with this passage is interesting. I well recall that one of the first verses I was urged to memorise as part of a topical memory system I used in the early days of my walk with Christ was the very last sentence: "I will be with you always, even until the end of the world." No mention was made of the context in which the promise was given and I understood it to be simple, straightforward and unconditional. I can also recall that this passage was read by most missionaries who visited our church on furlough and the impression it gave me was that it is only those who are called to go to all peoples who should take notice

---

232   Matthew 28:18-20.

of the instructions. We were doing our bit by praying for and giving to the missionaries who have gone on our behalf.

It was at Bible College that I discovered that the word 'go' should be read, not as a command to the few but as an instruction to everyone: "as you go to all peoples everywhere…". Jesus was therefore preparing his disciples for the time when intense persecution would scatter them across the known world. I understood that I too must take the gospel wherever God took me. Sometime later, as I added a charismatic dimension to my theology, I was pointed toward the fact that I possessed authority which had been given me by Jesus.

In more recent years I began to wonder what 'make people my disciples' meant. Like Rebecca Manley Pippert, "there was part of me that knew that evangelism wasn't something I wanted to do to a dog, let alone my best friend".[233] I had had my fill of manipulative methods of persuading people to 'accept Christ as their personal saviour' and knew that Jesus' call to lost people was more profound than making a 'decision' at the end of a rousing sermon. More recently I hit upon the phrase that blew everything apart: "and teach them to obey everything I have commanded you".

The way I now read these final verses of Matthew's Gospel is that Jesus is instructing the twelve to call others to follow him in the exactly same manner as he had done with them. Disciples should make disciples who can make disciples, who can make disciples…. This call of Jesus was intended to be normative. He is calling us all to a life of discipleship and mission and is suggesting that disciples are only true to their name when they have themselves become disciple-makers. Therefore if I am to call myself a true disciple of Jesus, this is the kind of life I should be living.

Making Disciple-making Disciples

So far we have seen that, outwardly at least, Jesus operated according to a fairly typical Rabbinic model.[234] Yet, by the standards of the day, the men he chose were a distinctly unpromising bunch of individuals.

233   Rebecca Manley Pippert - *Out of the Saltshaker: Evangelism as a Way of Life* (Leicester: IVP, 1980).

234   In Jesus' day the term 'Rabbi' was used to denote respect and did not become an official title until after the destruction of the Temple in AD70.

They were nobodies, with apparently few talents. We don't know much about most of them, which says a lot in itself, and what we do know does not inspire confidence. They included a former Roman collaborator..., a former member of a terrorist group..., and the brothers John and James, who were nicknamed 'Sons of Thunder" because they had considerable problems with anger management! And Judas turned out to be a huge embarrassment to the early church, because the one whom Jesus trusted as a treasurer ended up betraying him for money.[235]

The New Testament accounts of their ongoing fallibility stand in marked contrast to the heroic, and probably apocryphal, stories of Rabbi Hillel's disciples who brought him great honour by inspiring the rescue and rebuilding of Jerusalem following the destruction of the Temple. It was well known that Hillel had himself achieved his honoured status by playing close attention to his master's teaching. It was said that on one occasion he almost froze to death as he sat outside a lecture room in the snow because he couldn't afford the admission fee. Top marks for persistence must go to Rabbi Kahana who was "dragged out from under a bed where he was making notes about how his rabbi was making love to his wife".[236]

In keeping with the practice of the day Jesus had a group of close disciples who were sometimes accompanied by a larger group of followers. Three of these, Peter, James and John, seem to have been his core team. Hillel's closest disciple, Johanan, was known as "a plastered cistern which never spills a drop", meaning that he was known for his ability to regurgitate his master's teaching to perfection. Clearly Johanan had no need to repeat each new teaching more than 100 times in order to remember it word for word which was considered normal practice.[237]

Peter, in contrast, was appointed by Jesus to be the foundation stone of his church, but was also the one the gospels present as the slowest off

---

235   David Instone-Brewer - *The Jesus Scandals*, 93-4. Much of the material in the next few paragraphs was taken from by the Second-rate Disciples chapter.

236   Babylonian Talmud Berakhot 62a.

237   A disciple was considered lazy if this was not his normal practise according to Babylonian Talmud Hagigah 9b.

the mark. "Are you still so dull?"[238] says Jesus of his protégé, a description the foremost scholars of the day felt remained an apt summary of Peter in Acts 4:13. It seems that Jesus spent the best part of his three-year ministry investing himself in a small group of fairly ordinary men and at the end of this period he gave them the same authority to interpret scripture for succeeding generations despite the fact that they had not yet made the grade[239] How could he be so confident they would succeed?

I believe that Jesus knew that, if these men were to become like him, they had to allow themselves to be moulded by the same forces that he allowed to impinge upon him. They therefore needed to learn to see like he did, be guided as he was and be completely open to the indwelling presence of the Spirit. Using a phrase now familiar to us, Jesus was engaged in a *hearts* and *minds* exercise that was often conducted in public,[240] included hands-on participation - often along the lines of 'watch me, copy me then reflect, do it yourself'. He had also taught them certain general and transferable principles, again in typical rabbinic fashion, delivered in short and pithy sayings which they could draw on and expand after his death.

But all this preparation was, as yet, incomplete without the most important factor that set Jesus' disciples apart from their contemporaries. Heroic stories are told of Hillel's disciples but they are almost certainly gross exaggerations. Hillel's disciples were crafted into the celebrities of their day because the nation needed to feel positive about its future. Jesus is far more concerned to work on the character of the twelve men who were following him. So Peter's greatest kairos moment was probably the brokenness that led to his repentance after meeting the resurrected Jesus at the lakeside. Gone is the need to prove himself or make a mark. Peter doesn't even feel the need to hide his shock at Jesus' return or explain his actions. Jesus was not interested in feats of great memory or academic ability but required followers who were simply willing to rely on him, learn humility, receive correction and embark on a journey of change just as their master had done

---

238   Matthew 15:16.

239   Matthew 16:19 and 18:18.

240   In John 18:20 we are told that Jesus taught the same in public as he did in private which was in marked contrast to other Rabbis of his day. David Instone-Brewer cites examples in *The Jesus Scandals*, op. cit. P 98 and footnote 4.

when he allowed himself to be born as a human child and preoccupy himself with doing his Father's will.[241]

The Content of the Gospel

Let us examine this suggestion that Jesus expected all those who would call themselves 'disciples' in future generations to be doers of the same things he did. If this instruction was found only at the end of Matthew's Gospel we might be excused from wondering whether his words had been interpreted or translated wrongly or were instructions intended just for the first generation of disciples. John allows us no escape:

> ➤ *If you hold to my teaching, you are really my disciples. Then you will know the truth, and the truth will set you free.[242]*

> ➤ *Jesus replied, "The hour has come for the Son of Man to be glorified. Very truly I tell you, unless a kernel of wheat falls to the ground and dies, it remains only a single seed. But if it dies, it produces many seeds. Anyone who loves their life will lose it, while anyone who hates their life in this world will keep it for eternal life. Whoever serves me must follow me; and where I am, my servant also will be. My Father will honour the one who serves me.[243]*

> ➤ *When he had finished washing their feet, he put on his clothes and returned to his place. "Do you understand what I have done for you?" he asked them. "You call me 'Teacher' and 'Lord,' and rightly so, for that is what I am. Now that I, your Lord and Teacher, have washed your feet, you also should wash one another's feet. I have set you an example that you should do as I have done for you. Very truly I tell you, no servant is greater than his master, nor is a messenger greater than the one who sent him. Now that you know these things, you will be blessed if you do them.[244]*

---

241 Philippians 2:5-11. John makes numerous references to Jesus' orientation towards his Father's ministry: John 6:38-40, 43-58, 65; 8:49-50; 12:44-46; 13:18-19; 14:12-26; 15:1-17, 22-15, 26; 16:1-15; 17; 18:36; 20:21

242 John 8:31-32.

243 John 12:23-26.

244 John 13:12-17.

➤ *A new command I give you: Love one another. As I have loved you, so you must love one another. By this everyone will know that you are my disciples, if you love one another.*[245]

➤ *I tell you for certain that if you have faith in me, you will do the same things that I am doing. You will do even greater things, now that I am going back to the Father. Ask me, and I will do whatever you ask. This way the Son will bring honour to the Father. I will do whatever you ask me to do. Jesus said to his disciples: If you love me, you will do as I command. Then I will ask the Father to send you the Holy Spirit who will help you and always be with you.*[246]

➤ *I am the vine; you are the branches. If you remain in me and I in you, you will bear much fruit; apart from me you can do nothing. If you do not remain in me, you are like a branch that is thrown away and withers; such branches are picked up, thrown into the fire and burned. If you remain in me and my words remain in you, ask whatever you wish, and it will be done for you. This is to my Father's glory, that you bear much fruit, showing yourselves to be my disciples.*[247]

➤ *Now I am going back to the Father who sent me, and none of you asks me where I am going. You are very sad from hearing all of this. But I tell you that I am going to do what is best for you. That is why I am going away. The Holy Spirit cannot come to help you until I leave. But after I am gone, I will send the Spirit to you. The Spirit will come and show the people of this world the truth about sin and God's justice and the judgement. The Spirit will show them that they are wrong about sin, because they didn't have faith in me. They are wrong about God's justice, because I am going to the Father, and you won't see me again. And they are wrong about the judgement, because God has already judged the ruler of this world. I have much more to say to you, but right now it would be more than you could understand. The Spirit shows what is true and will come and guide you into the full truth. The Spirit doesn't speak on his own. He will tell you only what he has heard*

245   John 13:34-35.

246   John 14:12-16.

247   John 15:5-8.

from me, and he will let you know what is going to happen. The Spirit will bring glory to me by taking my message and telling it to you. Everything that the Father has is mine. That is why I have said that the Spirit takes my message and tells it to you.[248]

➤ *As you sent me into the world, I have sent them into the world.*[249]

➤ *We know that we have come to know him if we keep his commands. Whoever says, "I know him," but does not do what he commands is a liar, and the truth is not in that person. But if anyone obeys his word, love for God is truly made complete in them. This is how we know we are in him: Whoever claims to live in him must live as Jesus did.*[250]

I am well aware that there is much debate about the historicity of the person of Jesus and over the nature of the Gospel records. Since it is the assumptions we begin with that guide both our selection and interpretation of evidence, the place we begin from plays a large part in predicting what our findings will be. St Augustine is quoted as saying "if you believe what you like in the gospels, and reject what you don't like, it is not the gospel you believe, but yourself" and this well illustrates the tension at the heart of Christian theology. Faith in another always requires allowing the other to reveal themselves to you as they really are, not just as you'd like them to be and it follows from this that there will be times when it is necessary to believe, and to obey, in order to understand.[251]

This means that theology can never be a merely academic question if the figure at its heart is always calling the theologian to personal trust. This explains to me why, despite excellent bridging work done by scholars such as N. T. Wright, so much theology is and will always be academic – in both

....

248   John 16:5-15.

249   John 17:18.

250   1 John 2:3-6.

251   St. Augustine of Hippo is known for his belief that "faith seeking understanding" could be best captured in the statement "Crede, ut intelligas" ("Believe in order that you may understand"). In essence, faith must be present in order to know anything. In other words, one must assume, believe, or have faith in the credibility of a person, place, thing, or idea in order to have a basis for knowledge.

senses of that word. Clever people are no different from the rest of humanity in their propensity to resist truth that is personally inconvenient.

There is so much that is inconvenient about the call to discipleship. At the heart of the matter is the need to adjust to the fact that I will no longer be able to please myself. This means I will have to change – which is also a major battle because I have so much invested in remaining as I am. These are the honest facts behind G. K. Chesterton's oft quoted maxim: "The Christian ideal has not been tried and found wanting; it has been found difficult and left untried".

Start as You Mean to Go On

I touched upon the question of conversion in the last chapter because the way we begin the Christian life plays a large part in determining the shape it is likely to take. As I write I am watching the progress of building work right outside the study in which I am writing. We spent weeks clearing the ground where a conservatory is going to be built and our builders have put in many hours of back-breaking work digging footings, measuring dimensions and laying the foundations. As I stand on the newly-laid concrete slab I can just begin to picture what the completed structure is going to look like but, despite the fact that no walls have yet been built, it would be far too late if I were now to decide it should be larger or a door should be in a different place. The dimensions are set.

When Jesus talked about a kernel of wheat[252] being put into the ground and dying in order to produce fruit he was referring to his own impending death but was also defining the necessary dimensions of discipleship:

> **Anyone** who loves their life will lose it, while **anyone** who hates their life in this world will keep it for eternal life. **Whoever** serves me must follow me; and where I am, my servant also will be. My Father will honour the one who serves me.[253]

Likewise his teaching about the way his Father will prune parts of us that we may consider fruitful but he wishes to cut away.[254] This finds an echo

----

252   John 12:24.

253   John 12:25-26.

254   John 15:1-8.

in the way Jesus dealt with Nicodemus and the rich man who baulked at giving his wealth away. Everything of our own we bring to Jesus may need to be laid down in order to be recast according to a different pattern. John records that poignant moment following Jesus insistence that his followers should eat his flesh and drink his blood – possibly the most offensive thing for one Jew to say to another. Despite the fact that even those closest to him found these words impossible to understand or accept, Jesus refuses to back down. Many of his followers leave at this point and Jesus' turns to the Twelve, asking them if they want to leave too.[255] John records a similar showdown in chapter 13 when Peter refuses to allow Jesus to wash his feet. On this occasion Jesus insists: "Unless I wash you, you have no part with me".[256] If Jesus feels the need to remind the Twelve that they are following on his terms, we should expect him to do the same to us. This is a habit that is best learned at the start of the journey.

Yet how many people who have 'responded to the gospel' understand what they have done? It is alarming how many caricatures of the gospel there are out there, each one based upon an overplaying of a particular card. The Evangelical tradition, for example, tends to over-play the 'personal' card, rightly based on Jesus' encounter with Nicodemus in which the phrase 'born again' first enters our vocabulary. We have already seen that Nicodemus came to Jesus because, as a religious teacher with a keen desire to see God intervening on Israel's behalf, he had clearly recognised features of the promised Messiah in him. The tradition I grew up in has it right when it points out that Jesus was deft at turning a potentially academic discussion in a personal direction as he indicated that many of the acts of God cannot be understood simply through learning or logic. Whenever God enters a situation he demands that we consider the personal response that is required.

Yet, certain sub-sections of the evangelical community misrepresent the Gospel when they push the 'personal' metaphor so far that it appears as if God's gift is being personalised to meet the whims of each individual. In many instances the gospel that is preached is little more than the promise that heaven could be our eventual destination. Any simple word study on 'heaven' blows apart this popular misconception that Jesus was only concerned with our eventual destiny and yet millions of Christians seem

....

255   John 6:60-69.

256   John 13:8.

to be wedded to this severely limited view of the gospel. The cynic might suggest that such a neat package is deliberately designed to be convenient since it leaves me free to determine the course of the rest of my life with an insurance policy in my back pocket. It is, however, a travesty of the gospel of Jesus. The early Church had an opportunity to seek state protection under Roman law if it were willing to accept the status of *cultus privatus*, which was essentially a private religious society of those seeking their own individual salvation without reference to the wider world beyond, but it refused to do so even in the face of intense persecution.

I could do the same exercise with other limiting views of Christian initiation but my intention is only to illustrate my point by reference to the tradition into which I was converted to Christ, not to go on a general witch-hunt. I am concerned that we begin our journey with Christ in such a way that offers us early pointers to the kinds of practices that will help us mature and bear the kind of fruit Jesus intends. The alternative is that the church is simply viewed as a holding pen for the heaven-bound and everyone in Christian leadership knows what a pain restless and purposeless Christians can be.

Live What You Believe

Frost and Hirsch cite Marshall McCluhan's dictum 'The Medium is the Message' as a reminder to the church that "we shape our tools, and then they shape us."[257] This is of massive importance to the future of the church since, much like Israel in the time of Jesus, we are the embodiment of the gospel – the message people see. It also means that something is always shaping us whether we know it or not and that which we allow to form us determines what onlookers believe the Gospel of Christ to be all about. "Deeds thus create words".[258] If we maintain the refusal to change that typified our pre-Christian experience we find that the forces that have made us what we are continue to speak more loudly than our profession, thus confusing those Christ wishes to reach through us.

Jesus is not afraid to use stark imagery to invite us into the reformation process when he makes it clear that eternal life begins with the death of

---

257   Michael Frost and Alan Hirsch - *The Shaping of Things to Come*, 150.

258   Michael Frost – *Exiles*, 55.

self.[259] Paul says the same in Romans 6 when he reminds his readers that this was the truth they had declared at their baptism. New converts are, after all, immersed into union with Christ's death in order that we might share his life.[260]

If the first task of the disciple is to learn to crucify the tendency each of us has to go our own way, do our own thing and please ourselves, the invitation that follows it is to cultivate a habit of obeying Christ until we become people through whom he is able to live fully and freely.[261] Our Spirit-empowered actions then supplement our words and we become increasingly consistent witnesses to the gospel.

Frost and Hirsch quote Martin Buber:

> *"What is the sense of (rabbis) speaking Torah? Man should act in such a way that all his behaviour is a Torah, and he himself is a Torah... The aim of a wise man is to make himself into a perfect teaching, and to make all his acts as bodies of instruction; and where it is not possible for him to attain to this, his aim is to be a transmission of the teaching and a commentary on it, and to spread the teaching by each of his movements. The people in whom this Torah-nature fulfils itself are called **zaddiks**, 'the righteous', the law-full."*[262]

I recall the shock I experienced the first time I asked myself the following question: "how can someone give any meaningful assent to even a single doctrine about Christ until they have seen it put into practice?" Belief can never be just an intellectual exercise divorced from 'action that springs from faith',[263] which is why God's first invitation is to taste and see that he is good. This causes us to ask the next question: How did Jesus teach his disciples to follow his example?

....

259   I am thinking of the image of the grain quoted above but see also Matthew 10:38 and 16:24.

260   Romans 6:3-5.

261   Galatians 2:19-20.

262   Michael Frost and Alan Hirsch - *The Shaping of Things to Come*, 156.

263   See James 2.

Leading and Following

I have already suggested that Jesus had a distinct strategy when it came to coaching the disciples. All the passages quoted above indicate that Jesus intended the disciples to understand that he was imitating what he saw his Father doing and was expecting them to learn how to imitate him. This was the point of God becoming incarnate – humans can learn doctrine by decree but new behaviours can only be copied by example. A helpful way to illustrate the method Jesus used to teach the disciples is to consider a square like the one below.[264]

The Square has a flow indicated by the arrows and illustrates four phases of leadership. Each phase is experienced as a Leader (L1, 2, 3 and 4) or a Disciple (D1, 2, 3 and 4). Let us allow Jesus to take us around the square.

Phase One

When Jesus meets Nicodemus he tells it like it is. Likewise with the Twelve. He sets the standard and refuses to compromise. He often offers little by way of explanation and has no intention of letting the disciples set the agenda. This is D1 leadership. At the beginning of their journey with Jesus the disciples may have been under the illusion that Jesus had chosen them due to some inherent qualities they possessed and they were both enthusiastic and self-confident. Jesus knew differently.

Phase Two

The Feeding of the Five Thousand is the first occasion in John's Gospel in which Jesus toys with entering the second phase of leadership. At the beginning of chapter 6 we read "Jesus crossed to the far shore of the Sea of Galilee and a great crowd of people followed him because they saw the signs he had performed by healing the sick." It is Jesus who takes the initiative and he is the centre of everyone's attention. A few verses later Jesus turns to Philip and asks him a question: "Where shall we buy bread for these people to eat?" John also tells us that "he asked this only to test him, for he already had in mind what he was going to do". What follows is a miracle in which he involves all twelve of the disciples as his assistants. This would have served to reveal to The Twelve the full extent of the learning

---

264   See chapter 8 of Mike Breen and Steve Cockram – *Building a Discipling Culture.*

curve that was awaiting them which would have been underlined by the further experience of seeing Jesus walk on water.[265]

The rest of the chapter records the first occasion in which Jesus enters into significant dialogue with the disciples which is exactly what they would have needed at this low point in their journey. They are now unsure disciples who are faced both with the reality of the task ahead of them and their own inadequacies and they need a leader who is both accessible and full of encouragement.

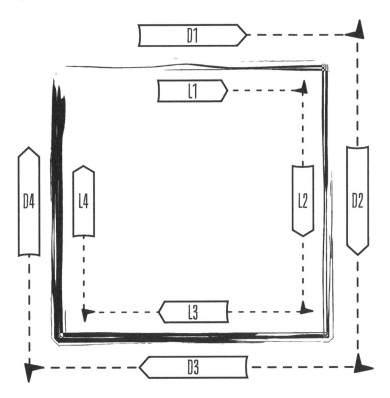

Phase Three

There is one little word in the first verse of John 9 that carries a great deal of weight: "As long as it is day, we must do the works of him who sent me". Can you imagine the double-take in the minds of the disciples the first time they heard Jesus talk like this. Did he really say "we"? Those who know the Gospel well are aware that Jesus talks later about his followers bearing

265   John doesn't mention Peter's attempt to do the same but readers would have recalled this detail from Matthew's Gospel.

fruit and doing works similar to those he did but all this is in the unknown future as far as the Twelve are concerned. The Disciples have entered phase three and are experiencing a greater sense of confidence that matches their growing experience. The time spent with Jesus in phase two has borne fruit and they have begun to learn to imitate their master. The synoptic gospels indicate that this is the stage at which Jesus sends them out ahead of him in pairs but we will come to this in a minute.

Phase Four

If truth be told, John's Gospel is not the ideal choice to illustrate phase four of the leadership square. Jesus alludes to the way the Disciples will pick up the reigns in that poignant section following the Passover supper in chapter 13 but the book of Acts is the pre-eminent example of delegation of both task and responsibility. Jesus has moved the Disciples from "I do, you watch" through "I do, you help" and "You do, I watch" to "You do, the Holy Spirit directs and I watch from afar". His coaching *mentoring* task is complete.

The Nuts and Bolts of Mission

We have to jump to Luke's Gospel if we are to complete this chapter on Jesus' Mission Strategy. In chapter 9 we read:

> When Jesus had called the Twelve together, he gave them power and authority to drive out all demons and to cure diseases, and he sent them out to proclaim the kingdom of God and to heal the sick. He told them: "Take nothing for the journey - no staff, no bag, no bread, no money, no extra shirt. Whatever house you enter, stay there until you leave that town. If people do not welcome you, leave their town and shake the dust off your feet as a testimony against them." So they set out and went from village to village, proclaiming the good news and healing people everywhere.

And the following chapter begins:

> After this the Lord appointed seventy-two others and sent them two by two ahead of him to every town and place where he was about to go. He told them, "The harvest is plentiful, but the workers are few. Ask the Lord of the harvest, therefore, to send out workers into his harvest field. Go! I am sending you out like lambs among wolves. Do not take a purse or bag or sandals; and

do not greet anyone on the road. "When you enter a house, first say, 'Peace to this house.' If someone who promotes peace is there, your peace will rest on them; if not, it will return to you. Stay there, eating and drinking whatever they give you, for the worker deserves his wages. Do not move around from house to house. "When you enter a town and are welcomed, eat what is offered to you. Heal the sick who are there and tell them, 'The kingdom of God has come near to you.' But when you enter a town and are not welcomed, go into its streets and say, 'Even the dust of your town we wipe from our feet as a warning to you. Yet be sure of this: The kingdom of God has come near.'

There are at least six learning points in these sections, each of which are designed to instruct the disciples in missional living.

Power and Authority

In Acts 17 we encounter Paul in Athens. He has sent a message to Silas and Timothy to join him and is waiting for them to arrive. In the meantime he visits the synagogue to engage the Athenian Jews and God-fearing Gentiles in debate, teaches daily in the public square and converses with a group of Epicurean and Stoic philosophers. All this leads to an invitation to address a meeting of the Areopagus. Paul has spent his time in Athens wisely and has noted that the outwardly religious Athenians have no great confidence they've covered all the bases as far as pacifying the gods are concerned. The problem with a polytheistic world-view is that you can never be certain just how many gods there are in the firmament, hence the reason Paul discovers an 'altar to the unknown god'. Paul takes advantage of the fear at the heart of their empty religion and proclaims the Father of Jesus to be this previously unknown deity.

The Athenians listened attentively up to the point where Paul mentions the resurrection of Christ, at which point

some of them sneered, but others said, 'We want to hear you again on this subject.' At that, Paul left the Council. Some of the people became followers of Paul and believed. Among them was Dionysius, a member of the Areopagus, also a woman named Damaris, and a number of others."[266]

266   Acts 17:32-34.

We then read that Paul leaves Athens for Corinth. With this in mind, Paul's first letter to the church at Corinth is revealing:

> When I came to you, I did not come with eloquence or human wisdom as I proclaimed to you the testimony about God. For I resolved to know nothing while I was with you except Jesus Christ and him crucified. I came to you in weakness with great fear and trembling. My message and my preaching were not with wise and persuasive words, but with a demonstration of the Spirit's power, so that your faith might not rest on human wisdom, but on God's power.[267]

I can't help but wonder whether the resolving Paul refers to was made whilst on the road. In Athens he had taken the opportunity presented by the Greeks' love of debate and the lack of assurance inherent in their superstitious religiosity. Once in Corinth Paul seizes the initiative, knowing that the death and resurrection of Christ has made possible convincing demonstrations of the power of God's love. All forms of cultural engagement are valid but it is as if Paul, whenever he is given the choice, defaults back to the reality that Jesus anointed all his followers with his power and authority and calls us, not to be salesmen of a gospel idea, but ambassadors of its fullness,[268]

The Kingdom is the Message

When I stepped down from leading a family of God's people it enabled me to visit and work with other communities of faith. The thing that dismayed me most during this transition was the discovery that most Christians seem to think the message Christ has entrusted to them is 'church'. The Big Church Day Out, Messy Church, Café Church, Open Church... all these seem to be about getting people into a building in order for us to prove to them that church can be fun, relevant or contemporary. At one level all these initiatives are to be commended. Praise God that creative people are skilfully building bridges to people outside the faith. But if those lost people begin to believe that our primary motivation is to fill our churches rather than introduce them to a lifetime of following Christ we are doing them, and the Kingdom of God, a disservice. "...tell them, 'The kingdom of

267   1 Corinthians 2:1-5.

268   2 Corinthians 5:20.

God has come near to you'" instructs Jesus. And he meant it.

Heal the Sick

I chose the sub-title The Kingdom is the Message above for a good reason. I started by writing The Message is The Kingdom but then realised that we talk about The Kingdom a great deal more than we demonstrate it. All the evangelistic sermons recorded in Acts were preached to the crowd that gathered following a healing or miracle. I have heard of church planting strategies that adopt a similar methodology, but never in the West. I will consider miracles and the gifts of the Spirit in the next chapter but it needs to be noted here that Jesus sends the Disciples out with express instructions to seek out sickness and bring healing as a means of preparing the people for his visitation. Jesus sees meeting people's needs as a key stepping stone to them entering the Kingdom.

Go Vulnerably

How wise Jesus was when he instructed his Disciples not to take anything with them they could rely on for assistance. When a salesman arrives at my door with a bag full of wares I am instantly on my guard. His agenda is to try and convince me that I need what he has and, all of a sudden, I act like I haven't a need in the world! That is the way people are and Jesus knew it. Far better to send us out with nothing but our faith that God may already be up to something amongst the people we are being sent to and the understanding that it is our task to discover what that is.

If I leave home with everything I need to sustain me and a credit card to buy anything I've forgotten, I display a sense of confidence that I have all my needs covered. This is exactly the attitude Jesus is trying to prevent. If I have all the bases covered I feel secure. Security breeds complacency and such people don't need to keep an eye out for God's provision. If, on the other hand, I have no idea what I'm going to eat or where I'm going to sleep I am going to be that much more alert to discover the way my Father is going to supply those needs.

The Person of Peace

Jesus calls the person who is most likely to meet our needs a Person of Peace. They are also likely to be our bridge into the community. In Jesus' day it was considered a religious duty to offer hospitality to a stranger and Jesus was making use of this custom to teach the disciples a key lesson. In our cultures where people are much more wary of strangers we may not be looking for food and a bed but to engage with people who see the needs of the community as we do and are willing to help us.

Stay Where You are Welcome

There is something fundamentally unsettling about this final instruction. The first instinct of many churches on moving to a new community would be to rent a meeting space with a view either to buying it or building their own. Having a place we can all our own and within which we can establish our own little corner of heaven feels the natural thing to do. Yet Jesus instructed his disciples to think entirely differently.

This does not mean that buildings are wrong *per se* but it is a sign that Jesus had far greater confidence in his missionary methods than we do. Let me illustrate by use of a metaphor. If you were the carrier of a friendly virus that would benefit every child, woman and man on the planet, would you build a walled colony and invite people into it one at a time or would you simply walk the streets and breathe out deeply? Jesus had taught the disciples to see themselves as carriers of the Kingdom of God and he had shown them how to bring Kingdom blessings to earth. Who needs a building?

Jesus knows that, if a new idea is to find favour in a new community, it has to be set free to do its stuff in real relationships. The best way to make such relationships is to live with people. Jesus knew that people who are willing to invite his disciples into their homes are also open to sharing deeper fellowship and that this attitude is the normal prerequisite to questions about faith. Go where you are invited and stay where you are welcome.

Churches that Live for The Kingdom

In the next chapter we'll see that signs and wonders were very much a double-edged sword in the ministry of Jesus. On one hand they attested to the powerful love of God and the reality of the Kingdom. On the other, Jesus is aware that people can become addicted to getting their needs met and miss where the sign is pointing. Just after Jesus fed five thousand people with the help of his disciples we read:

> Jesus answered, "Very truly I tell you, **you are looking for me,
> not because you saw the signs I performed but because you
> ate the loaves and had your fill.** Do not work for food that spoils,
> but for food that endures to eternal life, which the Son of Man
> will give you. For on him God the Father has placed his seal of
> approval." Then they asked him, "What must we do to do the
> works God requires?" Jesus answered, "The work of God is this:
> to believe in the one he has sent." So they asked him, "What sign
> then will you give that we may see it and believe you? What will
> you do? Our ancestors ate the manna in the wilderness; as it is
> written: 'He gave them bread from heaven to eat.'" Jesus said
> to them, "Very truly I tell you, it is not Moses who has given you
> the bread from heaven, but it is my Father who gives you the
> true bread from heaven. For the bread of God is the bread that
> comes down from heaven and gives life to the world." "Sir," they
> said, **"always give us this bread."** Then Jesus declared, "I am
> the bread of life. Whoever comes to me will never go hungry, and
> whoever believes in me will never be thirsty. But as I told you, you
> have seen me and still you do not believe.[269]

In a day and age when food represented hard work and would have cost
most people a far greater proportion of their income than many of us can
imagine, the thought of a never-ending supply of free food would have been
very tempting. The fact that Jesus distinguishes between the miraculous
sign and being fed is therefore significant. Matthew uses the sign as an
opportunity to record Jesus' promise that God knows our needs and will
commit himself to meeting them if we put his Kingdom first.[270]

I wonder if, earlier in the chapter, my comments about Christians
confusing getting people into church with preaching the Kingdom offended
you? "Surely church is the place where they will hear about Jesus and the
Kingdom" many will have thought. Possibly. I say this because much of what
I came up against in my battle to introduce missional thinking and practices
into a growing church was rooted in thinking similar to that above.

....

269   John 6:26-36.

270   Matthew 6:8, 11, 25-33.

When I was trained I was taught how to care for the flock, how to teach them sound doctrine and help them to live ethically coherent lives. It felt like pastor and people had entered into a mutually supportive contract in which I would serve them using my gifts and training in return for an income which kept me secure. This feels like a similar arrangement to the one Jesus calls into question when he denounces those who exercise control in the belief that they are acting as benefactors.[271] Paul Maconachie comments:

> Pastors in the Church seem to have entered into a 'benefactor agreement' with their congregations, where they are expected to be the providers of what people need pastorally and spiritually. We have 'taken hold of that for which the Church has taken hold of us' instead of taking hold of that for which Christ has taken hold of us. When we do this, we effectively become like a 'shell', insulating people from the life of discipleship that Jesus has called them into, instead of a skeleton supporting and helping people to disciple others. The church becomes like a crab or a wood louse, with the staff surrounding the people with care and teaching, catering to their needs. But what we want to see is the church operating like a human body; arms, legs and torso supported by the skeleton and working together to achieve the commission that the head gives it.[272]

It is vital that a church enables its members to provide pastoral care for each other and that God's people know the truth and are able to teach, encourage and rebuke each other. Those who are called to leadership roles should oversee any structures which may be necessary to achieve this whilst giving the majority of their time to their primary calling.[273]

> We can do this by 'pruning' out a lot of the management we do, and then **start living the life**. We form a core community, live life-on-life and reach out to others to bring them into the Kingdom. Like Jesus, we identify and call a group of disciples to go on the

---

271   Luke 22:25-26.

272   www.mikebreen.wordpress.com/2012/04/02/we-must-expect-different-things-from-pastors-what-america-can-learn-from-the-european-church-part-4/.

273   Acts 6:4.

journey with us and ask them to do the same.[274]

Living in a society where the consumer is king and where Christians leave churches that are not providing them with the experiences they feel entitled to presents us with a huge challenge. The denomination within which I was trained compounds this difficulty by insisting that all leadership must be 'servant leadership' and defines this as giving people what they vote for at church meetings. I know that this is a caricature and that, at best, Baptist church meetings are able to discern the will of God but every colleague I speak to knows the ideal to be a rare experience.

Churches that think like this are expressing, in the language of the square, that they prefer the experience of being in L3 and L4 and therefore don't want leaders who will go all L1 on them. It is therefore irrelevant that there is a new challenge to be faced and skills to be learned that require a season in D1/L1. Consumer Christians would rather duck a challenge than feel like they are having their choices taken away from them. If churches are to grow in discipleship it is essential not only that they appoint godly and gifted leaders but also that they allow those leaders to lead.

Empowered leadership is a crying need in many of our churches but this can never be something those in leadership can grasp for themselves. For this reason, if this is a challenge in your situation, the best way to broach the subject may be to share your impressions of the square with those closest to you and begin to share from the heart how it feels to lead or be led into D1/L1. It may be that there is more agreement amongst the body than you fear once it is understood by all that leadership has its seasons and the first stage will not last for ever!

---

274   www.mikebreen.wordpress.com/2012/04/02/. Op. cit.

CHAPTER 10
The Holy Spirit: Our Missional Partner

In this chapter I intend to explore the role of the Holy Spirit and signs and wonders in our Kingdom mission. The church is divided in many ways over questions such as these. There are, first of all, many long-running disagreements over some fundamental theological issues. For example: Does the bible describe actual miracles or just recount stories that have grown taller in the telling? If the Gifts of the Spirit were once made available to Jesus and the early church, have they ceased now that the scriptures are complete? My view is that the stories are honest attempts to tell the truth and all the Gifts are for today.

Assuming we are in agreement on these issues doesn't necessarily imply there are no further issues to debate and explore since there are many, more nuanced, questions and disagreements amongst those who accept that the Gifts are for today. If the Father is still operative through the Holy Spirit in ways similar to those in the New Testament why do we not see more miracles in our churches and communities? Why are preachers content to select freely from a range of miracle stories happening in distant continents but so few seem to be able to point to any they have witnessed, or initiated, themselves? How is it that Christians, like myself, who believe such things can happen today are so wary of revivalists who seek to create an environment in which a God of miracles seemingly needs to be wound up by an hour of fervent singing and then let loose?

Some sections of the church that would label themselves 'charismatic' are in crisis over these questions. If you don't believe me consider the fact that the editor of *Charisma Magazine* has estimated that there are "92 million believers world-wide who identif[y] themselves as post-charismatic".[275] In the same article J. Lee Grady writes:

> *Rather than watch our wounded brothers and sisters turn their backs on the faith or reject genuine spiritual experiences, those of us who identify with the charismatic renewal should determine to help rid our movement of its extra baggage.*[276]

In his study of late 20th Century Evangelical division and decline Rob Warner concludes that it is certain features of the charismatic-evangelical sub-culture that led to its demise. He concludes that "in the context of chronic church decline, a more credible orientation (is) needed... beyond the temporary mesmeric and beguiling but ultimately quixotic and untenable promises of the amnesiac entrepreneurs."[277]

I do not expect this chapter to offer all the answers to the questions above. Indeed, I expect some of my conclusions may be controversial. Whatever your position on such questions I want it to be understood that I am raising them because it is my belief that the ongoing confusion is stunting the growth of Christian disciples and thereby hindering God's mission. John's Gospel indicates that the role of the Spirit is crucial to God's ongoing mission and this is therefore a nettle that must be grasped.

My own story which includes a mixture of alienation, clarity, disappointment and faith will reveal itself as the chapter unfolds. I allude to it now in case it reassures any disciples of Christ who would describe themselves as part of the missional movement but are unsure about the

....

275   Rob McAlpine – *Post Charismatic?* (Eastbourne: Kingsway Communications, 2008), 19.

276   J. Lee Grady – *What happened to the fire?* (Grand Rapids: Chosen Books, 1994), 169.

277   Rob Warner – *Reinventing English Evangelicalism* (Carlisle: Paternoster, 2007), 144.

label 'charismatic'. Let us begin with a survey of the miracles of Jesus and the responses they elicit in John's Gospel.

The Problem with Signs

"Words mean what I want them to mean" said Humpty Dumpty in Alice in Wonderland. The same could be said, it seems, of the way people understood Jesus' miracles. We have already seen that things began promisingly. Just after Jesus' first run-in with the authorities John tells us that "while he was in Jerusalem at the Passover Festival, many people saw the signs he was performing and believed in his name.[278] In the following chapter we are told that Nicodemus' secret visit to Jesus began with the confession, "Rabbi, we know that you are a teacher who has come from God. For no one could perform the signs you are doing if God were not with him".[279] John then tells us that a whole Samaritan village believes in Jesus following the woman's testimony of his prophetic ability[280] and that he finds a similar welcome across Galilee for "they had seen all that he had done in Jerusalem at the Passover Festival."[281]

Yet, "Jesus would not entrust himself to them, for he knew all people. He did not need any testimony about mankind, for he knew what was in each person".[282] The first indication that Jesus is aware of the ambiguity of his miracles occurs in Cana, the town that had witnessed the turning of water into wine: ""Unless you people see signs and wonders," Jesus told [the government official who asked him to heal his son], "you will never believe.""[283] Although, in the NIV version of the text, it may seem that Jesus is expressing little more than mild frustration, the official takes Jesus' words to be a rebuke. Textual critics tell us that the form of words chosen by John is a traditional Hebrew expression which makes little sense when posed

....

278   John 2:23.

279   John 3:1.

280   John 4:39-42.

281   John 4:45.

282   John 2:24-25.

283   John 4:48.

as a question as the NIV does.[284] The official's son is healed and the whole household believes, but Jesus' deeper misgivings are clear.

In the chapters that follow, Jesus continues to meet needs powerfully,[285] crowds follow him as a consequence,[286] and many people believe.[287] He even points Jewish leaders to the signs as evidence of his credentials.[288] Yet, as we saw at the end of the previous chapter, it was the argument about the self-centredness of those seeking miracles that led to Jesus' insistence that those who considered themselves true followers should "feed on me" and "live because of me."[289] This is a watershed moment in the Gospel. Following this showdown John tells us that Jesus holes himself up in Galilee to the degree that his brothers taunt him: "Leave Galilee and go to Judea, so that your disciples there may see the works you do. No one who wants to become a public figure acts in secret. Since you are doing these things, show yourself to the world."[290]

Jesus knew that, despite being exposed to his miracles and his teaching, even his own brothers didn't have the faith that was required to be a disciple.[291] Onlookers continued to accept that he may be the Messiah but this judgement was merely based upon the subjective opinion that there were no greater miracles possible than the ones they had witnessed. I conclude that a faith based on miracles may be as commendable as it is understandable[292] but is also incomplete unless it also calls people to follow as a disciple.[293] As Jesus said to Thomas, admittedly in a different context: "Because you have seen me, you have believed; blessed are those who

---

284   e.g. C. K. Barrett – *The Gospel According to St John*, 207.

285   John 5:1-15; 6:10-13.

286   John 6:1-2.

287   John 6:14.

288   John 5:36.

289   John 6:57.

290   John 7:3-4.

291   John 7:5.

292   John 14:11.

293   John 2:23.

have not seen and yet have believed."[294]

The Spirit of Mission

William Barclay prefers to call the Gospel of John "The Gospel of the Holy Spirit",[295] not because he does not believe John to be the author but because "for seventy years John had thought of Jesus. Day by day the Holy Spirit had opened out to him the meaning of what Jesus said."[296]

The first of Jesus' teachings on the Holy Spirit following the 'watershed' in chapter 6 points ahead to the Spirit's availability to all who would believe:

> On the last and greatest day of the festival, Jesus stood and said in a loud voice, "Let anyone who is thirsty come to me and drink. Whoever believes in me, as Scripture has said, rivers of living water will flow from within them." By this he meant the Spirit, whom those who believed in him were later to receive. Up to that time the Spirit had not been given, since Jesus had not yet been glorified.[297]

If an event, or series of events, matching this description had not happened in the intervening years John could not have written these words in his gospel. Neither would the following passages have been deemed credible:

> "If you love me, keep my commands. And I will ask the Father, and he will give you another advocate to help you and be with you forever - the Spirit of truth. The world cannot accept him, because it neither sees him nor knows him. But you know him, for he lives with you and will be in you. I will not leave you as orphans; I will come to you. Before long, the world will not see me any more, but you will see me. Because I live, you also will live. On that day you will realize that I am in my Father, and you are in me, and I am in you... "All this I have spoken while still with you. But the Advocate, the Holy Spirit, whom the Father will send in my name,

---

294   John 20:29.

295   William Barclay – The Gospel of John, Volume 1, 23.

296   Ibid, 24.

297   John 7:37-39.

will teach you all things and will remind you of everything I have said to you.[298]

Very truly I tell you, it is for your good that I am going away. Unless I go away, the Advocate will not come to you; but if I go, I will send him to you. When he comes, he will prove the world to be in the wrong about sin and righteousness and judgement: about sin, because people do not believe in me; about righteousness, because I am going to the Father, where you can see me no longer; and about judgement, because the prince of this world now stands condemned. "I have much more to say to you, more than you can now bear. But when he, the Spirit of truth, comes, he will guide you into all the truth. He will not speak on his own; he will speak only what he hears, and he will tell you what is yet to come. He will glorify me because it is from me that he will receive what he will make known to you. All that belongs to the Father is mine. That is why I said the Spirit will receive from me what he will make known to you."[299]

Of course we know that an event did happen very soon in the life of the early church that marked the coming of the Spirit as Jesus promised. As the events of Pentecost were unfolding Peter understood them to be a fulfilment of Joel 2 and took obvious encouragement that Jesus' promise, which was later to be written down by John, was being fulfilled. I have heard Pentecost called 'the birthday of the Church' but surely this is misleading. It was a powerful enduing of the Spirit which enabled 'ordinary' men and women to declare truths about Christ to people from all nations. It also transformed the believers into an attractive community, thus propelling them into the world as witnesses and missionaries. The Spirit is God's gift to the world through the Church, whom he also transforms. This is the context in which the Gifts of the Spirit are to be rightly understood. Remember that the accounts we now read about in Acts were in the past when John wrote:

Believe me when I say that I am in the Father and the Father is in me; or at least believe on the evidence of the works themselves. Very truly I tell you, whoever believes in me will do the works I have been doing, and they will do even greater things than these,

---

298   John 14:15-20; 25-26.

299   John 16:7-15.

because I am going to the Father. And I will do whatever you ask in my name, so that the Father may be glorified in the Son. You may ask me for anything in my name, and I will do it.[300]

Let us be clear: the Holy Spirit is the prime mover in God's mission. In his summary of N. T. Wright's theological works, Stephen Kuhrt reminds us that the Spirit brings the 'advance payment' which "enables the church to implement the achievement of Jesus and be the channel of his salvation coming further into the world". It is also the Spirit who "call[s] people through the proclamation of the gospel" and then "brings these people, through baptism, into the Body of the Messiah". He also "inspires the Church and individual Christians to produce further signs of God's new world within the present one, anticipating their future reign over the earth as its 'priests and rulers'". In the meantime the Spirit enables the Church to "exercise within itself the judgement that it will one day have over the new creation" and display "the unity of its people across the normal divisions within the world of class, race and gender."[301] That, I'm sure you'll agree, is some CV!

The Gifts of the Spirit

In chapter two I wrote about my journey through Acts when I found myself asking who discipled Stephen and Philip and what the process looked like. I also wondered why Luke alludes to signs and wonders that seem to have been prime features of Stephen's ministry without naming a single one of them. The most significant thing about him, according to Luke, seems to be his defence of the faith before the Council and his martyrdom.[302]

John's gospel compares two Kingdoms when he calls Jesus the true, or *real*, light. He is also *real* bread and the *real* vine. This makes Jesus not only a figure in time but a window allowing us to see into a deeper reality, an opportunity to encounter the activities God is always doing. His acts thus become signs that demonstrate snippets of the glory of this Kingdom and his wonders therefore make us wonder. Signs, after all, point beyond themselves to what their originator can do if lives are placed at his disposal.

---

300   John 14:11-14.

301   Stephen Kuhrt – *Tom Wright for Everyone*, 58-9.

302   Acts 7.

The first thing the Spirit does is create authentic community. I am reminded of a fascinating conversation with a Russian interpreter whilst working with church leaders in Belarus. It had occurred to me that, whilst the Soviet system promised a society that looked like the church in Acts 2, it had delivered very little whereas the Holy Spirit managed to deliver the goods with no spin, manipulation or advance notice. Surely the first signs of the Spirit are not, as some suggest, flashy gifts and miracles, but the kind of community that can only flourish when previously self-centred, self-reliant and self-seeking individuals experience an inner revolution that makes such life possible.

It may seem to us that the letters of Paul exhort the churches to a depth of relationship with each other that is unduly intrusive. If you have not been challenged in this way I suggest you haven't appreciated the number of times the phrase 'one another' occurs in these letters and what this implies. We in the West, with our high value on individual freedom, need to listen carefully. We have also seen that almost all the promises contained in the New Testament are given to groups, not individuals. We know this because most occurrences of 'you' are plural, not singular. The implications of this are also profound and all this will be the subject of the next chapter.

In some charismatic circles you could be forgiven for thinking that the Holy Spirit is a gift-giver and little else. I have been asked to advise in situations where churches have become divided over charismatic issues and I sometimes ask a simple question: "If God gives you a Spiritual Gift who is it for? You or other people?" As we unpack the answer together it becomes clear that your gift of hospitality is for... others. The same with your gift of healing, preaching, administration etc. The only exception in the New Testament is the gift of personal tongues, which is why Paul criticises the Corinthians for using it to indulge themselves at a community event.[303] Tongues edify the individual and are only of wider benefit when an interpretation is given, presumably so that unbelievers who are present may then hear the message in their own language. Just like in Acts 2.

The positioning of 1 Corinthians 13 in the middle of this corrective passage indicates that Spiritual Gifts are most effective as signposts in the hands of believers who are becoming perfect in love, and are thus learning to share their all within community. That way God knows that whatever Gifts he gives will either strengthen the church or be given away to those outside

303   1 Corinthians 14:6-14.

the community of faith.

When Enthusiasm Takes Over

It was at university that I had my first encounters with the charismatic movement. The first part of me to be won over was my intellect. It was as if someone was reading from sections of the New Testament that it seemed to me had simply not been there before – accounts of groups of Christians in the early church era experiencing phenomena that Jesus had said should be part of normal church life. I had never heard these passages read in my home church and I now found myself involved with people who were convinced that the full range of Spiritual Gifts mentioned in the New Testament remained available to followers of Jesus today.

I became increasingly convinced by the logic of the arguments being put forward and could also see the need for the kind of gifts God had apparently promised to the church. It didn't take long to discover that not everyone was as ready to be convinced as I was. I recall listening to the vehement arguments of opponents of the movement who, for a variety of reasons, were opposed to any theology which taught that the Holy Spirit could or would want to be active today in ways similar to those he employed in the past. I was, and still am, unconvinced by those arguments that seem more rooted in fear and the desire to maintain the *status quo* than any desire to reach lost people.

I became part of a city-centre Anglican church which was known to be a centre of charismatic renewal. One evening, in response to a word of knowledge, I found myself at the front of the church being ministered to by members of the prayer team. I have already referred to my disability and the fact that I have short arms. Despite the fact that the word of knowledge I responded to had nothing to do with my disability I soon discovered that members of the prayer team believed God had told them that my arms were going to grow to normal length and strength as a result of prayer. We prayed. In fact a team prayed for me on many subsequent occasions. Nothing happened.

Looking back it is clear to me now how vulnerable we are when we believe something with a deep and durable conviction. In my own case I was led along by others who believed God had something for me that was apparently not the case. Those several months of seeking God for a miracle we believed had been promised but never came led to deep disillusionment and eventually depression. Although I remained intellectually convinced that the Spirit was the giver of good gifts, and I still hold that belief, I can see how my psychological defences against further disappointment became stronger at that point. I still wonder whether this event is the reason I have never personally experienced the kind of life-enhancing encounter with the Spirit of God that others I know and trust have been so transformed by. I learned to be, and I remain, wary.

I have reached a point in my journey where it is important to acknowledge this part of my own story. We all have weaknesses and failings but as long as we hide or minimise them they hold a hidden power over us. My dealings with churches of all different types and sizes has revealed a consistent pattern – the churches that are seeing the greatest fruit in terms of restored lives and significant community-based ministries are those that, at some point in their recent history, have been broken and remade by an ongoing encounter with the Holy Spirit. There is therefore no avoiding questions like these if we are to be involved in building churches that are fit to engage in the mission of Jesus.

Bringing my small story into the light has also brought a degree of insight into the bigger picture. I have been reminded of the key place the 'heart' plays in our walk with God. The Hebrew compilers of scripture understood the human heart (used figuratively) to be the very centre of our being, encompassing our feelings, will and intellect. This explains the frequent reminder that those who intend to follow God should cultivate a 'soft heart' – meaning that we should be humble, attentive, trusting and obedient. The opposite is the 'hard hearted' person known for a stubborn determination to do what he thinks best; and the damaged follower is frequently referred to as 'broken hearted', meaning that something is hindering them from walking freely in the path God has prepared.

Into this context the words of Isaiah and Ezekiel have resonance:

> The Sovereign LORD has filled me with his Spirit. He has chosen me and sent me to bring good news to the poor, to heal the broken-hearted, to announce release to captives and freedom to those in prison.[304]

304   Isaiah 61:1 GNT).

I will take away your stubborn heart and give you a new heart and a desire to be faithful. You will have only pure thoughts, because I will put my Spirit in you and make you eager to obey my laws and teachings.[305]

It seems that God's intention is either to soften the hard heart, win the wayward heart or heal the broken heart in order that each of us may become wholehearted followers of him, drawn by love towards a life of free and holy obedience. John Eldredge says: "the story of your life is the story of the long and brutal assault on your heart by the one who knows what you could be and fears it"[306] – and he is right. All sin (refusal to change) is ultimately rooted in fear – and our fears have their foundation in whatever wounds are part of our story. Until we find God's healing presence within that same story it becomes very hard for us to see ourselves as part of God's larger story within which ours derives its meaning and purpose. We need the gift of the 'Advocate' Jesus promised.

Miracles at the Time of Jesus

It surprised me to discover that miracles were as controversial in Jesus' time as they are today.

Healing miracles were a frequent source of scandal in the first century – in fact the whole subject of miracles was viewed with distaste. They were regarded as scams that were carried out on the gullible – a way to start a new religion and get rich quick.[307]

There is evidence that highly profitable religions could be founded on a good trick which was staged well. In fact, doing so became so common that Plutarch started a campaign against such money-making scams.[308] Lucian describes a very successful religion begun by Alexander the Prophet when he planted a bronze tablet in a temple of Apollus. The tablet foretold that Apollus and his son Asclepius would take up residence in Abonuteichos -

---

305   Ezekiel 36:26-27 (GNT).

306   John Eldredge – *Waking the Dead* (Nashville: Thomas Nelson, 2003), 34.

307   David Instone-Brewer - *The Jesus Scandals*, 27-28.

308   Many of the details below are taken from Magic and Miracles – a sermon on Acts 8:4-25 by Dr David Instone-Brewer found on his website www.visualsermons.co.uk.

which just happened to be Alexander's home town. When the spoof tablet was 'discovered' the townspeople started building a temple for them. Meanwhile, Alexander emptied a goose egg and inserted a baby snake through a small hole and secretly hid it in the foundations which were being dug for the new temple. He then feigned a fit of madness which drew crowds to him and during this fit he produced the goose egg and broke it open to let the snake out – declaring it to be a sign of the healing god Asclepius.

Alexander then set himself up as the prophet of Asclepius in a dimly-lit room with a large live snake on which he had placed a human head with a speaking tube inside. Lucian writes that a servant would hide himself in another room and would speak eerily through the tube, thus drawing followers to consult him – at a price of course! Alexander was said to have made about 70,000 drachma a year through this deception.

In Acts 8, we read about another magician who was equally adept at fooling people. Simon had learned to perform various magic tricks which the people in Samaria regarded as miracles, the result of which was that he was believed to be the agent of "The Great God". On Philip's arrival it seems that Simon's customers quickly deserted him for the more impressive acts performed by the disciple of Christ. With his own eyes Simon saw Philip expel demons and heal the paralysed and lame. As Simon made his own investigations he was shocked to discover that Philip wasn't claiming any glory for himself and was a simple 'deacon' - which was the Greek word for a servant who waited at tables; which, of course, is exactly what he was. What amazed Simon even more was that Philip, and later Peter and John, claimed to be doing these things in the name of Jesus - who apparently had been raised from the dead.

It seems to me that these simple insights into the world of the First Century help to explain why Jesus was so wary about using miracles to draw attention to his ministry. It is almost as if, each time he performed a miracle, compassion outweighed his better judgement. The earliest Church Fathers were also loathed to mention the miraculous side of Jesus' ministry in the knowledge that non-believers would be more impressed by his humility and self-sacrifice and the church that shared these characteristics than with more stories of miracles and wonders.

Lessons to Learn

In the West today there seem to be few miracles in evidence, despite many claims, and this may be the reason why many rationalists conclude that the New Testament accounts of healings and miracles are either fabrications or exaggerations designed to impress the weak-minded. The problem is that we still hear dramatic reports of miracles elsewhere in the world but, because they are difficult to corroborate, it is hard for us to learn any lessons from them.

Sadly stories of charlatans have also poisoned the minds of believers and unbelievers alike. Just recently, I watched a video clip of a well-known American evangelist proclaiming that all illness is against God's will and cannot fail to be healed if the sufferer has enough faith. I viewed the clip, not to traumatise myself afresh, but to view the comments that followed the clip, as a way of assessing its effect. It soon became clear that the adulation of a few followers convinces most thinking non-Christians that believers are mad to be deceived by such nonsense. Sadly such people are probably more immune to the claims of Christ as a result of such exposure to self-seeking charlatans.

I also recall watching Joan Bakewell assess the claims of Morris Cerullo as he visited the UK some years ago. Bakewell decided to scrutinise Cerullo's claims that Jesus was healing people through him and asked the evangelist to present his best cases so that she could investigate for herself. After a great deal of obfuscation, she was eventually given the names of twelve people who were convinced they had been healed and were happy to be interviewed. Bakewell visited their GPs, with their permission, to discuss their past and their progress since their encounter with Cerullo. She discovered that some of them only remained 'healed' for a short time and that in all the other cases the GP said either that there wasn't much wrong in the first place, or that their ailment was a condition which they expected to clear up by itself. Bakewell concluded that there was no evidence of any cases where anything miraculous could be reported.

Interestingly, Bakewell didn't stop there but was determined to look for other evidence of divine healing. She found a small group of Christians who prayed for seriously ill individuals and were led by a surgeon who wanted to do something for the patients he could not help through medical means. She noted that this group prayed intensely for a small number of people, without any publicity, and that they had seen a number of remarkable healings of incurable tumours which were all followed up with full medical investigations.[309]

It seems significant that the method of the small prayer group mirrors many of the healings of Jesus. Like him, they simply loved, listened to the Father and prayed. Conversely, I can't help linking the big healing crusades, in which the evangelist features so prominently, to the story of Simon the magician who had stage-managed everything for maximum publicity, seemingly for the evangelist himself. If people want to be healed they often have to come up onto the stage. If there is an exorcism it is done with loud shouting and gesticulations. If someone is to be filled with the Spirit, they have to stand up in order to fall down impressively. What is more, all this is frequently followed by repetitive appeals for money – once again, just like Simon the magician.[310]

It is vital that we are clear in our minds about constitutes a 'miracle'. We will all be familiar with 'conversions' that seem to be verified by strong emotions and meetings where people are seemingly overwhelmed by 'the power of God'. Having been brought up in a pentecostal tradition where these phenomena were routinely seen as proof that the Spirit was at work, part of Derren Brown's rejection of the Christian faith followed his ability to explain, and reproduce, the same phenomena through psychological means. In his recent tour labelled "Miracle" Brown spends the second half of his show parodying certain 'Christian' preachers and demonstrating convincingly how it is possible to generate an environment in which scores of people genuinely believe, and willingly testify, that they have experienced a profound bodily healing. Simon the magician gained a following because he produced results. The same is true today.

"Some people," writes Brian McLaren, "seem to develop an addiction to dramatic experiences that disrupts their life as other addictions would."[311] Addicts of any kind tend to be self-deluded and manipulative and we must do all we can to rid ourselves of any desire that the miraculous Gifts of God should somehow add credibility to ourselves or our ministry. The problem

309   These are recorded in Bakewell's book *The Heart of the "Heart of the Matter"* (London: BBC Books, 1996).

310   All these details have been observed by me and are not hearsay.

311   Brian D. McLaren – *Naked Spirituality* (London: Hodder and Stoughton, 2011), 16.

with miracles, if 'problem' is the right word to use, is that they place too much attention upon the possibility of 'gifted' people impacting other 'less gifted' recipients without the need for a long-term relationship that is necessary for discipleship to become possible. Jesus, I believe, wants to create close connections between people that result in changes that are, arguably, more profound than restored bodies. Signs, wonders and other extraordinary experiences need to point beyond themselves to a holy life if they are to glorify God and be of any service to humankind. If Jesus did all he could to ensure that the miracles that flowed from him spoke of purity of heart and the love of God, a truly Christ-like community must be ruthless in making such pure love its primary goal.

My God is so Big

A few weeks ago I received an email from a student who had been disturbed by Rodney Stark's book *The Rise of Christianity*. I was delighted to read the following:

> Stark seems to completely take God and the Holy Spirit out of the movement of the church. He seems to say that it was just the right movement at the right time that led to it flourishing... One of my arguments for believing in God in the past has been the rise of the early church, even in the midst of persecution. So when Stark takes away that argument and says Christianity was just a movement like any other movement it really unsettles me. I want to be part of something that is so big that the only explanation for it would be that God did it. Seems like Stark would just say that it was just the same as anything else though.
>
> Any thoughts? Is this just an outsider's perspective that is trying to explain away the movement of God?

It was such a well-phrased, brutally honest, question. My reply included the following text:

> I can see you are beginning to think deeply - and sometimes this can be very stretching. I wrestle with similar questions on a frequent basis and I think the answer lies in the realm of tension rather than extremes. I think we create the seeds of a future problem whenever we adopt a 'God of the gaps' approach typified by either-or thinking. Inevitably, that kind of 'God' becomes smaller

the more we are able to explain.

You see, whenever 'God' does anything it will always be perceived by us through our senses. Any move of God, if that is what we want to call it, will give rise to a number of very 'human' results - After Acts 2, for example, there was less poverty, more eating and drinking, songs and laughter. What gave rise to these things? A sense of awe and a rise of faith? Can these be explained? Not as easily, and therefore the recorded results can be 'explained' by writers like Stark but this doesn't reveal why these things happened.

So the question is this: why did the church act as it did, in such counter-cultural ways, and in ways that others didn't? Because they believed Jesus and sought to obey him? And did that result in blessing & growth? So how was 'God' involved?

Of course, the root concern is the natural desire we all feel to "be part of something that is so big that the only explanation for it would be that God did it". In my reply I also asked whether Jesus would have commended such a desire and whether his teaching on the Kingdom as 'yeast' and 'mustard seed' addressed this question.. Some weeks later the student replied, graciously affirming that I had provoked a *kairos* moment that was still being processed.

Gifts to Receive

Western society values its commitment to rationality and reason. Although many individuals in our society may not consider themselves intellectuals, Christianity will ultimately stand or fall on historic facts that can be verified and a theology which is coherent. That said, we have already seen that Jesus looked for more than this in a disciple. Works of the Spirit we may call 'signs and wonders' are only extra-ordinary to us because we are so unfamiliar with the realm within which God can be fully himself: the realm Jesus calls the Kingdom of God. Sometimes people who prefer the order they see in the modern versions of the religions Jesus despised need to be drawn from the shadows into reality. People who concoct forms of religion that deny the power of God through the Spirit know nothing of the way of Christ and, says Paul, should be avoided.[312] Humans need signs to

....

312   2 Timothy 3:5.

point us beyond ourselves and wonders to keep us slightly off-balance.

Jesus was wary of people who followed him for their own gain and those who demanded increasingly impressive proofs and we should be equally wise. On the other hand we have been given the Holy Spirit who unites us with God and enables our hearts and spirits to respond to the love of God like children to a Father. According to John, the first thing the Holy Spirit gives is himself. It is *he* who joins *himself* to a child of God. This is how disciples of Christ find themselves immersed in a transformative relationship within which they experience all the personal blessings promised by Jesus in the verses we have already mentioned. These may be called the 'Fruit of the Spirit' – the natural fruit that emerge in the life of every disciple truly joined to the Vine that is Christ. That same Spirit also gives Gifts, most of which are designed to be given away.

The Acts of the Apostles record a variety of signs and wonders, such as healing, and Paul, like John, insists that they are part of the Spirit's endowment to us today. If we are to walk in obedience to Christ, we will be shown how to take these tangible signs of God's love onto the streets. Samaria was a city in thrall to false magicians and its inhabitants needed to see that Jesus was Lord of heaven and earth and could point them both to earthly and heavenly realities. The community I live in needs similar demonstrations.

The sad fact is that, throughout the years the charismatic movement was at its peak, the focus of the teaching on healing and the Gifts delivered by characters like John Wimber was on 'Power Evangelism', yet most of us acted as if the gifts were for ourselves.[313] On researching for a Ph.D. on the charismatic movement several years ago I recall spending hours reading through the archives of the Fountain Trust.[314] The minutes of Trustees

....

313   I recall a story told by a friend who leads a church in the South of England. On hosting a talk given by a missionary from Brazil, he observed a number of spectacular miracles with his own eyes. The following night the hall was packed by people wanting to see a repeat performance and, by Sunday, the atmosphere was at fever pitch. My friend felt the need to calm things down, remarking to the church that 'signs are given to point to something greater than themselves and wonders are performed to make us wonder'.

314   The Fountain Trust attempted to promote the Renewal within the historic denominations whilst promoting a credible charismatic theology and resourcing churches that were becoming centres of Renewal.

meetings revealed growing misgivings amongst some trustees as they debated the reasons why many 'renewed' churches were slipping back into 'life as usual'. Very few seem to have noted the Apostles' obedience to Jesus instructions to do as they had seen him do and that Jesus' ministry was rarely contained within religious buildings. Sadly, during those momentous years, many charismatic Christians acted as if they were concerned only about their own health and well-being and the Gifts seem to have atrophied as a result.

Walking in the Spirit

The final question I want to deal with in this chapter is how, in the light of the mistakes of the past, can a church or missional community engage, in faith, with the promise that Christ in us desires to do greater works than those we find recorded in the New Testament?[315]

The early church needed none of the ingredients deemed necessary for modern-day charismatic gatherings but the Spirit was present. Even a basic understanding of psychology tells us it is possible to produce feelings of euphoria through the use of music, group dynamics and shared experiences, and I am convinced the entirely natural 'highs' so generated have often been mistaken for the presence of the Holy Spirit in meetings where I have been present. I am not necessarily alleging dishonesty or impropriety. The fact is that most of the time we are misled either by ignorance borne of a laudable desire to please God or by feelings generated by natural human enthusiasm.

I mention this simply because too many enculturated Christians are blind to the treasures practised by disciples of Christ from previous eras. Take, for example, the Celts who would journey into the wilderness to find God in the belief that, once found, those in need of salvation would be naturally attracted to the presence of Christ within them. Or the more contemplative orders who devised silent or liturgical practices through which they received intense revelations of God, or social activists like Mother Theresa who attest that in the poor we actually find Christ. These, and so many more, have discovered the real presence of God that transforms and renews but have engaged with him via routes which are perhaps more in keeping with their temperament and calling. The charismatic evangelical

---

315   I am assuming John means greater in number rather than greater in impact. I'm not sure how even Jesus could have gone one step further than raising the dead.

tradition desperately needs to uncover these rich traditions by re-engaging with the stories of our forebears.

"A way of life is formed by its practices. By practices, we mean doable habits or rhythms that transform us, rewiring our brains, restoring our inner ecology, renovating our inner architecture, expanding our capacities."[316] We have, thus far, encountered four LifeShapes: The Circle, The Triangle, The Pentagon and The Square. To close this chapter I am going to introduce you to two more shapes, both of which aim to bring balance to crucial areas of our lives: our prayer (breathing in) and our daily witness (breathing out).

The Hexagon is a way of breaking The Lord's Prayer into its six component parts: The Father's Character, The Father's Kingdom, The Father's Provision, The Father's Forgiveness, The Father's Guidance and The Father's Protection.[317] Jesus told us that disciples would preach but he left us with no instructions how to do it. He does, however, leave us with a model of prayer which indicates its key importance. *Building a Discipling Culture* suggests ways of using the Hexagon as a reflective tool, learning to reflect as we pray and pausing wherever the Spirit guides us to do so.

The main challenge for all of us who would seek to walk with God as Jesus did is to cultivate a sensitivity to his voice. The Hexagon helps us do just that. Until we learn what daily intimacy with God looks and feels like we are condemned to live according to our own limited awareness. The shape reminds us that intimacy with God is a posture. Just as the circle did, it begins with submitting to God in faith and asking him what he is up to and what is to be learned from every event and at the beginning of each new day. I will develop these thoughts further in chapter twelve but, for now, I will conclude with the observation that the Holy Spirit is the founder and guide to this way of life and that The Hexagon is an aid to reflective prayer.

The Octagon helps us see that the Mission of God is entirely a work of the Spirit, despite the fact that Power is only one of its eight faces.[318] We have already seen how Jesus taught that the key to missional living was being aware that God has gone before us and his Spirit has already found and prepared 'people of peace' who will act as bridges into a community

....

316   Brian D. McLaren – *Naked Spirituality*, 25.

317   Mike Breen and Steve Cockram – *Building a Discipling Culture*. See chapter 10.

318   Mike Breen and Steve Cockram – *Building a Discipling Culture*. See chapter 12.

or culture.[319] *Building a Discipling Culture* gives excellent guidance on discovering a Person of Peace and also explains the other seven facets of Spirit-led evangelism: Presence, Passing and Permanent Relationships, Proclamation, Preparation, Perception and Power. The Holy Spirit is our missional partner precisely because he is the member of the Trinity who seeks to glorify Jesus whilst convicting the world of its sin. He remains constantly committed to this task and calls us to co-operate with him as part of an authentic community of faith.

The Holy Spirit and Mission

In this chapter I have attempted to build a bridge between expressions of the Christian faith that, to my eyes at least, view the Holy Spirit as a hidden partner in mission and others for whom his signs and wonders seem both the beginning and the end of the story. By way of reflection on this chapter I would like to encourage you to examine your own story in order to determine whether you have any toxic memories that need bringing into the light. As I came to terms with the fact that my story was hindering me from engaging with the Spirit I have set myself the target of connecting with the teaching of people like Bill Johnson who have managed to combine both a credible and coherent theology and a culture of best practice within a local church context. I am still on that journey.

For me, the local church context is vital. The inherent dangers of 'specialist' or 'single issue' ministries is that they are sometimes founded upon a particular revelation which they then seek to normalise – implying that everyone may have the same experience if they attend a particular conference or practise the same healing technique.

This is not to say that there is no role for para-church ministries. Indeed, many who find themselves compelled to offer their gifts beyond the boundaries of a single church have much to teach us about the way we help Christian disciples to partner with the Spirit in mission. In recent years we have seen the growth of ministries like Healing Rooms, Healing on the Streets and the practice of Treasure Hunting which seek to follow the Spirit's guidance within safe and accountable boundaries.

It is my suspicion that the Spirit is far more willing to glorify Jesus than many of us have yet experienced. If I am correct that he desires that signs

---

319   See Chapter 9.

and wonders point to a holy life because such people best mirror Jesus, this implies that the questions touched on in this chapter are of crucial importance. I will be returning to this theme in chapter 13.

CHAPTER 11

The Transformational Role of Christian Community

Rob McAlpine lists the four primary reasons Christians who once called themselves 'charismatic' no longer wish to be labelled as such:

1. Abuses and elitism in prophetic ministry, coupled with a 'carrot and stick' approach to holiness that many find legalistic, manipulative and repressive.

2. The excesses of Word of Faith teachings (Health and Wealth, Prosperity doctrine) which clash with the emerging generations' concern for a biblical approach to justice and ministry with the poor.

3. Authoritarianism and hierarchical leadership structures that exist more to control people than to equip the saints for works of service.

4. An approach to spiritual formation (discipleship) that depends on crisis events - whether at 'the altar' in a church service, or in a large conference setting - but either neglects or deliberately belittles other means of spiritual maturation.[320]

....

320   Rob McAlpine – *Post Charismatic?*, 18.

I recognise every one of these descriptions, having been in meetings where I have shared the same misgivings. My maxim has been to resist a position where 'no use' of the Gifts of the Spirit is the favoured response to their widespread misuse, but it has sometimes been a tough position to hold in view of the damage that people who adopt practices such as those described above do, both to individual believers and the Body of Christ. As I have reflected on the list above I have come to see that, whilst it is indeed possible to describe such scenarios as resulting from an excessive preoccupation with the Holy Spirit or with his Gifts, they are, in fact, the result of failures within Christian community.

Sin, if it is left to do its worst, will divide people into the smallest possible social units. If I allow myself to be swayed by my basest instincts, my condemning mind and the law of the streets I will find myself ruled by jealousy, hatred, lust, bitterness, envy, greed and fear. Each of those passions will put barriers between myself and others until I become united with myself in a self-righteous, self-serving, self-referential unit of One.

As a pastor, I used to laugh at the wisdom of God who welcomes individuals to himself, all of whom have been influenced by such thinking, and the first act he performs is to place us in a close family relationship with others who share a similar history! It has been said that you can choose your friends but not your family and nowhere is this more true than the church. The kind of behaviour recorded in the list above points to a failure of Christian community simply because we are placed in relationship with each other in order that each of us might have the truth about our character pointed out to us with sufficient grace that it enables our transformation to greater Christ-likeness. The way Jesus ministered to others was diametrically opposed to the methods described above and we are called to do as he did but we cannot do so whilst our love of power, acclaim and prestige is still greater than the power of our love.

John called himself "the disciple whom Jesus loved". We understand him to mean that he was one of three disciples whom Jesus chose to spend most time with. His Gospel records many occasions in which Jesus drew his disciples into close orbit, challenging them individually when needed, teaching them about the Kingdom and truths about themselves. Using modern language, he mentored them, coached them, nurtured them and taught them; all as a means of preparing them for effective ministry to a lost world.

I am well aware that the various churches described in Acts and Paul's letters are a mixed bag, as every collection of redeemed humans will be, but we see plenty of evidence that the methods they employed drew from their experience of Jesus. We read of extraordinary generosity being practised and a high level of commitment to regular gatherings, both around the meal table and in prayer. They made decisions collectively, faced challenges squarely and didn't shy away from issues of internal discipline. All these are marks of a healthy community.

Trinity: The Only Basis for Christian Community

Some years ago I got to know Peter Holmes who, for many years, had been involved in building a Christian congregation which he was equally content to call a *therapeutic community*. In the book he wrote as an adaptation of his doctoral thesis, Holmes describes how Christ's call to discipleship can also be understood as a journey towards wholeness in relationship with others.[321] Holmes begins by challenging the way Western theology, now dominated by Hellenistic categories of thought, understands God. Convinced that it is the idea of God as Trinity that is the best lens through which to view his relationship with his creation, Holmes argues that the static and wholly transcendent model of Trinity that springs most naturally from classical Greek thinking is unable to describe God as he truly is.

This captured my attention because I had already become convinced that it was the Western tendency to view the Gospels through a Greek-influenced lens that blinded us to the core meaning of much of Jesus' teaching. For example, biblical Hebrew has far fewer words than the English language,[322] with the result that each word operates "like an overstuffed suitcase", with "many verbs...that we think of only as mental activities [also] encompassing their physical result."[323] This means that, at the time of Jesus, his hearers would have struggled "to find words for mental activities that we see as all-important" because every "thought is [automatically] tied to its

....

321 Peter R Holmes – *Becoming more human: exploring the interface of spirituality, Discipleship and Therapeutic Faith Community* (Milton Keynes: Paternoster, 2005).

322 Biblical Hebrew uses around 8,000 words, whereas English has more than 400,000.

323 Lois Tverberg – *Walking in the Dust of Rabbi Jesus*, 37.

natural outcome" by the very words Jesus used.[324]

Holmes looks to Cappadocian theologians from the Eastern Christian tradition to define for us a God whose very essence is "the dynamic of persons in relation"[325] or, to quote Basil of Caesaria, "a sort of continuous and indivisible community," in which "each person is only what they are by virtue of what all three give to and receive from each other".[326] The point of all this is to recover a theology of Trinity that is able to describe God in terms that would have been familiar to the First Century Hebrew mind and that are therefore truer to the nature of the God Jesus knew.

"We have this notion that God is among us as well as in us, so we understand him as being alive in our community, while also recognising he has a wider kinship with his whole creation."[327] Holmes contrasts this Hebraic world-view, which underpinned the language and culture of Jesus' time, with the way our Western-educated minds tend to think of God. As we do so it is shocking to discover that the culture that spawned the texts I read every day and find so familiar would have approached them with a different set of assumptions to those I have been taught are 'normal'. The Hebrew mind, for example, is unfamiliar with my dualistic (either-or; black-white; right-wrong) assumptions and my use of logic-bound fixed categories which I have been taught do justice to God's faithfulness and trustworthiness.

I can illustrate this by reference to a radio series I listened to several Easters ago in which John Humphries conducted a series of combative interviews with four eminent religious leaders, purportedly in an attempt to regain his faith in God. The two that struck me most forcibly were Humphries' conversations with Rowan Williams and Jonathan Sacks. Asked to present God to someone who has lost his faith, the Archbishop of Canterbury made a reasonable, balanced and thoughtful defence of God in entirely philosophical terms – without, I seem to recall, once mentioning Jesus. It was interesting but hardly compelling listening. The Chief Rabbi, on the other hand presented his faith as a journey and admitted to numerous unanswered questions. In every answer Sacks could not help revealing his

---

324   Ibid.

325   Peter R Holmes – *Becoming more human*, 49

326   Ibid. 50.

327   Ibid. 53.

core conviction that God can only be embraced from within a covenant relationship in which he must be allowed to reveal himself as he wills, despite the fact that, to our minds, this might involve agreeing to live with apparent contradictions. In challenging Humphries to allow the idea of God to remain unreasonable, to our definition of reason at least, I found myself intrigued as opposed to just 'interested'. If I had been on the search for a new religion I would have been much more likely to seek out a synagogue than a church on the basis of those presentations alone.

Holmes demonstrates how the Hebrew mind is therefore far better equipped to consider God as a *being* who is *becoming*. Instantly the Greek-educated mind jumps to the defence – probably because we conceive a *being* that is in the process of *becoming* as someone who is currently weak or incomplete and on a journey towards greater harmony and strength. It is interesting that even these words conjure up a certain sense of lack of movement and protection against change. So why does something in me feel insecure when presented with ideas of a God who is not always predictable and often refuses to 'make sense'? Surely, God exists within a tightly regimented heaven where everything is done his way and according to prescribed patterns – doesn't he?

> In Hebrew thought change is the matrix of all that was, is and shall be, the ground of all being and becoming, as with God himself... but under the increasing influence of Greek ideas it became exclusive... this made reality two dimensional instead of three dimensional: e.g. me and God, me and you, but not us in community. In Hebrew thought we see Yahweh's vibrant presence among His people.[328]

The very word God uses to describe himself in the Hebrew language: *hayah* signifies "becoming into existence" – suggesting that "one cannot be alive yet remain the same" because "to live is to continually change".[329] This is celebrated every Christmas with our focus on the incarnation and is the reason we find ourselves in prayer. The baby Jesus grew up in a highly unstable environment and the adult Jesus was moved to meet human needs. Only a dynamic God who desires to promote new beginnings and adapt to ever-changing scenarios can enter such a world as ours whilst

328   Ibid. 53, 4.

329   Ibid. 54.

retaining anything that approximates to sanity (assuming it is not considered blasphemous to anthropomorphise God in this way!).

The point at which these ideas begin to become almost profane to some people is the suggestion that our activity, whether co-operative or destructive, also brings about changes in God. There is some allowance made for thoughts like these within the belief structure I grew up in when the distinction is made between God's permissive and perfect will, but this carries with it images of an almost inevitable second-bestness to everything I attempt. I can't help engaging mental pictures of God unfolding his grand map and getting out a black marker pen to change 'Plan A' into 'Plan B' with a shrug of the shoulder or a knowing look whenever I miss the mark. But maybe God has no map and no marker pens. Maybe the keyword to creation is 'adventure', with God constantly taking love risks, entrusting people like me with glimpses of what could be – knowing I might crush the reality once I have grasped it, but also aware I'll pick myself up and reach out again if (when!) I mess up because the glimpse I had of God's intended future was life-transforming. Holmes says:

> Yahweh has the capacity to respond to a changing world, for change is His familial nature, and creation expresses and engages this. Continual change itself constitutes Covenant in process, and the Covenant in process enables creation in process. Thus the world is in process of becoming... put another way, the Hebrew way of living could be described as continual becoming in ourselves and in and through others.[330]

This is truly exciting: God has established a way of parenting the earth in a way that allows it to flourish in freedom and joy whilst also maturing along the way. I intend to draw heavily on Holmes' insights in this chapter because, more than anyone else, his ideas have influenced my understanding of the essential basis for true Christian community.

Sin is Unwillingness to Change

God's goal for humanity is maturity in Christ and, if this comes about as we conform to the image of God we carry with us under the direction of the Spirit, the end result is greater holiness. This is defined, not as a private inner experience similar to the warming qualities of *Ready-Brek*, but a

330   Ibid. 55.

growing ability to participate in the active, world-transforming Life of Christ. Holiness is therefore not best understood as a state but as a doorway to an abundant life. Under such a definition, "being *personally spiritual* is only truly *personal* when it becomes *public*".[331] Sin, therefore, is not just thinking and doing things that sully me and harm others but a deliberate and persistent choice to *be* rather than to *become*. Or, to put it another way, sin is a refusal to change – the one thing God is constantly doing and inviting me to share.

Embarking on a journey of change begins with a willingness to leave certain things behind in order to journey to new destinations. But sin refuses to move on. The path to maturity involves being taught to see people and things as they really are, embarking on fresh challenges that need hitherto untested resources held within the whole community. Fullness of life is seen as co-operating with others in Godly adventure – often the exact opposite of any traditional understanding of the normal Christian life. The truly horrific thing about sin defined in this way is that it results in a total blindness to what might be and a closed mindedness to partnering with God and others in adventurous mission.

If sin is best defined as a *refusal to change*, this even makes certain definitions of holiness 'sinful' since we are not human beings on an inward journey to becoming more 'spiritual' but are spiritual beings who are being drawn in ways that could teach us to become more fully human. Jesus is more interested in equipping us to engage with an unredeemed world than with giving us private experiences of serenity or elation. What is more, since God is community within himself (Father, Son & Holy Spirit) and is calling us to become increasingly like him, the Image of God is only fully possessed in us when it is lived relationally – in the same way as 'Christ among us' becomes a lived-out reality whenever we meet with other human beings (including those who possess the Image but do not yet know the giver of that Image).

To be even more explicit, this means sin is both a resistance to every move of God and to our own best interests, even though the sinful option is considered attractive because it claims to put self first. "Without personal change none of us can become more Christ-like".[332] I have just one life and my determination to continue to *be* rather than to *become* closes down

---

331   Ibid. 57.

332   Ibid. 60.

every adventurous and faith-filled use of that life. Our flesh nature, it seems, prefers a quiet, often solitary, life with its own familiar baggage intact, whilst the call of God is to 'follow', to 'obey', to exercise the "spontaneous inclination to seek to harmonise the self with Christ and others in the process of positive change,... to be more authentically human,... to be in a permanent state of becoming."[333]

Discipleship as a Journey to Wholeness

We are, by nature, spiritual creatures. The Hebrew scriptures describe every human being in the same terms – as body and spirit fully co-mingled together, two aspects of the single nature, a complete wholeness. We therefore inhabit a body, a fixed reality operating within structured and pre-determined parameters, inter-penetrated at every point by a spirit with unlimited capacity, "able to pass beyond itself, and in a permanent state of becoming".[334] Holmes understands this to be the essence of what makes us persons. It is this definition of what it means to be human that must be allowed to form our understanding of discipleship. Unless it does so we will not free ourselves from the misunderstanding that following Christ just relates to a 'spiritual' part of us that is going to heaven. Discipleship is an invitation to return to what is normal and find deep healing there.

So what is discipleship and how do we do it? Again we must begin by unpicking our Greek-influenced frames of reference. I have sat through countless church services where the main point, apparently, was that I should be reading the bible or praying more frequently, fervently or hopefully than before. The hidden assumption is that reading God's written word or speaking and listening to him produces a kind of change by osmosis, an essentially private and passive discipline by which it is hoped maturity will be cultivated. The problem is that the mind alone is not able to produce maturity. It may bring about changed actions through changed thinking, which is good in itself if the new thinking is better than the old, but often all we are doing is replacing one static idea with another...... static idea. This may be beneficial in the same way CBT is helpful, but it need not aid us in following Christ. Holmes sees Discipleship as "living in personal positive

---

333   Ibid. 61.

334   I L Gotz – quoted by Holmes. Ibid 76.

change,"[335] by which he means living life in such a way that we become able to attune ourselves to the call of Christ whilst being increasingly likely to act on what we hear.

The discipleship 'journey' thus includes a combination of practical support and guidance on how to let go of the baggage and sin of the past, together with "the actual <u>experience</u> of meeting and knowing Christ".[336] God has designed the community that is the church to be the ideal place for this to happen. Holmes names this process the *Rapha* journey – *rapha* being the Hebrew term God uses to introduce himself at Marah in Exodus 15. The word is normally translated 'heal' in our bibles but the word originally meant 'to patch or sew together, to unite or make whole'. Thus, right at the heart of the law we find God introducing himself as initiating "a unique relationship with his people, focused on a promise of freedom from disease through 'therapeutic' positive change, initiated by obedience to him."[337] The condition of God's promise is that his people listen, do what is right from his perspective and live in obedience – meaning that, in a very real sense, it is the right action of God's people that sews them back into every dimension of right relationship – otherwise called 'wholeness'.

Any study of Jesus' dealings with his disciples and others, the letters of Paul and also of early church history, reveals that those who followed Christ in the early days of the church were expected to change radically. It was only after Constantine adopted the Christian faith as his national religion that 'Christian' became a cultural label and 'discipleship' became defined as learning new concepts and ideas rather than a lived-out life-long journey of continuous change in relationship with others. Holmes proposes a return to the appreciation that discipleship is a journey toward wholeness, that this is something we "must do *for* ourselves and *to* ourselves" and that it is the only way we will "live fully while living Christ".[338]

Discipleship for Everyone

Peter Holmes insists that, in his experience, the *Rapha* journey is

335   Ibid. 81.

336   Ibid. 84.

337   Ibid. 91.

338   Ibid. 109.

effective for everyone, by which he means it works both for people who claim to know God and also for those who have no belief in God or desire to know him. This claim initially aroused my suspicions and I suspected that this amounted to an admission that what Holmes was teaching had to be merely a set of psychological techniques operated within a loving community, the majority of whom happened to be Christians. I could then picture the scenario in which individuals submitting themselves to the *Rapha* journey found help through insights from modern psychology and discovered God by forming an attachment to the majority belief.

Peter demolished my false categories first of all by pointing out that we perceive God through our everyday senses: the same senses we use to perceive everything else. I thus needed to appreciate that the techniques and insights of psychology do not sit outside the framework we use to understand the way God works and speaks, but within it. I also discovered that *Rapha* is *more than* psychology, initially via the Exodus 15 text but also because, although Peter is open about the fact that he finds it easier using the language of psychology than theology when describing his model to newcomers, he does this only in order to bypass the popular misconceptions about biblical words such as conversion, sin, repentance, forgiveness and the like.

Take his definition of 'sin' as an example. If, on first meeting Peter, he was to use the word 'sin', several things may happen – none of which would be helpful. For a Christian, the chances are that their limited definition of the word floods into the unfilled space and they are then predisposed to misunderstand much of what follows. For the non-Christian a similar process would unfold and whatever mental images the word conjured up may come packaged with ideas and feelings of judgement, hell and rejection, or popular misapprehensions that sin is somehow all about the enjoyment of sex. I discovered that Holmes was simply trying to describe the reality of theological concepts using terminology that is less 'loaded' to the modern mind and that he is happy to leave the Holy Spirit to connect (in this example) the word 'sin' to experienced reality. It is, after all, not the word that is important but the truth behind it.

What sealed it for me was the example of Jesus who was frequently willing to do good to people before they made a decision to follow him. Some who experienced blessing failed even to thank Jesus. Others went away sad because they knew their brush with the Kingdom was going to be nothing more than a fleeting one because they were not prepared to change in order to continue the journey. They had been blessed by an encounter with the Son of God but had passed up the invitation to become his disciple and thereby begin a journey through which they would learn how to be shaped by God into a fully human being.

What excites me in the context of this book is that an invitation to experience and enjoy wholeness thus creates missional opportunities. This resonates with my experience of using the LifeShapes. When they become part of the vocabulary and operating system of a church the Shapes become catalysts for reflection and change. They are equally effective when drawn on a table napkin in a pub before a group of agnostics because they describe faith in God using terms that are neutral and therefore full of adventurous possibility. The principles also work for everyone, as I have proved on a number of occasions. Becoming a 'Christian' may no longer be attractive to some seekers after truth but 'following Christ' expressed using the Circle rightly seems like a journey worth trying.

Community is the Essence

If a young elephant is tethered at an early age by means of a chain or rope attached to its leg it soon learns that it cannot break free and stops trying. I recall seeing an adult elephant with a slender rope loosely knotted around its foot and secured to a small wooden stake sunk into the soil. The huge elephant was held, not by the power of the rope, but by its learned behaviour and its resultant unwillingness to test its own strength.

The same thing, sadly, is true of the church. Søren Kierkegaard once wrote a parable that told of a community of ducks whose custom it was to attend duck-church every Sunday. Every week they would waddle into the sanctuary, take their seats and wait for the service to begin. Each time the fare would be the same. They would stand to sing rousing songs written by their duck forefathers extolling the power of flight. There would be readings telling of what it was like to have wind under their wings and poems that waxed eloquently about looking down on forests, rivers and hills from above. The highlight of the service came when the preacher addressed them, reminding the ducks of how God had given them wings with which to fly. "With these wings", he would say "there is nowhere we ducks cannot go! There is no God-given task we ducks cannot accomplish! With these wings we can soar high in the sky!" Shouts of amen were quacked throughout the duck congregation. The preacher concluded his message by exclaiming, "with our wings we can fly through every circumstance of life! WE...... CAN.....FLY!!!!" More ducks quacked out loud AMENS! in response. Every duck loved the service. In fact all the ducks that were present commented on what a wonderfully uplifting message they had heard from their pastor. At the end of the hour the ducks would say their farewells and waddle their way home.

Kierkegaard's target was the moribund Danish People's Church and the idea of Christendom that had birthed a stereotype of Christianity that he believed was far more pleasing to man than to God. Kierkegaard is not alone. Church history is littered with stories of people whose passion for the church latches them on to one or more of its failings and are driven to found denominations or renewal movements aimed at restoring this missing ingredient. Driven by a desire to restore one or more features of early Christianity as described in the New Testament, church restorers frequently see the need to locate a moment in history at which the church underwent some kind of 'fall'[339] together with the existence of a divine plan, hidden from all but the most conscientious and diligent believers, whose task it now is to deliver a full reformation of the church according to their own prescribed pattern.[340]

For every existing group or denomination that began in this way there are others that flourished and died, sometimes after the demise of their founder or as a result of internal divisions brought about by disagreements over just how radical 'radical' should be. It is fascinating to observe how visionaries can devote their lives to birthing and nurturing movements that are so clear about the benefits that will follow the restoration of their own preferred feature of early church life whilst also being apparently unaware of previous attempts to pursue similar goals or blind to other missing features that others were equally prepared to make it their own life's work to restore.

I can still recall the beginning of my love affair with Church History as I made my way through theological college. Up until that point I had very

---

339   See D. Durnbaugh - *The Believers' Church: The history and character of radical Protestantism* (New York: Macmillan, 1970), 212-16.

340   My own Doctoral research analyses the heady days of the Restoration Movement in the UK. All these features are present and it is not difficult to feel the energy and breathless enthusiasm 25 years on.

little time for any kind of history but I can well remember what it felt like to be gripped by the gradual realisation that in the book of Acts there was a story that, if true, was unlike anything I had ever read before. This kind of church had huge potential to transform people and communities. In my early days as a new Christian, church had been a place to go to on a Sunday, the building where I'd meet my new group of friends and endure an hour or so of singing, praying and listening before the evening youth group began. As I entered college I had experienced no desire to work in a church and no expectation that it was what I'd end up doing with my life. But I came to see that 'church' is, above all else, a community of faith and that this was the creator's preferred way of demonstrating himself to a world that had lost connection with him. I reasoned that, if God was willing to inhabit such a community in similar ways today, this kind of church was worth giving my life to help build.

In the Acts of the Apostles and the letters of the New Testament we catch glimpses of a variety of Christian communities which, whilst differing in structure and facing a variety of challenges and opponents, clearly had a life and vitality which set them apart from the society in which they lived. So, of the church in Jerusalem Luke writes:

> They spent their time in learning from the apostles, taking part in the fellowship, and sharing in the fellowship meals and the prayers. Many miracles and wonders were being done through the apostles, and everyone was filled with awe. All the believers continued together in close fellowship and shared their belongings with one another. They would sell their property and possessions, and distribute the money among all, according to what each one needed. Day after day they met as a group in the Temple, and they had their meals together in their homes, eating with glad and humble hearts, praising God, and enjoying the good will of all the people. And every day the Lord added to their group those who were being saved.[341]

Later glimpses of this church suggest that what struck onlookers was that theirs was a 'total way of life'[342] embodying values that were extremely attractive to onlookers searching for authenticity. These churches were

---

341   Acts 2:42-47.

342   N. T. Wright – *The New Testament and the People of God*, 120.

distinctly counter-cultural and even subversive. Yet they were also one step too far for some outsiders who could not face the challenge of discipleship they saw lived out before them.[343]

If all the evidence we had to hand was this single account written by a sympathetic observer, we may be justified in concluding that this was a high point in the life of a particular church located in the distant past. The problem, for those who hold this point of view, is that the New Testament contains a series of letters written to a number of churches over a considerable span of time which contain specific references, teachings, encouragements and words of correction, many of which teach a normative standard of behaviour and presuppose that many of the features we read about in Acts should be evident in all Christian communities.

So, the fact that the phrase 'one another' appears so many times in Paul's writing and in so many different contexts, implies there was a depth of commitment to each other's growth in Christ which goes far beyond the warmth and friendliness found within non-church social groupings. We also have a number of letters containing teaching that makes it clear that God distributes spiritual gifts to everyday believers and expects worship to be ordered in such a way that every member is enabled to minister to each other whilst also ensuring that non-believers receive what they need from God.

The Christian community I was involved in leading spent a great deal of effort morphing a formalised membership structure into something that expressed the language of partnership, thus seeking to foster a culture of belonging. We altered our leadership structures so as to give permission to people with giftedness and passion to try new things. We did our best to encourage creativity, thus ensuring that people were valued and could find a role. This led to us carving out spaces in our community life where we could explore the practical implications of the texts we studied on Sundays and where we could be real with each other and have fun.

We made these changes in the belief that disciples were formed within community and that such communities don't happen by accident. As I look back at everything we changed, the picture of the elephant held by a piece of string looms large. We removed all sorts of shackles and chains and yet

....

343   Following the punishment of Ananias and Sapphira, Acts 5:13 records: Nobody outside the group dared join them, even though the people spoke highly of them.

many members of the church acted as they had always done, apparently unable to break free. To use another analogy from the animal world, it is said that tame geese will flap their wings and run when wild geese pass overhead but it has rarely been known for tame geese to return to the wild. All this points to the need for more than a compelling vision that is shared by the whole church community and a clear strategy by which the vision can be achieved. It requires leaders who are prepared to model the change they desire and this is a theme I will return to later.

Transforming Church Culture

Culture change takes time, especially when the values we are trying to normalise are considered foreign within the culture that predominates within wider society. For example, many people who lived in the community around our church moved to Norfolk to retire. They therefore had made an investment in keeping things as they were. I also found native Norfolk people to be fairly traditional in their outlook[344] and many of them were also supported by strong family networks that also tended to value the *status quo*. I have also come to understand that, what others perceived as unfriendliness on the part of the 'natives', was actually a mixture of contentment and fear. Contentment because the family network provided safety, security and social cohesion and fear because newcomers were often better educated and came with a more eclectic world-view. All these observations are supported by social trends statistics.[345]

If, as I have suggested previously, our natural human tendency is to resist change (sin) and we live in a society that is resistant to change of any kind due to fear, becoming a disciple in this environment is going to require a huge degree of tenacity and social discomfort until the new culture becomes perceived as the normal way of being church.

About halfway into *Becoming More Human* I had a profound sinking

....

344   I observed that native Norfolk people tended to prefer the local Parish Church, whereas incomers were more amenable to making their home with us.

345   I am referring to neighbourhood statistical data. I am also mindful of the 'NFN' designation reputedly used by professionals in the County. In my opinion 'Normal For Norfolk' has been used unkindly to poke fun at native Norfolk dwellers whereas it was probably intended as a way of acknowledging that the native sub-cultures simply thought and behaved differently.

feeling. I was beginning to discover that all this theory had practical implications to it and was finding it hard to imagine the most liberating features of a *Rapha* community becoming normal within our church for the reasons above. I wrote in my own journal:

> *I was with Peter - in theory - until he described the depths of openness within his community. Why am I threatened by such honesty? Is it just that I fear our church couldn't live with such a high level of disclosure or that I am afraid to ask it of them and lead them there? I actually don't know how to do so either. I must ask Peter.*

I was perturbed by a section in which Holmes describes a group of men who met weekly - apparently a different sub-section of men each time – to declare to each other things God had revealed to them in the previous week. This 'spiritual surgery' was apparently far more effective when carried out with others because whilst "modern psychology examines us not as God sees us but as others or we ourselves see us", being in a place where we can hear "Christ speak to us about ourselves is preferable to any therapist."[346] If it is true that "we, rather than others, have brought most of the disorder into our own lives – we are our enemy and we need no other."

It is because "we conceal the real narrative about ourselves with a 'cover story' which we choose to let others believe, while we ourselves only half believe it" that we need to be part of a loving community of fellow disciples inhabited by God's spirit and committed to truth. Such a community is the best place within which to "expose our hidden/ unconscious self" so as to limit the degree to which the "combination of self-deceit, our gravitation towards the darkness within us, as well as our ignorance of our true nature" is able to continue to exert its invisible forces upon us.

Sadly, the damage often goes deeper than this since our tendency to forget our new nature and our propensity for self-deceit will have impacted the relationships with all those we may have blamed for our plight before Christ revealed that it is we who are, in fact, the primary authors of our own fate. It can take time to rebuild trust in people in order to allow those whom God will use to heal us to get close.

....

346 All the quotations in the following three paragraphs are from Holmes, op. cit. 119-121.

Holmes believes that it is within a healing community that "the process of positive change is compressed... The key issue here is that none of us knows instinctively how to change, so it must be 'caught' from others." For most of us, our healing involves engaging with feelings which have become our enemies. Holmes believes that "aspects of the dark side of our nature are often most easily identified at an emotional level, whereas much of our self-deception is more often cognitive."

Since most of us engage our emotions far more freely with people who love us rather than when we are alone (witness a funeral in a country where people are far more liberated in expressing their feelings or how a lump comes to the throat or tears flow when recounting your pain to others) what many of us may be in most need of is a company of trusted friends with whom we can release "the pain that keeps toxic memories alive". And, of course, I haven't even begun to unpack the benefit of community in regard to helping us rewrite 'unhelpful scripts', design alternative schemas[347] and helping us stick to our resolutions.

Holmes describes himself as a "reluctant convert" to the necessity of community as a place where disciples are formed. Many of us will need to correct some of the false stereotypes we have of community, much like Holmes does when he describes his "flawed assumption...that being church automatically created community" and his previously held belief that community is for weak people, especially women. It may be surprising to us how many of these false assumptions arise from the hidden values that underpin our own culture or out of a mistaken fear that communities always tend towards unhealthy extremes.

Once again, Holmes believes Greek-influenced thought has been the root of the problem, specifically Cartesian "I think therefore I am" self-oriented individualism. Holmes affirms John Macmurray as a philosopher with an antidote because he draws upon Hebrew thinking as his inspiration. Macmurray "suggested that Cartesian man, and his dualism, made it impossible to argue for personal knowledge of another, because it is not what we *think*, but instead what we *do*" that has to be the "starting point of

---

347   Holmes borrows these terms from modern psychology – scripts and schemas being mental patterns or actions, often in the form of words that we repeat to ourselves so frequently that they become almost sub-conscious.

all knowledge" of another.[348] If this is true, the goal God is calling us towards can "only be realised in and through fellowship or community". Our sin, therefore, is "making self the centre of our world, rather than the community or God" – which is exactly what we find echoed throughout scripture where so many passages about following Christ are addressed to communities rather than individuals.

We miss this fact because, as I have said before, in the English language, the word 'you' can refer either to a singular or plural object. In both Testaments we discover that the sinful action of an individual is revealed first and foremost to be sin against the integrity and life of the community because it damages relationships between its members (e.g. Ananias and Sapphira). This is worth saying a number of times: the most devastating effects of sin are always relational. In his book *The Secret Message of Jesus*, Brian McLaren argues that wilful sin that persistently damages the body of Christ is the only transgression that scripture teaches as meriting the ultimate sanction – namely, a person being excluded from that body.[349] This underlines the fact that it is the health and integrity of community life that is the most fundamental activity of God on this earth, meaning that church is the only place where the watching world is likely to find a consistent demonstration of true love in action. It is also the ability of the church to unite and produce mature believers that God delights to brag about as the powers of darkness dare to doubt his wisdom.[350] God draws people to himself as individuals and puts them into a wholesome community because only there can we become all we were created to be.

Embracing a Hebrew World-view

It is worth summarising how the Hebrew understanding of community was formed. Holmes suggests that the distinctive factors that formed Hebrew thought about community were its Theocentricity, together with a derived understanding of kinship. By this he means that "Yahweh was himself the common cause, the cohesive centre" and "when covenant was broken with Yahweh, so was the motivation and power to live community...

....

348   All the quotations in this paragraph are from Holmes, op. cit. 169-171.

349   Brian McLaren - *The Secret Message of Jesus*, (Nashville: Thomas Nelson, 2006). See chapter 18.

350   Ephesians 3:10.

Restoration of covenant was first needed through corporate obedience, releasing a certain power to sustain Theocentric community."[351]

The drive to actively embody a Theocentric community thus emerged from the nature of Yahweh himself. In its early days, Israel "knew nothing in any situation or at any time of a religious individualism granting a private relationship with Yahweh". All this changed with the call for a King to rule them, from which time worship became more ritualised and Yahweh more distant.

Holmes sees Jesus forming the disciples into a community of a very similar type, though sometimes using very different terminology. Jesus demonstrated a distinct style of Theocentricity throughout his life, retreating to commune with God in a manner Richard Rohr insists can only have been understood by every Christian prior to AD313 as deeply mystical and intense. Yet he also built community around himself.

> *Christ and his disciples clearly saw themselves continuing in the tradition of Hebrew ideas, of both community and spiritual heritage. Christ restored something largely lost. He practised the concept of community Assembly where community is the leader, and each person contributes their own unique gifting toward it... For about three years he travelled, taught, loved and rebuked these disciples, forming a core community based on radical Kingdom principles that created a **koinonia** [fellowship], ultimately capable of shaping human history. He demanded personal integrity, the willingness to speak truth at all times, and the importance of one's personal reputation before others... Christ's strategy was to consolidate all aspects of their worlds into one, in bringing a unity reminiscent of a way of life in the early settlements. But to do this he needed every one of them to change, maturing the way he saw wholeness, through his words spoken to them about them.[352]*

Many of the very first Christian churches were brought into existence by one or other of the earliest disciples and many also looked to Paul for spiritual guidance. Paul's assistance was often a mixture

> *of Hebrew thought, Christ's own teaching and the wisdom of*

----

351   All the quotations in this paragraph are from Holmes, op. cit. 176-179.

352   Ibid. 181-2.

*common sense in responding to practical problems... Théocentric communities were built, focusing on **charisma** (the exercising of spiritual gifts) within flat organisations by a living **koinonia** honouring both men and women... Paul, in turn, emphasised the need to build up the Body of Christ by deepening relationship with Christ, but all the time being mindful of the vulnerability of the weaker brother or sister... Being baptised into Jesus Christ signalled for Pauline converts an extraordinary thoroughgoing re-socialisation in which the sect was intended to become virtually the primary group for its members, supplanting all other loyalties.*[353]

It must be remembered that each church met in a home and was probably no more than thirty people in number. Whenever the church met

*Paul saw Christ as truly present... which is theologically essential, for it endorses the Theocentric possibility of full relationship with Christ for everybody... It is important to note that most of the time, when Paul spoke of maturity, he addressed the issue corporately... and that one major distinctive of this new divine Assembly of all members was the strong culture of personal change demanded of every new disciple... Since such spiritual growth is a gradual thing, the fruit of a person's life in Christ, within community, it becomes incumbent on all of us to minister into the lives of others... Also, for Paul, people did not go to church to 'worship'. Instead Paul saw one's whole life as worship... Paul saw the purpose of meeting corporately together as the spiritual strengthening of one another. This is done through sharing gifts in mutual ministry or **charisma** with one another, exercising gifts for the benefit of all present... Each person, through the **charism**, heard Christ for themselves and this released the **charismata**... The fullest expression of this love within the community was around the Eucharist or Breaking of Bread – the bread during the meal, the wine at the end and in between the experience of eating the food of warm relationships. Communion is a community meal, focused around a proper family event, usually with guests.*[354]

---

353   Ibid. 183-4.

354   Ibid. 187-190.

Church as Holistic Community

In a later book Holmes develops the idea that, as people created in the Image of God, human beings are most fully human when we model a community-held theology that resembles Trinitarian reality, where there is no being without belonging, and no being without giving oneself, as the Trinity has always done.[355] This enables a community of faith to hold two seemingly contradictory truths together: the idea that whilst the priority is common purpose (all doing the same journey, toward the same end, together) we can, at one and the same time, honour our uniqueness whilst learning the voluntary interdependence of authentic community. Trinity is the only place where persons can act freely, maintain their uniqueness, and also be totally united. This can be our experience because the Spirit that inhabits Trinity lives within each church.

In order to describe the component parts of such a community Holmes uses Haigh's five characteristics of the "quintessence of a therapeutic environment" which he sees as coherent with Hebrew community principles. These, he suggests, are the essential features of a life-enhancing, wholeness-inducing faith community. He also adds his own sixth characteristic to the list.

Attachment: the culture of belonging

In contrast to other forces in society at large where the tendency is to label in order to distinguish and separate, a healthy church perceives a deeper common identity that binds it together. We know and experience Christ who is our head and distributes gifts which help define the unique contribution each of us may make to that body. Holmes also demonstrates the importance of shared values and 'social rules' which, whilst unwritten, bind it to the deeper common goal.

1. Containment: a culture of safety

Holmes has learned from experience that most broken people "know and understand their problems already, and merely need the opportunity and space to articulate them. Personal growth occurs as these two forces play out in relationships." But people will only trust this culture of safety where it

....

355   Peter R Holmes – *Trinity in Human Community: Exploring congregational life in the image of the Social Trinity* (Milton Keynes: Paternoster, 2006).

is demonstrable that there is a "deep capacity... to absorb bad behaviour", freedom of self-expression and a focus on "growing wholeness".[356]

2. Communication: a culture of openness

There is a belief among many churchgoers that congregational life should be warm and friendly, rather than a more authentic place of discipline and painful ongoing self-reflection, as the Rapha journey sometimes requires. Psychiatrist, Denis Martin sees "much Christian 'love' as little more than a "superior brand of human kindness, based upon the suppression of bad feeling". A culture of openness is willing to question motives, challenge defences and explore relational dynamics in some depth – because, just as the Apostle Paul describes, we have finally accepted that nowhere else but the church do we stand a hope of someone loving us enough to 'provoke', 'challenge' and 'spur us on' in the understanding that "much pathology is the person's inability to 'talk out' what they fear, or what it is that entraps them. Implicit in this practice is the concept that when one openly 'confesses' a matter, its power is usually broken, whereas if one allows to remain hidden by keeping it 'confidential', it retains oppressive power over us."[357]

3. Involvement: a culture of participation and citizenship

"Citizenship in Hebrew community depended upon a number of factors, including personal integrity, a reputation for being just and a willingness to change, learn and mature." In truly Christian communities "newcomers are takers, whereas full citizenship in the community means one is an acknowledged giver... they are honoured for who they are, not what they can do... Most newcomers are given up to six months to begin to change, and acknowledge they need help. They need to begin to get honest with the community. If, during this period, they show no signs of progress and effort at change, they will find themselves at the edges, where less and less people will give them time... The leadership team has to let this happen: if they do not they risk creating a culture of dependency, where the community becomes responsible for alleviating sickness... A belonging culture has

....

356   Holmes – *Becoming More Human*, 208.

357   Ibid. 211.

conditions attached to it for the benefit of everyone."[358]

4. Agency: a culture of empowerment

"Agency means everyone is empowered to do whatever they need to do in order to change. What they suffered from in the past is not important, because the power to shed it is presumed... Living is a process of breakdown and repair in relationships: discord followed by increases in understanding. It is a strenuous process but we become empowered together as we search the basis of our own personal agency, and the negative authorities over and in us... In effect, the combination of the person's increasing knowing of themselves, drawn out of themselves with the help of others as part of the community social process, allows the person to begin to refine their perception and behaviour of what was previously 'sick' in their lives. The community appeals to the healthy part of each person, calling them away from their toxic pasts, while acknowledging its trauma and pain. The new member begins to believe they can change, like everybody else already is, by taking responsibility for their lives, thereby becoming who they are meant to be and not who they have previously been."[359]

5. With Christ in our midst

"Church, to be authentic community, must... have an acknowledged pathological dimension to its culture, with people being honest enough to admit they are sick, needing help and needing to change."[360] All this is possible because God is present and it is he who 'meddles' in our lives, reminding us what should be 'normal' and what is therefore not yet complete or not wholesome. It is God, remember, who offers to heal us and it should therefore be God who is allowed to define what sickness is and how we can be healed as the love of Christ is demonstrated through one another in such a way that we "enter into Christ together in a way we cannot achieve privately".

How does this work? As I understand it, there are two dynamics that come together within a wholesome Christian community. The first is that

---

358   Ibid. 213-214.

359   Ibid. 215.

360   Ibid. 217.

we know ourselves perfectly known and loved by God. William Barclay is saying something profound when he writes: ""We never see ourselves until we see ourselves through the eyes of Jesus. We never see what our lives are like until we see them in the light of Jesus. Jesus often drives us to God by revealing us to ourselves."[361] The way this truth is most frequently experienced by us is if those who represent God to us are open to God's revelation and are loving enough to act as a mirror for what Jesus sees.

Lisa Graham McMinn, recalls the passage in Ecclesiastes 4:

> *You are better off to have a friend than to be all alone, because then you will get more enjoyment out of what you earn. If you fall, your friend can help you up. But if you fall without having a friend nearby, you are really in trouble. If you sleep alone, you won't have anyone to keep you warm on a cold night. Someone might be able to beat up one of you, but not both of you. As the saying goes, "A rope made from three strands of cord is hard to break... We often miss opportunities to be present to each other as Christ loved us, laying down his life for us. As we do so, our stories are woven into a living tapestry of human struggle and perseverance in the context of a community. We open ourselves to blessing in our extended family, faith community, neighbourhood or work community when we humble ourselves to need others and be needed by others."[362]*

The second dynamic is that our churches know themselves to be healing communities that understand how lives that are broken can be mended. In his ground-breaking book *Connecting*, Larry Crabb writes:

> *A community that heals is a community that believes the gospel provides forgiveness for all sin, a guaranteed future of perfect community forever, and the freedom now to indulge the deepest desires of our hearts, because the law of God is written within us - we have an appetite for holiness. Communities heal when they focus on releasing what is good.[363]*

....

361   William Barclay – *The Gospel of John, Volume 1. Revised Edition*, 46.

362   Lisa Graham McMinn – *The Contented Soul: The art of savouring life* (Downers Grove: IVP 2006) 54.

363 Larry Crabb - *Connecting* (Nashville: W Publishing, 1997), 38.

All too often it is our fear and pride that prevent us from achieving the levels of depth the New Testament seems to indicate are necessary if we are to grow in Christ. If you are experiencing any tension after reading this chapter I predict that this is where its roots lie. For many of us the implications of this kind of community being formed under our feet are deeply unsettling, but hopefully the theory is more scary than the practice. Holmes warns us that "if openness or 'transparency', as we call it, is promoted too aggressively, it closes people down, causing reactance."[364] Any steps we take must therefore be baby steps and must first be modelled by those in leadership before they be embraced more widely.

The Key Features of Missional Communities

I picture this final section as the small glass beneath the pipe that runs from the condenser in a whisky distillery. I have found it necessary to explore the Hebrew concept of community in such depth because, until the church in the West sees the full picture, we will never be able to make the kind of disciples our societies need. Jesus set the standards for discipleship in an era in which every Jewish child would have been an apprentice to his or her mother or father from the age of twelve and would have learned what it meant to follow God within an extended family-sized synagogue made up of people who knew them well.[365] The 'one-anothers' of Paul's letters assume a similar depth of relatedness within the churches he fathered. The disciplines of submission, openness and accountability are just words until we build the kind of communities that nurture these as vital realities.

Using the language of The Triangle, this chapter has been strongest on the "up" and "in" corners with a smattering of the "out" dimension. It has, maybe, felt more like a therapist's waiting room than a preparation for mission. In the context of the whole book such a judgement would be hasty since my reading of the New Testament suggests the existence of an equation that reads (Up + In) x Community = Out. Healthy people make up healthy churches and healthy churches are essential for holistic mission. I also believe that the Spirit of God is inspiring a move toward growing the Kingdom through missional communities and humans cannot do effective mission with others they do not know well and trust deeply.

....

364   Ibid. 211.

365   If you want to research the cultural background in more detail I commend Ann Spangler and Lois Tverberg – *Sitting at the Feet of Rabbi Jesus*, Chapter 4.

The book of Acts records that people were won to Christ because they had such a deep respect for the way Christians conducted their lives.[366] Surely such communities are what Jesus envisaged as he prayed to the Father in John 17. Notice the way he includes communities of Christians within a trinitarian relationship with himself and the Father. Marvel too at the foresight that places such communities of radical love at the vanguard of God's missional purposes:

> I pray also for those who will believe in me through their message, that all of them may be one, Father, just as you are in me and I am in you. May they also be in us so that the world may believe that you have sent me. I have given them the glory that you gave me, that they may be one as we are one — I in them and you in me — so that they may be brought to complete unity. Then the world will know that you sent me and have loved them even as you have loved me.[367]

You go first... No, after you...

Twice in this chapter I have noted that unless leaders model what it means to live in accountable relationships it is unlikely that God's people will discover how to do it for themselves. Brené Brown believes that disengagement is endemic within society and "is often the result of leaders not living by the same values they are preaching... Faith minus vulnerability equals politics, or worse, extremism. Spiritual connection and engagement is not built on compliance, it's the product of love, belonging, and vulnerability." If we are expecting the disciples who are following us to follow the ways of Jesus for themselves "what we are matters immeasurably more than what we know or who we want to be".[368] This involves calling people close and teaching them to imitate you.

One of the key skills we teach as we run Learning Communities for church leaders is how to use the Learning Circle as a template for running discipleship huddles. We also huddle church leaders as they look to embed principles of discipleship and mission into their church communities. A huddle is simply the means by which individuals who have responsibility for

366   Acts 5:13-14.

367   John 17:20-23.

368 Brené Brown – *Daring Greatly*, 176-7.

leading others remain real with and accountable to God and each other.[369] The pattern for each meeting was taken from the one adopted by John Wesley for his class meetings.

When a group huddles the leader will focus the group on a question, or a list of questions, and each individual will be invited to share what the Holy Spirit is currently saying to them. The leader's role is to facilitate a process whereby each individual, herself included, is assisted, with the help of the group, to go around the six stages of the circle. Once each individual decides on a suitable plan they invite the group to hold them accountable for the action they commit themselves to and may request support as they put the Spirit's call into practice.[370]

369   See the web site www.3DMEurope.com for huddle resources and for details of Learning Communities.

370   This, already long, chapter would be incomplete without some reference to the book Family on Mission (Pawley's Island: 3DM, 2014) which explores the crucial connection between a healthy family and holistic mission.

CHAPTER 12
Preparing the Church for Discipleship and Mission

'To worship is
...to quicken the conscience
...to feed the mind with the truth of God
...to purge the imagination by the beauty of God
...to open the heart to the love of God
...to devote the will to the purpose of God'
　　　　　- William Temple, Archbishop of Canterbury 1897

It has been open season for critics of the church in the last decade or so and, although there have been many helpful words written on the subject, many of the evangelical critiques seem to suggest little more than repackaging the same contents in a more attractive container. In the midst of these, some wise voices have emerged. Michael Frost, for example, suggests what he believes to be the 'bare minimum' requirements for a bunch of Christians to consider themselves a church.[371] Frost and Hirsch paint a captivating picture of our ongoing relationship to Jesus, designed to ensure that our Christology determines our Mission and our Mission then

---

371　　Michael Frost – *Exiles*, 143-157.

forms the Church and not the other way around.[372] Finally, Alan Hirsch coins the word *communitas* to

> describe...the type of communality or comradeship that was and is experienced in the phenomenal Jesus movements... a deeper form of community than the one we have become accustomed to".[373]

The theme of the previous chapter is possibly the most important thing the Spirit of God is reminding the church in the West in these days. If a community of faith is to be true to its calling it must be passionate in its devotion to God (Up) and radical in its community life (In) in order to be zealous in its mission (Out). I say 'in order to be' because, unless our community life somehow approximates to the picture found in Acts 2, our 'devotion' to God invariably becomes in-grown and self-serving. Such an unhealthy orientation can never produce communities of faith that are attractive to lost people. Neither can it birth Christ-like expressions of mission.

Take another look, for example, at the beginning of John 14 and note the way the questions that follow Jesus' statements are framed:

> 'Do not let your hearts be troubled. You believe in God; believe also in me. My Father's house has many rooms; if that were not so, would I have told you that I am going there to prepare a place for you? And if I go and prepare a place for you, I will come back and take you to be with me that you also may be where I am. You know the way to the place where I am going.' Thomas said to him, 'Lord, we don't know where you are going, so how can we know the way?' Jesus answered, 'I am the way and the truth and the life. No one comes to the Father except through me. If you really know me, you will know my Father as well. From now on, you do know him and have seen him.' Philip said, 'Lord, show us the Father and that will be enough for us.'[374]

....

372   Michael Frost and Alan Hirsch – *ReJesus: A Wild Messiah for a Missional Church* (Peabody: Hendrickson, 2009), Chapter 7.

373   Alan Hirsch – *The Forgotten Ways: Reactivating the Missional Church* (Grand Rapids: Brazos Press, 2009), 218. I commend the whole of chapter 8.

374   John 14:1-8.

Did anyone notice the "we" and the "us"? Can you honestly say that this image of a house with many rooms and the "no one comes to me..." statement has been viewed by you as anything other than a personal, individualised, promise? Yet Thomas and Philip, having been knitted together by Jesus into a close band of brothers, cannot see any future for themselves as anything other than brothers in Christ and fellow-heirs of the Kingdom. It is in this spirit that I want to attempt to pick over the pieces of what most of us consider to be 'church' in order that we may reflect on the kinds of community practices that will be essential building blocks of the high quality lifestyle we described in the previous chapter.

Structures: The Medium is the Message

Misunderstanding about what the favour of God actually looked like was right at the heart of the factionalism within Israel at the time of Jesus. Just as today, the Jews of Jesus' time believed that God had given them a land to settle in with distinct boundaries and they thus understood the favour of God in terms of religious and political independence. The fact that this land was occupied and ruled by the Romans throughout Jesus' lifetime gave rise to much heart-searching and head-scratching – why had God taken their land from them? Some saw it as a matter of cowardice and insisted that they had a right to secure what was rightfully theirs. The Zealots, as they were known, insisted that God would help them if they trusted him enough to rebel against their overlords. History tells that many different groups attempted to do just this and found themselves crushed. Other groups (such as the Pharisees and the Essenes) were of the firm opinion that lack of purity was the reason God was displeased with his people. The Essenes withdrew from society whereas the Pharisees pressed for stricter observance of the Torah and increased vigilance against law-breakers. There were also groups of Jews who had been given prestigious posts by the Romans and were, unsurprisingly, fairly happy with the *status quo*.

Each of these groups believed in their particular story as to why God was displeased and had a credible vision of a future in which things would be different. What none of them realised was the degree to which their preferred view of reality was influenced by factors they were blind to – such as their cultural, temperamental and religious presuppositions. God had different ideas altogether. He chose to send Jesus: who made it clear that Israel's problem was a lack of discipleship and mission. I want to suggest that the Western church has something to learn from this historical lesson.

It is a very risky business even to attempt to analyse what others understand worship to be or what they believe themselves to be doing or experiencing during 'worship services'. It is my observation that Christian communities seem as confused about what it means to enjoy God's favour as the Jews were at the time of Jesus. At one level the answer in both contexts seems straightforward since both the Old and New Testaments declare that loving God and loving others are pretty much all that is demanded from any of us – and that obeying these commands perfectly would be the most pure and acceptable worship we could offer to God. This means that, strictly speaking, there need be no church buildings, hymns, prayers, songs, video clips or anything else for us to be engaged in acceptable acts of worship every minute of our lives.

The problem is, of course, that we are not perfect and will never be so. My natural tendency is to please myself and to refuse to change. This separates me from God and from others and necessitates a call from God spoken into the deepest places of my being to revive me enough to see the state I am in.[375] As I respond to God I find myself drawn towards him and also to others, which is where the church comes in. Just as sin separates, grace unites. God is Persons in community and I am created in his image – which means I too am created to live in community with God and others. Without community I cannot be fully human. So church becomes the place where I learn who God is, how to please him and find life. It also becomes the community within which I find my place and discover my calling.

Church is a family that loves me enough to draw me close so that all kinds of people can demonstrate the boundless grace of God toward me in ways I need to experience.[376] I am thus encouraged to live an increasingly transparent life because I know I am accepted and loved, even when I find myself challenged or corrected.[377] Church is experienced as the community within which I find full acceptance and the desire to change. Church is the family in which what I have to give is accepted and from whom I am able to receive what I need. Church is where God prefers to work amongst his people.

375   Ephesians 2:1-5.

376   I have already referred to the long list of 'one anothers' in the New Testament that make this very clear.

377   1 John 1:6-7.

So how has what we call 'church' become centred on a shared event that happens in an unusual building once a week? What is it we think we are doing when we sit in rows singing the same song, saying 'Amen' to the same prayer or listening to the same sermon on a Sunday morning – especially where there may be little evidence it is producing the kind of disciples Jesus expects? Why has the stage-managed Sunday morning event become the focal point for what we call 'worship' when, if pushed, most of us would confess our awareness that the worship God requires is rooted in whole-life discipleship?

It is my belief that the categories the Christian church uses to understand what it means to enjoy the favour of God are very little different to those employed by the Jews in Jesus' day. There is something deep within our national psyche, for example, that equates church with the *status quo*, with order and stability. If the Jews of Jesus' time understood the favour of God in terms of religious and political independence, it seems we are tempted by our culture to view personal freedom as our touchstone – freedom to hold services without persecution, freedom to determine our own lives, freedom to worship in a style we prefer, freedom (if we are honest) to be what we want to be whilst occasionally being kind to others in ways that rarely require huge amounts of personal sacrifice. And the way we engineer church supports this understanding of the way church should be – no matter what brand of church we become affiliated with.

Most churches gather most frequently in 'services'. I have wondered for a very long time why we use the word 'service' and what we mean by it. Judging by what happens when these services occur it seems that what we really believe is that there is a certain form of arranging gatherings that God likes better than a family party or the meal table. By doing these as well as we can, we believe we are doing God a 'service'. We also seem to think that teaching and learning happens best through one-way communication and that 'fellowship' is best facilitated by rows of chairs/pews. The fact that the focal point of most churches is either the priest, minister, worship leader or other 'professional' is also theologically ambiguous. The fact that some brands of church refer to a 'priest', as if we need another human to mediate anything between ourselves and God, is both erroneous and alarming.[378] We

---

378   God's people, it seems, prefer the Old Testament model of someone going to God on their behalf to the New Testament understanding of the priesthood of all believers. Is this not similar to Israel saying to Moses that they wanted to hear God through him rather than go to

are supposed to believe that the New Covenant established by God through Christ is better in every way than the old and needs no repeating.[379]

To return to our Jewish categories, the caricature above suggests to me that many Christians apparently believe that surroundings similar to the Jewish Temple are necessary in order to construct the experience we call 'church'. This is despite the fact that Jews in Jesus' day met far more frequently in the local Synagogue.[380] The Temple was deliberately designed by God to reinforce the message that something of eternal value was being performed on behalf of the worshippers by a caste of set-apart individuals who would never be 'ordinary' members of society. Although Christ is better than all this, there is still a place for the larger gathering in our post-New Testament era because such occasions have significant potential to unite and galvanise a large group of disciples, and maybe even a movement, around a vision. The Temple-style gathering is not, however, the best model to use if we want to facilitate discipleship and mission.

As the early church was gradually expelled from Jewish places of worship it had two models to base its patterns on: Temple and Synagogue. Not having its own buildings meant that there were fewer places where large numbers could gather, although we read about many such meetings in Acts. Yet it chose the synagogue model as its primary vehicle for mission; refined, as Paul began to plant churches in places with no Jewish heritage, into the *oikos*, or household of faith. Since the best way to celebrate the New Covenant is to live it out within the world God loves, the most obvious place to support such mission is the nurturing environment of a truly counter-cultural community. This does not necessarily preclude holding 'services', but I am convinced it forces us to question whether it is the best model for doing everything Christ has commanded us to do.

It so happens that the word 'service' may be more helpful than I have implied thus far. In the Hebrew language the phrase *The Avodah* is the term used to describe the collection of activities that comprised worship

God themselves?

379   Read the whole Letter to the Hebrews!

380   I am contrasting the more formal and ritualistic elements of Temple worship (the need for a special building, the role of the priest etc.) with the more informal, participative nature of the early Jewish Synagogue which often met in homes and was based around the extended family.

in the Temple. The root is the single word *avodah* which means "work" or "service". This has prompted William Bjoraker to reflect:

> An **oved** is a worker... Work involves the idea of serving someone. **Avodat Elohim** is the service or worship of the true God... Worship of the true God in Messiah Jesus through the Holy Spirit and in truth is hard work. It demands expenditure of energy. Worship is not mere camp-fire singing. It requires focus and concentration of our faculties. "Be still, and know that I am God" (Psalm 46:10). Worship requires an inner humbling, a surrender of self-will, a repentance of sin, and trust. It requires cultivating the presence of God. It ascribes to Him the supreme value of who He is and acknowledges His worthiness (worth-ship) in words, deeds, and posture. Worship is hard work. Work (labour, enterprise, exertion) is always serving. For the worshipper of God, the believer in Jesus, it is serving God. "And whatever you do, whether in word or deed, do it all in the name of the Lord Jesus" (Colossians 3:17).[381]

Content: Songs as Truthful Expressions

In my early days as a Christian I went 'to church' so I could attend the Youth Group afterwards. As I became responsible for what went on most Sunday mornings I went 'to church' because I took my role seriously and was confident that the Spirit had given me things to bring to the gathered congregation. In more recent years, now I no longer lead a church, I have been free to attend services in other places and have been drawn to reflect differently on the Sunday morning routine. In what way do I believe I am going to meet God that is different to a Monday morning? Am I expecting God to do something to me or am I bringing myself to him? How will I recognise his presence and what difference will it make? Am I that much different to most other people who turn out for worship on a Sunday morning? Have we encouraged a culture of passivity and low expectation by packaging our services as we do and might we have we lost sight of the fact that 'worship' is a form of acceptable 'work'?

I wonder how often God finds himself unable to approach us because we feel we are doing the outward form of worship fairly well but are not interested in following the cues he is giving us to a more Kingdom-oriented

---

381   William Bjoraker – *Word Study: (AVODAH) — Work/Worship*. The full article can be found on the website http://ag.org/top/church_workers/wrshp_gen_avodah.cfm.

life. I also ask myself why in some places Christians rarely experience what they believe are direct interventions from God as they meet in his name whereas other groups of Christians imply that such encounters are what the whole show is all about and do their best to arrange all the elements of the 'service' in order to ensure this appears to happen as frequently and as dramatically as possible. Such questions led me to an intriguing study of Vineyard church culture in which the author writes:

> Congregants must learn to take their model of God – given content by the individual but also reinterpreted by the understanding of God within the church – and then use that model to reshape their own emotional worlds. This is an awkward task because one cannot just decide to feel Christ-like love, as if deciding what wallpaper to use in the living room. As a result, much of what people do and say at the Vineyard resembles psychotherapy. The insight at the core of psychoanalysis and psychotherapy is that we cannot change our emotions deliberately... clients experience their emotional lives as flawed, and they go to therapists to learn from them a healthier model of self and healthier patterns of response, and then to imitate those models.[382]

If you look around a typical charismatic-evanglical church on a Sunday morning my prediction is that there will be a huddle of worshippers (normally towards the front) who seem to be experiencing the kind of elation they are singing about. And if you turn up at the same church the following week my guess is that those same people will be having a similar experience all over again. If you study the faces of the congregants elsewhere in the room this will confirm Luhrmann's further conclusion that "not everyone seems to be able to have these experiences, even when they want to."[383] Couple this simple observation with recent studies on religion and autism.[384] The data shows that individuals with high-functioning autism are less likely to believe in God, not simply for intellectual reasons, but because their ability to visualise and relate to a being they cannot see is severely hampered by

---

382   Tanya Luhrmann – *When God Talks Back: Understanding the American evangelical relationship with God.* (New York: Vintage Books, 2012), 110.

383   Luhrmann, 188.

384   See, for example, http://csjarchive.cogsci.rpi.edu/proceedings/2011/papers/0782/paper0782.pdf.

the different wiring of their brain. "Everyone in church believes that those who pray are more likely to experience God", says Luhrmann, "but...it is the capacity to use your mind in certain ways that allows you to experience an invisible God as if he were present."[385]

I have to be brutally honest when admitting my belief that the switch I once favoured from old, dusty hymns to new songs has, largely, failed to deliver much in the way of substantial benefit apart from the fact that such songs are more like the popular songs which are the preferred idiom of the age. Michael Frost likens these "pop-style love songs to Jesus" to the adolescent, immature 'love' that "pop-idols sing [about] to a boyfriend or girlfriend."[386] The call of God to us is not to fall 'in love' with Jesus again and again on Sunday mornings but know ourselves so utterly one with Christ that we do the Father's work with every step we take. Maybe there is an overlap between the kind of mystical awareness of God testified to by generations of disciples who have been burned, but not consumed, by the fire of God's love and feelings of elation felt by some in a Christian gathering but we must be careful not to confuse the two.

There are times when I have found myself uneasy when I am invited to sing songs in public worship that either assume an intimacy with Christ that I am not experiencing or force me to express a depth of faith that, if I'm to be brutally honest, I cannot muster up in the few minutes it takes to sing a song. On one hand I believe in the vital discipline of finding strength in the truth of God's Word and in the promises he has given me. For this reason it can be a positive benefit to sing songs that declare certain eternal truths whether or not this is our current experience. At all times, and in all seasons of life, we need to bolster our faith by doing just this. Yet, singing words that describe the experience of a biblical character at a certain high point in their journey with God as if it were the current experience of everyone in the room, is not always helpful. If such songs are chosen week in, week out, presumably to try and create a feeling of resonance within a congregation, the whole worship event can begin to feel manipulative. Even those who are able to give themselves freely to such experiences on a regular basis may, in fact, be doing more harm than good if at some level within themselves they are making such fervency the object of their attention rather than Christ's still small voice. This is how seeds of future discontent are sown.

---

385   Luhrmann, 196.

386   Michael Frost – *Exiles*, 22.

I also recall times when I found it increasingly hard to sing songs that celebrated realities I was trying to introduce into our church life but were being resisted by the people of God. At such times I knew we were not prepared to address the issues that underlay our lack of authenticity and the songs stuck in my craw. An example of this were songs that confidently assured us that God heals all our diseases. The fact is that, although Jesus never turned away a request for healing and we will all be whole one day, Jesus does not always heal all our diseases today and redemptive suffering is a current reality however much we'd like it not to be the case. In such a context songs like these were not achieving anything except sowing seeds of unreality and frustration, thus making the gap between what we say we believe and what we are actually doing ever wider.

On such occasions I found myself thinking similarly to Paul as he addressed the church at Corinth over the issue of tongues: what is a newcomer to think? I'm not saying there is no place for worship songs like these, although the few that are factually untrue should go, however wonderful the tunes may be. My feeling is that those songs that describe God's intimate dealings with us should be used carefully and in settings where they might actually help us to experience this reality – assuming, of course, there is a reality to them that people of differing temperaments and capacities are able to experience. Likewise, those songs that are more triumphant in their emphasis. Let not our current limited experience stop us from using them but let us make sure we actually want the things we are singing about to happen and that we are willing to become people who will make the required journey. I am simply arguing that we should guard against the kind of worship experience that implies we 'have arrived' and currently have it all. Oh how I long that sung worship might sometimes include a greater degree of mourning, in recognition that one-third of the psalms are laments. Surely there is a need to express our longing for justice and breakthrough with the highest degree of integrity and honesty we can muster.

For a long time I put my unease down either to my temperament or perhaps to being in a different place with God to other worshippers. I then came across a psychological term known as 'cognitive dissonance' which shed some light on the issues I express above. Wikipedia describes the phenomenon in these terms:

> "Cognitive dissonance is a psychological state that describes the

uncomfortable feeling between what one holds to be true and what one knows to be true. Similar to ambivalence, the term cognitive dissonance describes conflicting thoughts or beliefs (cognitions) that occur at the same time, or when engaged in behaviours that conflict with one's beliefs."[387]

If we apply this insight to what happens within us when we are invited to sing worship songs that do not truly represent our beliefs, feelings, or our present experience it is not difficult to see that, if this effect is being experienced by just a single individual on a Sunday morning, the impact on them could be extremely discomforting. I would suggest that this phenomenon partly explains the mass opt-out observed at weddings, civic events and even school carol services where the congregation are invited to sing words that were designed to be sung as acts of worship. In church services something more complex is happening because, as good Christians, we are all supposed to believe the things we are singing and not opening our mouths is thus felt to be an uncomfortable option. What is more, others are obviously feeling the emotional highs they are singing about – aren't they? Many may comply outwardly with a request to 'sing as if you mean it' but compliance is not heart-felt worship. The dangers of conformity are illustrated in the following example:

In an experiment conducted in 1963 Aronson and Carlsmith studied what happened when children were forced to comply with an action that made no sense to them. The experimenter would question the child on a set of toys to gauge which toys the children liked the most and which they found the least tempting. The experimenter then chose a toy that the child really liked, put them in a room with it, and left the room. Upon leaving the room the experimenter told half the children that there would be a severe punishment if they played with the toy and told the other half that there would be a moderate punishment.

Later, when the punishment, whether severe or moderate, was removed, the children in the moderate punishment condition were less likely to play with the toy, even though now it had no repercussion. When questioned, the children in the moderate condition expressed more of a disinterest in the toy than would be expected towards a toy that they had initially ranked high in interest. Alternatively, the desirability of the toy went up for the children in the severe punishment condition.

387   Wikipedia entry on Cognitive Dissonance accessed in February 2008.

This study laid out the effect of over-justification and insufficient justification on cognition. In over-justification, the personal beliefs and attitudes of the person do not change because they have a good external reason for their actions. The children threatened with the severe punishment had a good external reasoning for not playing with the toy because they knew that they would be badly punished for it. However, they still wanted the toy, so once the punishment was removed they were more likely to play with it. Conversely, the children who would get the moderate punishment displayed insufficient justification because they had to justify to themselves why they did not want to play with the toy since the external motivator, the degree of punishment, was not strong enough by itself. As a result, they convinced themselves that the toy was not worth playing with, which is why even when the punishment was removed they still did not play with the toy.[388]

Cognitive dissonance therefore breeds ambivalence. This, to a worship leader who feels duty bound to lead rousing worship, may give rise to a cunning plan to choose more strident or impassioned songs next time around, thus upping the stakes even higher.

My response, on reflecting on this process, is that we need to learn to admit, and thereby connect, with our true emotions in worship. And I think the term 'learn to... connect' is the appropriate one since I'm not sure many of us are aware of the emotions we carry with us, especially in church. The fact is, of course, that sometimes the emotions we bring to worship are not positive at all. If we are honest, many of us will admit to being in situations where the emotion we bring with us to gathered worship (or may keep us away from gathered worship) is one we feel just a bit guilty about. Maybe we are angry with God, disappointed in him, confused by him or just simply distant from him. So we keep quiet - despite the fact that David, writer of the psalms, which are referred to by some as the hymn book of the Old Testament, poured out his feelings to God, often as a way of moving towards greater clarity or even resolution. It may feel as if I am making an incongruous suggestion since I seem to be implying that we should come to worship God and begin by admitting we are disappointed with him. Of course, this would be a crazy thing to do if God were unpredictable and if

388   Elliot Aronson and J. Merrill Carlsmith. "Effect of the severity of threat on the devaluation of forbidden behavior." *The Journal of Abnormal and Social Psychology*, 66.6 (1963): 43584.

we were able to keep our true feelings from him. But is he not patient with us? Does he not know the thoughts of our hearts in any case?[389]

Unless we derive some masochistic pleasure from turning out to praise God's greatness whilst secretly doubting whether it is true, my reading of the scriptures, together with a growing understanding of what it means to be mentally healthy, tells me that God receives very little honour if we are singing through gritted teeth. By doing so we are simply adding to our own inner fragmentation if we feel forced to wear a mask in order to worship the one we believe knows us intimately and loves us perfectly. My fear is that, unless we address the issues above, the whole worship event will eventually become meaningless and all we'll be left with is the thrill that comes from a community sing-song.

Outcome: Event-driven Discipleship

Rob Warner sees warning signs when "ecstatic intensity is presented as a universally attainable and repeatable spiritual experience. The ecstatic becomes normative. All believers can become a Saint Teresa d'Avila with none facing a dark night of the soul... The church triumphant is but a song away."[390] As one who was deeply involved in the Charismatic Renewal before becoming disillusioned, I get the feeling that Warner is alluding to his own "mephistophelian price tag" in his observation that "those who marry their Christian faith to a specific cultural context are destined to self-marginalisation when that culture fades".[391]

His reference to St Teresa is helpful because it reminds us that those who know most about the process of Christian formation attest to the fact that an enriching, life-transforming journey with Christ invariably involves seasons of brokenness and self-emptying as part of the Christ-formation process.[392] Experiences of exuberance certainly have their place but if we become addicted to the natural high that is created by a particular mix of

389   If you want to explore the idea of emotional health and church life I commend Peter Scazzero – *Emotionally Healthy Spirituality: Unleash a Revolution in your Life in Christ* (Nashville: Thomas Nelson, 2006).

390   Rob Warner - Reinventing English Evangelicalism, 83-4.

391   Rob Warner, op. cit., 65.

392   We will consider the role of personal spiritual disciplines in the next chapter.

songs and confuse this with the presence of God we risk falling prey to the idea that following God is always going to be exhilarating.

I recall a particular meeting I attended at which I found myself on the raised stage, facing the majority of the crowd during a time of worship. The worship band was of the high octane variety and the crowd in attendance had clearly come ready to give themselves fully to the experience. Not long into the extended worship session my eye was caught by a particular girl, probably in her mid 20s with brightly coloured clothing. She had her arms raised in typical fashion and looked enraptured. It was as she began to wave her arms that I noticed the white letters FCUK emblazoned on her red top. The letters were huge and, as these advertising gimmicks are intended to do, they stopped me in my tracks. The utter incongruity of the facial expression and the deliberately mis-spelt word hit me with huge force. Whilst trying very hard not to stand in judgement upon the wearer of the red top or doubt God's overwhelming love for her, I found I had some work to do over the next few days not just to remove the image from my mind but also to understand what may have been going on.

As someone who rarely feels exhilarated about anything, let alone worship, other people experiencing powerful emotions during worship initially confused me. I then went through the frustration stage, followed by resignation, explanation (mainly by developing an understanding of temperament), cynicism (it was all hype and hysteria) and finally revelation. As I evaluated this experience over the course of many months, it was as if all the things I already knew about worship connected themselves together in an entirely new way.

Worship is not about us, but about God. Worship need have nothing to do with songs – which may also have nothing to do with worship. Worship cannot be evaluated by the way it makes us feel – in fact sometimes our feelings can switch the focus from God to ourselves and thus be unhelpful. Going deeper still, the vehicle we use to 'worship' will invariably create an altered state of consciousness, but this must not be thought of as 'God'. This altered state is simply an explainable and observable fact, is well documented by psychologists of religion and is experienced in many cultures and within all religions and also via practices that are not religious in any meaningful sense. The fact that a feeling can thus be explained does not demean the state, but it does mean we must be careful not to assume it is necessarily God producing the feelings we are experiencing.

The tendency to jump to the conclusion that feelings of elation are proof that God is present can be potentially disastrous to our faith, our credibility and our mental and emotional health. They can also be dishonouring to God if we are either distracted by them or led in any way to conclude that how I feel is God's chief concern. This is not to say that God may not occasionally overwhelm us, move us or otherwise impact us, but we must not think that the feeling of being overwhelmed was the point of the exercise or is, necessarily, of any lasting value. It is important that we see these altered states of consciousness as simply by-products of the practices we are using to focus our hearts and minds on God and recognise that the symptoms we are experiencing may also be utterly explainable to someone who understands the way the human mind and body works.

The whole point of setting time aside to focus our attention upon God, through whatever means we use, is to put us in a place where we can hear God tell us things about himself and ourselves in order that our response to him is as apt and reverent as it can possibly be. These are the pearls to be sought and they can be found scattered throughout our lives if we develop the ability to perceive them. Every event of life can thus become an encounter with God which has the capacity to be life changing.

Given the fact that the New Testament suggests that a mid-sized *oikos* community is the optimum sized unit for Christian discipleship to happen, and all we have said about the dynamics of the larger event, this calls into question the common assumption that the disciple needs a more powerful experience of God in order to become a more fruitful disciple and that they need to be touched powerfully by God in order to minister more effectively to a lost world. Praise God for experiences like the one Heidi Baker testifies to when she was lain flat under the power of the Spirit and emerged transformed. When the Spirit of God comes close, humans experience the backwash. We are reminded by Paul that the church is the "the fullness of him who fills all in all,"[393] and its members have the same spirit who raised Christ from the dead living in them[394] and also have the capacity to "be filled with all the fullness of God".[395] Those facts remain the same even without experiences to underline them.

....

393   Ephesians 1:23.

394   Romans 8:11.

395   Ephesians 3:19.

If changed lives are the desired outcome, I am forced to wonder whether a simpler form of gathering may be a more effective format to help frame the kind of occasion in which those who are truly seeking to follow Christ can learn to listen to and receive the Holy Spirit. He is, after all, available and waiting to search our lives, awaken us to deeper dimensions of God and distribute gifts and guidance for the benefit of the world. I suggest this because I can recall times when I have received a word from God at a large meeting that thrilled me at the time but, as I tried to act on it by myself, I lost my way. Disciples need other disciples to help them grow in God and large meetings may deliver short-term impetus but cannot provide those vital, long-term, human connections. I wrote about this in the previous chapter.

Purpose: A Culture of Discipleship

Let's face it, not everyone who attends a public worship event knows what it means to be a disciple of Jesus or has made the decision to follow him. In fact, as I think more deeply about it, I actually find myself hoping that many of those who attend our public gatherings are there out of curiosity. There is no shame in this since, like the Jerusalem church in Acts, new people should be added to the fringe of these Sunday events because they are being attracted by something they see under the surface of our community life.

It has been said that if teachers were only allowed to teach that which was their current experience meetings would be a great deal shorter and we would all be more honest. Again, it is the division we have created between knowledge and practice that needs to be healed. The Greek-influenced mind sees discipleship as getting facts about God straight. Hence the silly statement I come across time and again that a person has 'sat under the ministry of...(insert the name of a teacher)'. That myth was dispelled for me when I witnessed the fate of a very well-known church that 'sat under' a brilliant bible teacher for years but had clearly absorbed so little that when he left (in entirely honourable circumstances) the church split amidst much acrimony. I fear that Christian TV may also be unwittingly supporting a generation of church-less Christians who have a similar mindset.

Jesus teaches that we don't actually believe something until we are putting it into practice consistently and effectively.[396] So what does this say about what we can hope to achieve at a Sunday gathering? The church

396   Matthew 7:24-27.

I was leading as I begun to reflect on these themes agreed to a bold experiment in which, once a month, we inserted LifeGroups into our Sunday schedule. In practice this meant meeting in homes for one Sunday a month. The focus of these groups was on trying to help people live out the truth of the message of the previous week. The reason they happened on Sundays was because we wanted to send the message that discipleship was so central to our thinking that we wanted to make it possible for everyone to engage in the process. The experiment was a limited success because I had not done the harder work of establishing a culture of discipleship but I learned a great deal about in the process.

In John 15 Jesus uses the image of a vine – something which would have been very familiar to his hearers, many of whom will have tended one themselves and done so for just one purpose: to cultivate a crop of grapes. A vine has no other purpose except, maybe, that of giving shade. So when Jesus speaks of pruning dead wood which is disposed of and describes the process of cutting back live growth to facilitate a greater crop, the point of his message is clear – God expects us to bear fruit and we can bear *none* without knowing how to receive everything we need from our life in God. Fruit is the necessary sign that we are disciples but, like grapes on a vine, it is expected to appear naturally as we draw nourishment from Christ.[397] Where there is no fruit we are therefore not entitled to make the claim that we are connected to the vine who is Christ.

Observing the regular cycle of feasts and obeying the fourth commandment every seven days provided the structure within which Jesus' disciples would have understood his teaching very clearly. In a culture more familiar with the protestant work ethic, we often need to be reminded about the importance and meaning of rest, rhythm and season. The Semi-circle is the LifeShape that deals with the balance between abiding and fruitfulness and is a much-needed reminder that productivity is not a direct result of endless activity.[398]

Some years ago I was leading a group in our church and teaching them the ancient *Lectio Divina* method of scripture reading using this passage. During this process I learned that one of the most faithful members of our church had been taught during childhood that, since Christ is no longer with

---

397   John 15:8.

398   See Mike Breen and Steve Cockram – *Building a Discipling Culture*, Chapter 6.

us, it is the church that now plays the part of the vine and not Christ directly. A second person had been told that the fruit Christ was looking for would only come about by their fervent evangelistic activity. Despite the repeated insistence that the Father is the vine and fruit is produced naturally as we learn to remain vitally connected to him, these teaching points had been completely obscured by poor theology.

So fruit production is the necessary mark of a disciple and, according to Jesus, there are also seasons in which disciples will be pruned in order to stimulate more vigorous growth on the branches the Father wishes to promote. This is a mysterious work done inwardly by God whose nature it is to replicate himself.

> Jesus also said, 'This is what the kingdom of God is like. A man scatters seed on the ground. Night and day, whether he sleeps or gets up, the seed sprouts and grows, though he does not know how. All by itself the soil produces corn – first the stalk, then the ear, then the full grain in the ear. As soon as the corn is ripe, he puts the sickle to it, because the harvest has come.'[399]

If these images teach us anything it seems that the spiritual dynamics underlying our growth in Christ-likeness are made up of a mixture of factors. The first, and most important, is that we are individually connected to Christ who is the Vine. It is he who causes us to bear fruit as we live in him and obey him. There will be times and seasons to our fruitfulness because Jesus will choose to cut off branches that are unprofitable and are draining energy from the vine, along with other branches that have borne fruit but need to make way for more growth in the next season. Whenever God calls us to a season of rest or abiding, my experience is that it rarely makes sense at the time. Just as Jesus teaches us in the second parable, all the farmer is called to do is prepare the ground and that is what we will consider next.

Focus: Making Disciples

Willow Creek Community Church is well-known for its distinctive seeker-sensitive approach to presenting the message of the gospel to the unchurched. Dig below the surface and it becomes clear that it is also a church that is equally committed to excellence in leadership, spiritual fruitfulness and Christian discipleship. Several years ago Willow began

---

399   Mark 4:26-29.

asking whether it was possible to measure the kind of growth that is a result of the unseen work of the Spirit in order that the church leadership could ensure they were investing their resources in the right places.

This huge project was launched only after some of the best minds in statistical research had convinced the leaders at Willow that it was possible to establish a robust methodology for measuring spiritual growth.[400] After conducting 5000 detailed surveys from within their own congregation and six other churches from various denominations, sub-cultures and regions of the United States, Willow published their initial findings and then surveyed a further 157,000 people in more than 500 churches across the USA and Canada.[401]

Willow had begun with three hypotheses which summarised the assumptions that had underpinned their discipleship programmes up to the point of the study:

1. There is a migration path for spiritual growth based on church activities

2. The most effective evangelism tool is the spiritual conversation

3. Spiritual relationships are the key driver of spiritual growth

Their research findings led to some head-scratching and can be summarised thus:

1. Involvement in Church activities may affect outward behaviour but does not increase love for God and others

2. Spiritual Growth is a function of increasing relational closeness to Christ

3. The church as an institution is most important in the early stages of spiritual growth

4. Personal spiritual practices are the building blocks for a Christ-

400   This is fully explained in Appendices 1 and 2 of *Reveal: Where are You?* (Willow Creek Resources: Barrington, Illinois, 2007) and Appendix 2 of Greg Hawkins + Cally Parkinson – *Follow Me – What's next for you?* (Willow Creek Resources: Barrington, Illinois, 2008).

401   In the years since Reveal was published many churches in the UK and Europe have also been surveyed to demonstrate that these findings transcend the North American culture.

centred life

5. A Church's most active evangelists, volunteers and donors come from the most spiritually advanced segments

6. More than 25% of those surveyed described themselves as spiritually 'stalled' or 'dissatisfied' with the role of the church in their spiritual growth

The first thing they recognised was that, whereas churches tend to measure success by numbers, Jesus seems not to have concerned himself with gaining a large follower-ship. Whilst numbers can indicate whether people like what you are doing, maybe opposition ought to be a far better test that you are making headway. Having also discovered that there was no direct correlation between increased church activity and spiritual growth[402] (growth as defined by Jesus, namely: love for God and one's neighbour) the research project began asking what attitudes, activities, and practices were statistically significant.

As they probed deeper the data began to suggest that no simple pattern was discernible but also it became evident that people at different stages of spiritual growth were saying similar things. Further analytical work seemed to suggest to the observers that four clear bands were evident within the data, and this became the foundation for the suggestion that it was helpful to depict the spiritual growth path taken by growing and fruitful Christians as a journey which has four distinct stages:

➤   Stage 1 - Exploring Christianity

➤   Stage 2 – Growing in Christ

➤   Stage 3 – Close to Christ

➤   Stage 4 – Centred on Christ

The very suggestion of a growth continuum is demonstrably scriptural and makes a great deal of sense. The idea that there are observable stages through which we pass is implied by Paul and the writer of Hebrews when

----

402   The study is careful to make clear that increased level of activity is not a predictor of greater love for God, which does not mean that people involved in church activities do not love him.

they talk about the need to progress from milk to meat[403] and by John who uses the Greek terms for children, teens and fathers as markers of spiritual maturity.[404]

The broad lessons to be learned from the *Reveal* research seem to be that discipleship is a life-time journey that passes through distinct stages. The key to growth at each stage is increased relational depth, both with God through the Holy Spirit and with others. Our relationship with God is deepened as we engage in spiritual practices that align us with him, making us more sensitive to his presence and leading. Our connection with others may begin within relatively structured settings such as church services and small groups but must be allowed to mature as we form closer connections with fewer people with whom we can share our journey and may also offer us a degree of personal mentoring.

One of the most surprising features of the research was the large number of 'stalled' and 'dissatisfied' Christians they had in their midst. On further examination it was discovered that these were followers of Jesus who had been taught that the church would be able to serve them at every stage of their growth. The staff at Willow were forced to accept, not just that growth was dependent on the development of personal spiritual disciplines, but that later-stage disciples needed to be involved in mentoring younger Christians and in outreach and evangelism if they were to continue their growth. What we see, in this extensive research, is that there is significant statistical evidence that confirms everything we have been saying about discipleship. It is not something that happens by osmosis as Christians engage with church events since growth towards a balanced life represented by the Triangle requires a carefully structured environment similar to the one Jesus created for the Twelve.[405]

Re-Defining Discipleship

As we draw towards the end of this book how much have you been forced to re-evaluate as you have walked with me through John's Gospel? The leadership of Willow Creek took a great risk in telling the world they had

---

403   See 1 Corinthians 3:2 and Hebrews 5:12-13.

404   John 2:12-14.

405   *Follow Me* focuses on the catalysts that progress a disciple from one stage to the next.

it wrong, precisely because they had such a high profile and a reputation for excellence. Are you prepared to bite the bullet and initiate a process of honest re-evaluation? Are there things you have been teaching and ways you have been leading that now need to change? What are the next steps you need to take to equip yourself and your church with the necessary tools and relationships that will facilitate true spiritual growth?

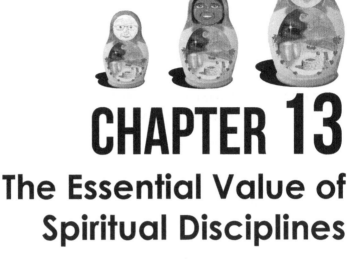

CHAPTER 13
The Essential Value of Spiritual Disciplines

At the beginning of the previous chapter I found two references to community in a passage that has been interpreted, almost exclusively, in individualistic terms by Christians who have been moulded into consumers by our present culture. This is not to deny the fact that we are each called to follow Christ as individuals and, as we saw in the *Reveal* research, if converts are not taught to feed on Christ for themselves they will fail to grow into fruitful disciples.

Several years ago I was preparing for 'Covenant Sunday', the occasion when covenanted partners of our church community re-signed their covenant commitment to God and each other for a further year. In the days leading up to the gathering my car had been experiencing problems starting and I was told by the garage that the recent 'jump starts' I had given the old battery had been fatal. The battery had died. The engineer had told me that it is far better for a flat battery to be 'trickle charged' rather than 'jump started' and this got me thinking.

As I began thinking about how to open the Covenant Service gathering I began asking myself why it had become normal practice to begin each Sunday meeting with a 'bang' usually made up of strident, faith filled songs and a stirring scripture reading. I had just learned that jump starting a car may be the method to use when we are in a hurry but it ultimately damages the battery. The more healthy way is to trickle charge a flat battery for many hours. I began to wonder whether the 'jump start' method of approaching God may not be good for our long term spiritual health if the message it is sending is that we need these outward stimuli to get us into the 'worship' groove. I have already suggested that such an approach to 'worship' risks confusing the natural 'high' generated by all the carefully chosen features of a worship event with the real presence of God. I am now suggesting that such confusion may militate against the establishment of the spiritual disciplines that are required for disciples to walk in the shoes of Jesus.

In the days that followed that service I began to hear murmuring. People were telling me that my suggestion that we spend the coming year learning some of the classic spiritual 'disciplines' didn't sound attractive, despite me rooting the word in Christian history. My desire to help God's people embed wholesome spiritual disciplines into their everyday lives was spurred by a principle I had picked up from John Eldredge: Teach a man a rule and you help him solve a problem; Teach a man to walk with God and you help him solve the rest of his life.[406] I was now discovering that God's people were being put off by a word that sounded too much like hard work.

I had read the following book review just before this Covenant service and it seemed to summarise our 21st century challenge:

> As a pastor, rarely do I ever read a book twice. But I picked up King's book again the other day because... I think King not only provides a much needed critique of evangelical youth ministry, but also a path forward. In his book, King quotes Os Guinness who was asked by a non-Christian foreigner, "How come when I meet a Buddhist leader I feel like I am in the presence of a holy man, but when I meet a Christian leader, I feel like I have met an entrepreneur, a mover and shaker, a wheeler dealer?" King's book seems to offer evangelicals a way to regain some much needed credibility by rediscovering spiritual practices that have been practised by Christians for generations long before we began writing them off because of divisive nuances in our

---

406   John Eldredge – *Waking the Dead*, 96-97.

ecclesiologies.[407]

Set Apart For God

I have assumed throughout this study that the discipleship journey has to begin with a desire to become like Christ. This may seem blindingly obvious since the Twelve were taught to see as Jesus saw, do only what they were directed to do and minister to others using the power and authority supplied by another to whom they were in submission. It becomes an entirely different question when we wake up to the fact that present-day disciples are also expected to learn to do the same things the Twelve were taught to do and that the only way of learning to act like someone else is to live as they do.

This "indicates that Christians are not merely called to be nice people, but to appropriate holiness as a distinctive way of life".[408] Holiness is both our current identity and our distinctive calling.[409] "Real holiness is not the special calling of a few. It is God's will for all believers."[410] Since holiness is our calling, the first step of faith is to believe that "what God wants from [us], he makes possible".[411]

In popular understanding the word 'holy' is thought to refer to having high moral standards, being upright or righteous, whereas the word really means being 'set apart' for the use of God and thereby withdrawn from common use.

This popular view is close to that held by the Pharisees whose static definitions of right and wrong were used to judge the behaviour of others

....

407   Mike King - *Presence-centered Youth Ministry: Guiding Students into Spiritual Formation* (Downers Grove: IVP Books, 2006). The review is from www.amazon.com.

408   Peter Holmes and Susan Williams – *Becoming more like Christ* (Paternoster; Milton Keynes, 2007), 4.

409   By this I mean that, as redeemed Saints God assures us that the holiness we were called to has already been achieved through our unity with Christ (Ephesians 1:4), and yet we are also commanded to live lives characterised by holy practices (Ephesians 5:1-20).

410   Jack Bernard – *How to become a Saint: a beginners guide* (Grand Rapids: Brazos Press, 2007), 24.

411   Jack Bernard – *How to become a Saint*, 25.

with the aim of ensuring outward compliance and correct behaviour. Jesus continually demonstrated the wrong-headed nature of such a system every time he clashed with the Pharisees on a minor point of the Oral Teachings. Jesus was simply revealing how static, defensive, hypocritical and moralistic man-made rules can be in comparison to the Torah which was intended to be an instrument of blessing. The fact that the Pharisees came to view Jesus as satanic[412] according to their definition of holiness goes to show just how easy it is to be zealous for God whilst entirely missing the point.

There is a huge difference between being fervent for something – in this case being counted amongst the 'chosen' people – and pursuing someone (i.e. God) whom we come to know as we cultivate a pure heart.[413] Jack Bernard is right when he says that holiness "has more to do with learning to trust God than with learning to be good."[414] Whilst our attention is upon ourselves we will never be able to please God, especially if we are preoccupied with sublimating our sinful desires. Trying harder to please someone whose nature we will never be able to match will never lead to success.

The right place to begin is to remind ourselves that everyone who is *In Christ* has already been made holy. We are therefore placing our faith in a God who has truly begun his work in us and promises to refine our desires as he renews us from within. At this point Peter Holmes' definition of sin comes into play once more. Sin, we recall, is best defined as 'consistent refusal to change' – refusal to become more like Christ, or more perfectly human. Our inward resistance meets a desire for holiness which comes from God and we get to decide which side wins.

This reminds me of an old American Indian proverb:

> *An old Cherokee was teaching his grandson about life: "A fight is going on inside me," he said to the boy. "It is a terrible fight and it is between two wolves. One is evil - he is anger, envy, sorrow, regret, greed, arrogance, self-pity, guilt, resentment, inferiority, lies, false pride, superiority, and ego. The other is good - he is joy, peace, love, hope, serenity, humility, kindness, benevolence,*

---

412   Matthew 12:24.

413   Matthew 5:8.

414   Jack Bernard – *How to become a Saint*, 26.

empathy, generosity, truth, compassion, and faith. This same fight is going on inside you - and inside every other person, too." The grandson paused to think about what he had heard and then asked his grandfather, "Which wolf will win?" The old Cherokee simply replied, "The one you feed."

Everything we need for victory is received by us within our spirit. The power to be holy must come from God in order that it might lead us toward him[415] and our role is to cooperate with God by allowing our attention to be increasingly devoted to him. Bernard sees humility as the key secret to growth in holiness since

our... problem stems from the fact that we do not face the truth. We are, in fact, frequently and passionately dedicated to just the opposite. We struggle with an inner drive to see ourselves as not only important but as superior, at least in some way, to others around us and base our sense of value on our superiority.... The standard trick of pride is to protect oneself from facing reality by always claiming unrealised potential.[416]

So, when I feel like I should be doing better, this itself is rooted in a kind of pride that really believes I can succeed by my own efforts. Bernard tells the story of Therese of Lizieux who

despite the limitation of being nothing at all, helped reform the whole church's understanding of holiness... she came across the scripture in which Jesus says: 'Let the little children come to me'... taking God at his word and assuming that every little and faltering thing she attempted to do for God he was pleased with.[417]

Surely this is how Jesus sustained himself. By this I mean that Jesus knew himself fully accepted, trusted his Father perfectly and was therefore inclined towards him and attentive to his Father's voice. Avoidance of sin is a natural result of being entirely focused upon and captivated by God simply because it is impossible to give yourself to two opposing masters at

---

415   Ibid. 29.

416   Ibid, 38.

417   Ibid, 40.

the same time.[418] John Piper puts it beautifully: "God is most glorified in us when we are most satisfied in him" for "sin is what you do when your heart is not satisfied with God.[419]

So, if we are to follow the desire for holiness that God produces within us "we have to allow ourselves to be taken hold of by the Holy Spirit."[420] God reveals, we agree (confess he is right), we respond as required (repent) and experience the freedom that results in us being able to live freely. "Real righteousness comes about by walking (living) according to or in the power of the Holy Spirit,"[421] and the Spirit brings life.

Bernard concludes that it is impossible to "seek holiness and the appearance of holiness at the same time" and that the only way do this is to "stop trying to manipulate how people think of you."[422] This only becomes possible as we learn to deflect our attention from ourselves and toward God in the power of the Spirit and is where the spiritual disciplines become essential if we are to live a holy life. Bernard says:

> *Disciplines are not for the purpose of driving us to do something we ultimately do not want to do. If we really have no heart for the things of God we need to go back to step one and face the choice of whether we want to give ourselves over to God or not. Spiritual disciplines will not help us if we are not willing to do this. Spiritual disciplines are founded on the assumption that we at least want to want to live in and for God. Disciplines are devices to help us transcend our feelings of the moment and get on with what we ultimately want to do. For the most part, spiritual practices are boring, not exciting. The point is to open ourselves to God on his terms, not to entertain ourselves. Spiritual disciplines usually involve setting aside specific times each day to pay attention to God rather than ourselves. If we won't do that. it is ludicrous to think that we will pay attention to God's will in the midst of*

418   Matthew 6:24 and Galatians 5:16.

419   John Piper – *Future Grace* (Leicester: IVP, 1995), 9.

420   Jack Bernard – *How to become a Saint*, 34.

421   Ibid, 33.

422   Ibid, 43,4.

everything else.[423]

Making Space For God

It is a brave decision to initiate a season of abstinence from sung worship, especially when your worship leader is a nationally known figure and his songs are a major attraction for visitors to your church, but this is exactly what St Andrew's Church in Chorleywood decided to do some years ago. In his song *'Heart of Worship'*, written during that period, Matt Redman writes about how easy it is to miss the point, especially when we find ourselves caught up in an exhilarating experience. There are times in our lives when it is necessary to close down avenues of stimulation in order to attune our senses to the voice of the Spirit. Seasoned disciples have learned that the Spirit fine-tunes our trajectory by whispering to us moment by moment and that it takes years of practise to tune out other, competing, voices.

Surely this was the lesson learned by Elijah after the momentous display of the power of God recorded in 1 Kings 18. In the following chapter we find Elijah empty and exhausted, ready to surrender his life, but not as a result of failure and defeat. Elijah's readiness to give in was a natural human response to the accumulated pressure that had built up as he had allowed himself to be forced out on a limb, needing God to act to ensure his own survival. Elijah had been vindicated, but in a manner that brought severe opposition from the most powerful woman in the land. What Elijah needed was not another demonstration of power but for God to meet him at his place of deepest need:

> *"Go out and stand before me on top of the mountain," the LORD said to him. Then the LORD passed by and sent a furious wind that split the hills and shattered the rocks - but the LORD was not in the wind. The wind stopped blowing, and then there was an earthquake - but the LORD was not in the earthquake. After the earthquake there was a fire - but the LORD was not in the fire. And after the fire there was the soft whisper of a voice. When Elijah heard it, he covered his face with his cloak and went out and stood at the entrance of the cave. A voice said to him, "Elijah,*

---

423   Ibid, 96.

what are you doing here?"[424]

I believe we need to find ways of creating similar spaces where we force ourselves to curb our addictions to endless stimulation. Generations of Christian disciples have understood the need to create 'desert spaces' into which God can speak to us about himself and thus renew our minds and our lives. These are the places where we discern God asking the questions our souls need to hear and which allow the Spirit to draw more of what will be our future into the present. These are also the means by which we discover that, in the long run, rhythms and routines are more significant to our growth in Christ-likeness than programmes and meetings.

Attentiveness To God

In the week leading up to Easter many of us turn our attention to Jesus' experience of anguish just before the betrayal that led to his crucifixion. The account is graphic and full of pathos as Jesus faces his final hours alone but not unsupported. Luke writes:

> *Jesus went out as usual to the Mount of Olives, and his disciples followed him. On reaching the place, he said to them, "Pray that you will not fall into temptation." He withdrew about a stone's throw beyond them, knelt down and prayed...*[425]

The disciples are unable to offer Jesus their support because they are unaware of the fate that awaits him and are clearly exhausted. Despite being alerted to the section of the pattern prayer that was most apposite to the moment, they miss the cue and fall asleep.[426]

For Jesus, such times with his Father had become routine. This was just one of many regular trips to the Mount of Olives to commune with his Father. John, it seems, managed to stay awake for longer than the others since he is able to record Jesus' prayer in great detail. He hears Jesus pleading with his Father that those whom he was about to leave, and all who followed them subsequently, would know their new identity, the source of

---

424   1 Kings 19:11f (GNT).

425   Luke 22:39-41.

426   Look back to Chapter 10 for a summary of the six sections of the Lord's Prayer.

their security and the importance of remaining 'sanctified', or 'holy'.[427] The risen Jesus, we now understand, remains in prayer on our behalf.[428] The question remains how many of his earth-bound disciples are awake enough to receive the answers to his prayers.

"The main reason for God's calling us to obedience is not for an imposition of discipline for discipline's sake... [but] to keep us spiritually perceptive, open to God, attentive to his voice."[429] John Westerhoff writes of his experience of a form of Eastern Christian retreat known as *poustinia*.

> *Its purpose is to help us experience the desert, that lonely silent secluded place where God cares for us... I went to a small, windowless room with only a mattress on the floor. For forty-eight hours I was alone in that room. I read my bible by the light of the candle and lying prostrate on the floor waited in the dark silence for God to come. It was in these moments of self-emptying or what might appear to be escape that I found enlightenment and unity with God, myself and all humanity.[430]*

This, I think, is an example of being made holy by allowing godly desire to well up within us. Such an experience is not something that can be worked up. It emerges from deep within us as we allow the Spirit to breathe life into our spirit and we give godly desires the permission to emerge into our felt consciousness. I think *permission* is a good word because too many of us have become over-stimulated by 'worship' practices that assail us. In generating 'feelings' on such occasions we have, perhaps, closed the door to our emotions in our communion with God.

Westerhoff recalls a Russian Orthodox priest telling a group at his college that he did not understand their way of praying that spent so much time concentrating on the words. "Is not the aim of prayer", he asked, "to be in God's presence and to hear God's voice speak through images and emotions?" Peter Holmes said to me some time ago that "unless you can

---

427   John 17:17.

428   Hebrews 7:25.

429   Michael Frost and Alan Hirsch - *The Shaping of Things to Come*, 141.

430   John Westerhoff and John Eusden – *The Spiritual Life* (New York: Seabury Press, 1982), 45.

imagine something you will never feel it." I believe that our godly imagination is only as strong as our communion with God in the secret place that is our Gethsemane.

In the previous chapter I suggested that learning to mourn in 'worship' could be an important discipline for Christian disciples for the sake of their mental and emotional health. What a challenge it would be for many evangelical Christians to admit to themselves that there are places within that do not correspond to the shiny, happy stereotype that is often presented as the default mode for all true Christians. Lois Tverberg suggests that the rabbis of Jesus' day would have considered the command of the *Shema* to love God with all our hearts to be an instruction to love him "with the angry, sad, mourning part of our heart as well" as the happy part.[431] The only way it is possible to do this is to direct our minds to notice the small and frequent blessings we normally take for granted which, once again, is a traditional Hebrew practice commended by Paul,[432] and is the means by which we regain our balance. So it is only as we allow ourselves to mourn that the discipline of giving thanks truly makes sense.

Knowing God

Both Jesus and Paul make it clear there are different ways of knowing truth. Just as the prophet Isaiah distinguished between knowledge and wisdom[433] and Jesus indicates to Peter that he receives insights directly from God,[434] so Paul unpacks this mystery in greater detail. In the first chapter of his letter to the church at Corinth he distinguishes between the wisdom of God and the so-called 'wisdom' of humans who can understand, and therefore believe, only that which makes sense to their minds. We might call this an 'educated awareness'. In the following chapter Paul writes about the need to be taught spiritual things spiritually and insists that such revelation produces a wisdom that human knowledge simply cannot test.

Richard Rohr explains that in the early church era these two streams of knowledge were denoted as *Logos* (gk: 'word') and *Sophia* (gk: 'wisdom')

---

431   Ann Spangler and Lois Tverberg – *Sitting at the Feet of Rabbi Jesus*, 93.

432   Ephesians 5:10; Colossians 3:17; 1 Thessalonians 5:17-18.

433   Isaiah 11:2.

434   Matthew 16:17.

and were held together fairly successfully until the Christian faith was adopted as the favoured religion of the Roman Empire in around AD313.[435] From this moment the church adopted power structures to mirror the Empire, was given favoured rights, set up its own universities and learning centres and also convened numerous councils to rule against those it deemed heretics. In many cases they were acting wisely in opposing many strange doctrines but the Church also found itself opposing mystics it simply didn't understand because such individuals were discerning truths the Church was no longer equipped to receive. The *Logos* stream (which had always been described as if it were masculine) was now the only way of *knowing* the new, powerful, (male) leaders of the Church would accept as valid.

God, however, continued to speak using both 'languages' and the two distinct traditions diverged, rarely coming into contact with each other. The dominant mode became known as Kataphatic Tradition ('According to Images' – speaking through symbols, words and descriptors) whilst the Apophatic Tradition ('Beyond Images' – knowing by intuition) flourished in more remote locations such as caves where hermits would dwell, or desert places where small prophetic communities would locate themselves. In coming centuries individuals like St Patrick, Francis of Assisi, St Bonaventure, Julian of Norwich, St John of the Cross and Theresa of Avila became known for their intense devotion and often had hugely influential ministries – but always from the edge.

Equally, characters like Anthony, Aidan, Benedict and many others formed monastic orders based around a distinct rule of life and these became communities to which seekers would go to receive wisdom, prayer and direction. Some of the cities and towns we know today were built around these places where the presence of God was deemed to have come close (they were called 'thin places'). It is said, for example, that town names beginning 'Kil...' are so named because they were built around a 'cell' where a holy man lived.

Once the Church lost touch with this deeper way of seeing taught by Jesus and Paul it seems it became unable to distinguish between the benefits and pitfalls of Hellenist-influenced ways of thinking and reasoning. Much Western thought is thus based upon definitions of reality based upon

....

435   The following paragraphs draw from Richard Rohr's DVD set - *Holding the Tension: The Power of Paradox*.

opposites: black or white, good or bad, positive or negative, wrong or right, for us or against us, friend or foe, heretic or saint.

This means that, as far as we have been influenced by this way of thinking, we have learned to go through life excluding, denying, opposing, tied in by absolute truth claims to which others must adjust if they are to gain our approval. To be right is to be considered godly whereas to be deemed wrong is to be excluded and damned. The problem is that once we find ourselves in this *quid pro quo* world it becomes so difficult to love as Jesus demanded because it is nearly impossible to exercise grace, show mercy or truly forgive people who seem to be getting their just deserts.

It is also impossible to understand and therefore live by, many of the sayings of Jesus, such as the concept that the first can be last, the fact that we find ourselves by losing ourselves, that death is really life, weakness is the ultimate strength, the poor are rich... the list goes on and on. If Christian disciples really believed these things the world would be a hugely different place but we struggle because we are so steeped in an non-biblical world-view. Only the things that make sense within the framework we are most familiar with are readily accepted as true and, even then, are 'true' only in the sense that we give mental assent to them. As in Athens at the time of Paul, Greeks are very good at deploying strategies to stop them from living according to the truths they apparently believe.[436] In living as good Greeks, we are thus surrendering the ability to receive wisdom which must be lived if it is to be experienced as true.

So, for generations, the Church has taken stands against trends and behaviours it doesn't agree with, has endlessly divided itself into opposing factions, many of which have appointed themselves as defenders of certain bodies of truth – as if 'truth' can ever be a body of knowledge or set of ideas that need to be defended as if lives depended upon it. Meanwhile, many of the more esoteric sayings of Jesus appear to this same mindset as riddles because such people are unable to hold together thoughts and ideas that are deemed to be opposites within their restricted frame of logic. Unless we are somehow able to escape this constricted world in which it is so easy to become trapped, much at the heart of Jesus' teaching remains a mystery to us, even while we seek to defend various things we believe about his person.

---

436   Acts 17:19-21.

Jesus, remember, rarely answered a straight question with a clear answer. When asked which mountain God found most acceptable, Jesus directed the Samaritan woman beyond the issue of when and how 'worship' rites are best performed. Instead he taught that we come to God thirsty and find ourselves fully satisfied by the living water that flows from within us. He thus turns a potential argument into an invitation. Likewise, Nicodemus found himself mulling over the image of the Spirit who is wild, unpredictable and leads people away from empty religious structures and fruitless debates. Each of the images around which John's Gospel has been constructed attempt to achieve the same feat.

What we have learned about the Apophatic Tradition demonstrates that it is far closer to the spirit of John's Gospel, and to the Hebrew way of thinking and living, than the Greek categories of thought many of us have been taught to live by. The Hebrew mind is able to live with paradox because it does not see the same need to reconcile every seeming contradiction. It is content to live with mystery and this is rooted in the deep conviction that if we think we understand something fully it cannot be God. God will be whom he will be and sometimes we need to let go of the need to know in order to see things as they really are. As Einstein famously said: "No problem can be solved with the same consciousness that created it". If we are to be part of the solution to the human problem we will need to allow ourselves to be drawn into an entirely different mindset.

The Hebrew mind has developed the capacity to hold two or more seeming opposites and live with the tension. I am told that two Jews in dispute may achieve this as they seek a 'reconciling third' option – which will often contain elements of the previous opinions of both combatants, formed into a new mix which neither had envisaged before. Rohr is keen to point out that this Hebrew way of thinking is not anti-intellectual since it actually requires us to sharpen our minds, not abandon them. We are, it seems, being invited to perceive differently, from at least three places within ourselves at the same time – our spirit and both halves of our brain.

The way we learn to enter this different level of consciousness is through contemplative prayer – where contemplation becomes the path into the moment. This is what Westerhoff experienced in his windowless cell. The mind, says Rohr, is only able to take us either to the past or the future – but never the present. The spirit is endlessly present and enables us to perceive the greater depth underlying the reality around us. We might suspect all this mystical talk sounds more like Buddhism than Christianity, but this is only because we are so unaware of thousands of years of Christian tradition. The only way to recover this authentic experience, according to Rohr, is to realise that many of the rules by which we have lived life thus far don't work. We need to change by re-engaging with the Apophatic tradition.

Without the ability to access wisdom, education simply provides us with more criteria by which to judge and divide. The critic can never be happy because he feels forced either to deny the darkness in himself, excuse it or project it onto others. Remember, says Rohr, the only prohibition in the Garden? To choose to know in preference to receiving God's word on trust. The only other path is for us to develop a humility about not knowing and discover Christ's compassion for ourselves and for others. We have to fall into that mystery, and contemplative prayer is the trapdoor.

Missional Communities

I reordered my bookshelves fairly recently and experienced a perverse delight in placing John Piper's books next to those by Rob Bell. Both are my friends – why should I have to choose between them just because the authors cannot agree where the boundaries of God's love lie? Just as Jesus found God working in places others thought he couldn't (and shouldn't) be found, so we must learn to cultivate a similar expectation.

> We are called to be **fruitful** (John 15) but are only able to be so if we are rooted in Jesus. We are commanded to go and preach the gospel (Matt 28) but first we must come to Jesus' side... John Skinner, founder of the Northumbria Community, describes a monk as "one who separates himself from everybody in order to be available to everyone".[437]

Freeman and Greig explain the degree to which the Houses of Prayer they have established are dependant upon the disciplines I have described in this chapter. They describe the formation of communities in which all three dimensions of the Triangle are lived, along with a rhythm that helps its members balance the Martha/Mary or the abide/bear fruit dimensions of a Jesus-oriented life. Being available to everyone is just part of the picture. Becoming attractive to those to whom we are available is equally

....

437   Andy Freeman and Pete Greig – *Punk Monk: New Monasticism and the Ancient Art of Breathing* (Ventura: Regal Books, 2007) 94, 111.

important and this is where the disciplines are essential. Freeman and Greig have discovered that these qualities are formed in the quiet places and are attractive to the lost:

> *Too often my attempts at evangelism resemble a person trying desperately to pass on to others an illness that I'm not carrying... if I'm not carrying it the virus will not spread. It is only when I spend time breathing in the presence of Jesus that I catch his contagion and I become infectious with the gospel... What the world needs are people... who have spent so much time in the presence of God that their very life has become a form of blessing.*[438]

The calling of missional disciples is to create centred communities[439] united by a clear vision of what Christ has called us to become and an awareness of how such disciples are formed. Such communities are made up of individuals who know how to sustain their lives in Christ, have a healthy rhythm and are supported by leaders who are living examples of change in progress.[440] Our calling is then to go beyond the idea of mission as intervention and to allow God to incarnate himself in the world through people like us, living in communities that embody the features of a discipleship culture found in Acts 2:42-47.

---

438   Ibid, 95-96.

439   The difference between a Centred Community and a Bounded Community is best described by reference to sheep farming in Australia. A rancher with a centred set mentality pays far more attention to providing food, water and safety at the centre of the ranch in the knowledge that sheep will not stray when they are provided for. The alternative is to spend huge effort and resources on maintaining hundreds of miles of fence.

440   The theory and practice of Missional Communities is best researched by reading Mike Breen and Alex Absalom – *Launching Missional Communities: A Field Guide* (Pawley's Island: 3DM, 2010) and Mike Breen - *Leading Missional Communities* (Pawley's Island: 3DM, 2013).

PART 3

Jesus' Commission

CHAPTER 14
John's Great Commission

In the opening chapter we noted the masterful manner in which John constructed the first few verses of his gospel using a mixture of Jewish, Greek and pagan thought-forms. In doing so he provided himself with a broad foundation upon which he was able to introduce the Messiah to all nations and cultures. The fact that people from most cultures and nations have become followers of Christ in the millennia since Christ walked the earth has affirmed the validity of John's conviction.

Sadly, what passes for 'Christianity' today is often a lukewarm version of the original faith.[441] This makes it hard for us to appreciate what an uphill battle it must have been for the Apostles as they sought to point to a saviour who was both firmly rooted in the soil of Judaism and had his sights set on a truly radical and transformative vision.

There is something delightful about the fact that all Mary has to hear is her name called in a certain tone for her hope to spring back to life. Likewise

....

441   Of course, one person's 'nominality' is another person's sincere belief. I am referring here to the fact that it is possible to be labelled 'christian' without it making a great deal of difference to a person's everyday decisions and values.

the way the disciples find instant comfort in the common greeting *Shalom aleikhem* spoken by a voice they recognise. Jesus' resurrected features may have been unfamiliar but his manner was not. They know him so well. Thus begins a phase in which the male disciples enter a period of rehabilitation, in stark contrast to Mary who is ready to do Jesus' bidding straight away.

Once again, it is important to pay attention to the exact words Jesus uses:

> Again Jesus said, "Peace be with you! As the Father has sent me, I am sending you." And with that he breathed on them and said, "Receive the Holy Spirit. If you forgive anyone's sins, their sins are forgiven; if you do not forgive them, they are not forgiven."[442]

Note the similarities between these instructions and Jesus' last words as recorded by Matthew: "As the Father has sent me, I am sending you" refers to the manner in which the Disciples were to engage with God's lost world and "If you forgive anyone's sins, their sins are forgiven; if you do not forgive them, they are not forgiven" is the content of the message they are told to embody. It was typical for a Rabbi to give fully trusted disciples complete freedom to apply the principles they had been taught to new situations and this is exactly what Jesus is doing here. This second instruction may be couched in familiar language but was entirely different in content to any instruction other Rabbis of the day would have issued. Jesus is not instructing them to teach doctrine as he taught but permitting them to minister God's grace as they had seen him do. In other words, the very same activities that got Jesus into trouble (acting like God by forgiving people's sin) have been entrusted to those who will follow him!

Eight days later we read that the disciples are gathered together once more. Thomas hadn't been present when Jesus appeared to the others and clearly his faith was so shredded that he could not bring himself to believe the testimony of his closest friends. Jesus addresses him by name, inviting him to see, touch and believe. There follows the clearest statement of Jesus' divinity recorded in the Gospels: "My Lord and my God!".

> Jesus told [Thomas], "Because you have seen me, you have believed; blessed are those who have not seen and yet have believed." Jesus performed many other signs in the presence of

---

442   John 20:21-22.

his disciples, which are not recorded in this book. But these are written that you may believe that Jesus is the Messiah, the Son of God, and that by believing you may have life in his name.[443]

There follows a textual dilemma in verse 31 that delights me greatly. Ancient manuscripts are divided over whether John wrote "so that you may continue trusting", which would imply that the Gospel was written to help readers retain their faith, or "so that you may, at a point in time, come to trust", implying that the book is for unbelievers.[444]

I find the problem a delight because each option reminds us of a key truth we have already seen to be deeply embedded in the Gospel. The first reading reminds us that 'believing' who Jesus is must lead to the kind of believing that leads to life – namely, putting what we believe into practice and thus experiencing blessings we can pass on. The second reading underlines the fact that the early chapters of John record Jesus reframing his Father's intention to save the world as he reveals himself through his chosen people. I therefore see no need to choose between the two options.

Fishers of Women and Men

The section of the gospel that we denote as chapter 21 reads like a clunky extension to a document that felt complete at the end of chapter 20. It has been suggested that the section was added to correct a misunderstanding. We know that a story was in circulation that Jesus had promised he'd return in glory within John's lifetime and it seems that John feels the need to correct the rumour. He is, after all, the only one still alive who had heard both Jesus' actual words and their context. So John invites us to listen in to another appearance by Jesus to a sub-set of the twelve, most of whom had been first introduced to us in John 1 at the point at which they became followers of Jesus. There is even a second mention of the fact that Nathanael was from Cana, the place of Jesus' first miracle.

It is early in the morning. Jesus has slipped amongst them but they are unaware that it is he. We are, by now, familiar with this key discipleship

---

443   John 20:29-31.

444   David H. Stern – *Jewish New Testament Commentary* (Clarksville: Jewish New Testament Publications, 1992), 212-3.

lesson – it is easy to miss God's presence, especially when we feel we are on familiar ground. I find it so encouraging that these characters who knew Jesus best still needed their Lord to introduce himself to them despite all they had been taught over that three year period and the fact that they'd already met him in his resurrected body. Each day is a new day and God is always going about his business. The disciples, some of whom knew everything there was to know about fishing, had been out in their boats but had caught nothing. The question: "Friends, haven't you any fish" is a blunt way of stating the reality of their situation – the experts had pooled their skills and drawn a blank.

The early chapters of the gospel had also introduced us to two images of fruitfulness: a vine and a fig tree. In this final chapter we are presented with fish and a non-fisherman who not only knows where they are hiding better than the professionals but is also able to supply instructions that result in them ensnaring more fish than they are prepared for. I don't think I am reading too much into this story when I suggest that John is underlining some key truths here: the wisdom of the Kingdom is greater than human wisdom and the methods Jesus has taught his followers are guaranteed to yield better results than conventional methods, no matter how professional the approach.

I cannot help thinking back to John's version of the Commission in 20:21 - "As the Father has sent me, I am sending you" and linking that to Simon Peter's first encounter with Jesus at which the Messiah had said "Don't be afraid; from now on you will fish for people."[445] Yes, this encounter would have jogged Peter's memory right back to the moment when Jesus called him, borrowing his boat as a pulpit from which to teach the crowd. I think there is even more to the story. Jerome delightfully informs us that, at time of Jesus, it was popularly believed that there were exactly 153 species of fish in the sea[446] and Augustine of Hippo and other scholars suggest the number 153 represents totality.[447] The point is that the number has significance. The 153 fish could well have been understood as Jesus reminding the disciples of his command to preach the Gospel to all nations.

445   Luke 5:10.

446   Robert Grant – *Early Christians and Animals* (Abingdon: Routledge, 1999), 23.

447   See http://prophecynotes.blogspot.co.uk/2006/05/prophecy-of-153-fish.html and http://prophecynotes.blogspot.co.uk/2006/05/prophecy-of-153-fish.html for full explanations.

Broken and Healed

In Jesus' day the bond between Rabbi and disciple was viewed as stronger than that between a son and his father.[448] Despite his protestations of loyalty, Peter had let Jesus down and was understandably devastated at the way he had betrayed his Rabbi. When John admits that Simon Peter had slipped back into the comfort of old routines we can understand why. After sharing breakfast with the team Jesus seeks out Peter and initiates a painful conversation.

It seems to me that Jesus' opening words are significant. He begins by tempting Peter to assert his self-reliance once again: "Simon, son of John, do you truly love me more than these?" He is clearly referring to Peter's earlier boast recorded in Matthew 26:33 that he would not abandon Jesus even if the other disciples were to desert him.

Many commentators resist making too much of the fact that Jesus asks twice whether Peter loves him with the strongest form of love (*agape*) and hears Peter reply with an affirmation using a weaker form (*phileo*). Surely it is significant that the third time Jesus asks using the weaker word and hears the same word in positive response. I feel that there is something deliberate in the choice of words simply because it takes Peter back to the last time he and Jesus were sat around a *charcoal* fire (the type of fire is also mentioned deliberately). This was the occasion on which he made his rash promise and repeated it three times. This adds an extra poignancy to Jesus' thrice repeated question here in this final chapter, suggesting to me that the choice of words must also be deliberate:

> Peter, do you still feel the need to boast to me about the strength of your love?

> Peter, are you still tempted to see yourself as better equipped than everyone else?

> Peter, do still you think I am looking for more from you than you can give me?

> Peter, are you prepared for me to work through you?

This, it seems, embarrasses Peter and he tries to shift the attention to

---

448   See Ann Spangler and Lois Tverberg – Sitting at the Feet of Rabbi Jesus, 57-61.

John who is standing nearby; "Lord, what about him?" Jesus' reply draws Peter back to himself and his own calling and we learn our final lesson about following Jesus. We each have our own distinct set of gifts and circumstances and, even if the way we serve Christ looks very different from the way others are called, we must resist comparing ourselves with them. "You must follow me".

Feeding and Leading the Sheep

Peter's unique 'follow me' was to 'feed my sheep'. It may be worth reflecting what this call to feed the flock means to those of us who are charged to lead churches, disciple Christians or reach the lost. I have implied in earlier chapters that much of what Christ's sheep have been fed in the generations that preceded ours seems to have made them fat, lazy and complacent. I had a conversation with someone just the other day whose church was altering its style of Sunday delivery in order to facilitate closer fellowship and more meaningful interaction. In short, she was bemoaning the shortening of the sermon which she had earlier admitted she'd forgotten by the time she got home but was still convinced should be the prime means of helping her to grow. I asked: "So, are these sermons helping you to act as Jesus did?" "No, not really", was her reply but she still insisted she was being discipled every Sunday morning by the Pastor and that any failing was hers for not listening intently enough.

What do we do when the call to 'feed my sheep' means offering them food they aren't used to and don't like? Maybe the thing many church leaders fear most will happen: the flock will go elsewhere. Perhaps they will. What have you lost if they do? The most significant loss is likely to be financial and this cost certainly needs to be counted. When I stood down from paid church leadership I was convinced that God had said to me that it would be at least a year before I knew what was coming next. It was a difficult decision to make but I also knew I wanted to be obedient and reminded myself that God had promised he would supply the needs of all who sought the Kingdom of God before all other considerations. I am still here and my family were provided for.

During my period in church leadership, each time we made a decision that affirmed our intention to establish a more missional culture we lost a few people who wanted to remain comfortable in their conviction that the church should serve their need of pastoral support or 'deep teaching'. After processing the pain of losing some folk who may have been lovely people but were never going to be persuaded, I had to remind myself that it was no great loss to the mission of God to let people go who may say and sing the right things but the message they were sending by their actions is that they'd arrived at a destination that suited them.

Having faced the worst case scenario – people might leave – it may equally be the case that those lovely people in your church who don't seem to want much personal challenge aren't the obstructive people they might seem to be. Mike Breen and Steve Cockram draw a graph with four quadrants. The vertical axis measures 'Invitation' and the horizontal records level of 'Challenge'.[449]

In his dealings with his disciples Jesus varied the mix of invitation and challenge to take account of his followers' level of understanding and maturity.[450] Breen and Cockram observe

> *Left to our own devices we tend to gravitate to either the High Invitation/Low Challenge quadrant or the High Challenge/Low invitation quadrant, depending on our personality... If you are a leader within one of the denominations which has historically functioned as traditional, it is far more likely you will be functioning in the Chaplaincy Quadrant. If you happen to be a leader within a strongly evangelical and pioneering tradition, it is far more likely that you will be functioning in the Stressful Quadrant.[451]*

Many leaders who are engaging with Jesus' call to make disciples in churches like the one I used to lead find themselves in the High Challenge/Low invitation quadrant whilst their people appear content to remain in the High Invitation/Low Challenge area of the graph. In my experience the whole church is unlikely to welcome a radical shift in focus, especially since the journey towards the High Challenge/High Invitation quadrant will inevitably lead through the Stressful quadrant with everyone experiencing a degree of discouragement, often for different reasons.

....

449   Mike Breen and Steve Cockram – *Building a Discipling Culture*, 12.

450   We have referred to this before when acknowledging the way Jesus shifts through the four stages which begin 'I do, you watch' and end 'You do, I watch'. Breen and Cockram explain this process as they unpack Leadership Square in chapter 8 of their book.

451   Breen and Cockram. Ibid, 12.

Most churches facing this scenario will want to begin by helping the few who want to become fruitful disciples make the necessary shifts. What is needed to begin these experiments is a church that has established a culture of permission. For example, I led a Baptist church whose understanding of its own ecclesiology assumed that every major decision had to be agreed by a church meeting and the phrase 'would turkeys vote for Christmas' was part of the Baptist joke book.

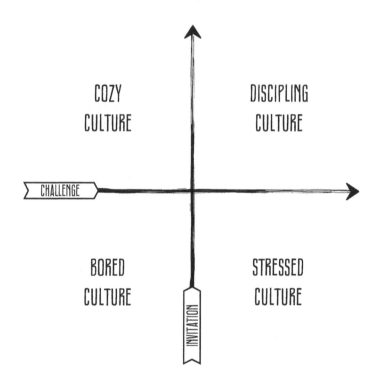

COZY CULTURE

DISCIPLING CULTURE

CHALLENGE

BORED CULTURE

STRESSED CULTURE

INVITATION

You may have reservations about the way Baptist ecclesiology can become a culture where the strongest our loudest voice wins the day, and I may share them, but the fact is that, unless there is a widely felt appetite for radical change, we are forced to use the models we currently have to change the prevailing culture. Once the culture has begun to shift it is then wise to revise church rules and constitutions to take account of, and embed, the new reality.

For us this meant developing a culture of permission within which church partners were able to express their delight at allowing others to take experiments that need not involve them. I have been part of churches which lurch from one make-or-break, all-or-nothing vote to another simply because it is assumed that everyone must agree about everything that anyone does. Such a culture is always going to be stressful for those who are naturally late adopters of any new idea. What these less pioneering folk may need is simply to see something modelled by others before understanding how they can become involved but, once they have voted against it, it is less likely that this will happen.

In my experience it is churches that tend to place great stress on some sort of voting mechanism as a means of discerning God's will that have most to benefit from by this shift in focus. My blood runs cold when I recall certain Deacons meetings many years ago in which the talk would be about getting an issue 'through the church meeting'. We felt entirely justified in the language we were using because our experience was one of being frequently stymied by members of the church who seemed to delight in keeping things the way they were. I now realise the degree to which our methods of engineering a vote in favour of the direction we were convinced was God's will must have appeared so full of unwarranted conviction as to appear desperate and therefore deeply suspicious.

The first step towards changing the decision-making culture of a church has to be to locate the unity of the church in John 17 rather than in its ability to agree over every decision. Although I understand the need for some kind of mechanism to discern the way people believe God is speaking, using a vote to do this is often cumbersome and counter-productive. This is because a ballot creates winners and losers, together with the implication that some have heard God and others haven't. And if those engaged in the vote are not mature enough to separate their own strong feelings from God's voice it is always going to be difficult to debrief afterwards. This may ratchet up the pressure next time and the temptation to over-promise in order to swing a vote may kick in, thus creating the inevitable disappointment which will ultimately lead to cynicism about the whole system. Voting is also very heavy-handed – by which I mean that it can deliver a verdict on a single, simple choice very well: do we want red or blue? What it can't deliver is any kind of nuance: would another colour be a better choice than both red and blue? Does every wall have to be painted the same colour?

A culture of permission is created by the way we ask questions and the kind of questions we ask. So, to request people's prayer support for an experimental venture that has arisen out of a youth group prayer time is far more likely to engage a wide range of interested responses which may pave the way for some funding being made available. To turn it into a test of whether or not God is in it or to begin with a request for money is to risk polarising the opinions of people who have nothing invested in the experiment. To take this illustration further, it is far more disarming to invite the support of the church at an early stage in the discernment process than at the point where the project has been fully defined and decided by an enthusiastic leadership team. Meetings of church folk often contain a huge amount of accumulated wisdom and imagination if they are handled wisely.

Jesus' Global Mission

John's final words remind us that Jesus said and did a great deal more than he or others felt obliged to recall. They also remind us that Jesus' work through the twelve and those who followed them has continued across the centuries into our age. In my opening chapter I skipped rapidly through the Old Testament pointing out how God's intended global mission was thwarted as the people he had chosen repeatedly fell short of their calling and pursued a trajectory that took them further from his heart. In closing I want to demonstrate how we can use the same pattern to indicate the way in which the mandate Jesus gave to the twelve and all who followed them covers the same bases as the original plan.

We can begin by taking Jesus' claim to be one with the Father at face value and putting his name at the top of our new diagram. John 14:6 contains probably the most complete self-designation by Jesus of his ministry. He is the way to the Father, a perfect image of the Father and the one in and through whom the life of the Father is experienced. We could use many passages from the other gospels and the letters of Paul to state this more explicitly but, when held alongside John 3:16, I believe this verse is the most profound way of stating the fact that the effects of the fall have been truly reversed and that the benefits can be enjoyed by the whole world through Christ.

Normality then becomes defined by Jesus as life in the Kingdom of God. No longer are we condemned to find security, significance and a modicum of purpose in what we can achieve through our own wisdom and strength. We have a Father who promises that whenever we put the Kingdom first he will supply all our needs and will equip us to bear abundant fruit.[452] It is,

452   Matthew 6:33 and John 15:1-17.

after all, to Kingdom minded people that Peter declares: "You are a chosen people, a royal priesthood, a holy nation, a people belonging to God, that you may declare the praises of him who called you out of darkness and into his wonderful light".[453]

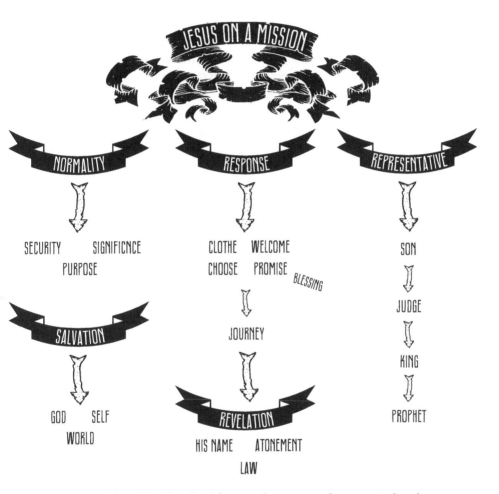

In the parable of the Prodigal Son we have one of many stories Jesus tells that illustrate his Father's response to the estrangement between himself and the world.[454] Notice the way the Father rushes out to welcome the lost son, how he clothes him with a new robe and gives him the family ring, symbolising both restored identity and authority. Having reinstated the privileges of son-ship to the wayward son the Father is then forced to

453   1 Peter 2:9.

454   Luke 15:11-32.

remind the elder son that he too is entitled to enjoy the same benefits but is choosing not to do so.

We have already seen how Jesus' choice of twelve men to journey with him for 3 years was both similar and different to the usual rabbinic practice of his day. Jesus spent three and a half years with them because he knew how long it would take them to tune in to the rhythm of God in order that they could engage with his larger mission. We have also seen how Jesus calls us first and foremost to know him, and through him to come to know the Father. He invites all his disciples to have intimate fellowship with him because this was the way the Twelve got to know their teacher and were taught to imitate him.[455] As our likeness to our Lord becomes a more natural way of living we also discover, as the Twelve did, that Jesus entrusts us with greater authority.

This is what Jesus meant when he told Peter in Matthew 16:19 and the whole crowd of disciples in Matthew 18:18 that he was giving them authority to 'bind' and 'loose' or 'forbid' and 'permit'.[456] The principles of the Kingdom of God demonstrated by Jesus to the Disciples were often diametrically opposed to those of the religious system that also claimed their allegiance. Jesus was expressing his confidence that the Twelve now had a sufficient awareness of the general principles of his teaching to apply them to a wider variety of situations. This is so different to Western models of discipleship which often involve little more than learning doctrines and devotional practices in a church or classroom.

As the New Testament progresses, and Paul is forced to conceive new images that connect with the non-Jewish world, the term 'disciple' is dropped in favour of pedagogue, apprentice and son. The Greeks and Romans understood the role of the extended family in nurturing a child and Paul is not afraid to choose a new image in order to affirm Jesus primary message: there is one way of becoming a follower of Jesus and that is to use the same training methods he used.

So, returning to our diagram, the source of our revelation is through our relationship with Jesus who is the Ideal representative of the Father.[457]

....

455   2 Corinthians 3:18.

456   David H. Stern – *Jewish New Testament Commentary*, 57.

457   John 14:8-10 (CEV).

The whole book of Hebrews explains how the atonement won by Jesus is infinitely better than the Old Testament forerunner and we have seen earlier how and why Jesus completely reinterprets the law. So, who needs a patriarch when you have a Son? And the Son described in the New Testament wraps up the mantles of Judge, King and Prophet in himself. Jesus covers all the bases set out in the Old Testament and, in so doing, takes upon himself the core mission of God. The events of the Old Testament were God's response following the fall – his mission to win the world back to himself. Having seen Israel turn their backs on their calling and noted how exile and exclusion were the inevitable result, the ministry of Jesus becomes the Father's perfect attempt to re-establish a people of promise and do an inside job.

Israel and the Church

For three and a half years Jesus took upon himself the task of forming and training the disciples so they could pick up the reins and pass on those same skills to succeeding generations of Christ-followers. God's mission has thus become the mandate of the church. To us the closing section of Paul's letter to the Romans is a warning:

> Am I saying that God has turned his back on his people? Certainly not! I am one of the people of Israel, and I myself am a descendant of Abraham from the tribe of Benjamin. God did not turn his back on his chosen people. Don't you remember reading in the Scriptures how Elijah complained to God about the people of Israel? He said, "Lord, they killed your prophets and destroyed your altars. I am the only one left, and now they want to kill me." But the Lord told Elijah, "I still have seven thousand followers who have not worshipped Baal." It is the same way now. God was kind to the people of Israel, and so a few of them are still his followers. [458]

We are meant to ask "Why did the God whose idea it was to establish a covenant reject his people?" The italics I have added to the following section answer that question:

> Do I mean that the people of Israel fell, never to get up again? Certainly not! Their failure made it possible for the Gentiles to be

---

458   Romans 11:1-5 (CEV).

*saved, and this will make the people of Israel jealous. But if **the rest of the world's people were helped so much by Israel's sin and loss, they will be helped even more by their full return**. When Israel rejected God, the rest of the people in the world **were able to turn to him**. So when God makes friends with Israel, it will be like bringing the dead back to life. If the roots of a tree are holy, the rest of the tree is holy too. You Gentiles are like branches of a wild olive tree that were made to be part of a cultivated olive tree. You have taken the place of some branches that were cut away from it. And because of this, you enjoy the blessings that come from being part of that cultivated tree. My friends, I don't want you Gentiles to be too proud of yourselves. So I will explain the mystery of what has happened to the people of Israel. Some of them have become stubborn, and they will stay like that until the complete number of you Gentiles has come in. The people of Israel are treated as God's enemies, **so that the good news can come to you Gentiles**. At one time you Gentiles rejected God. But now Israel has rejected God, and you have been shown mercy. And because of the mercy shown to you, they will also be shown mercy. All people have disobeyed God, and that's why he treats them as prisoners. But he does this, so that he can have mercy on **everyone**.*[459]

The letter to the Romans was written to a church made up of Jewish and Gentile Christians. The Messianic Jews were attempting to force their Gentile brothers and sisters to adopt certain Jewish customs in order that they might become better Christians and Paul was writing to correct this nonsensical notion. In Christ there is a level playing field. God's desire is for the whole world to become his children once again, living under his blessing. God chose Israel to be the means through which the whole creation was to be restored to fellowship with himself but it became necessary for him to turn his back on His people because they had become an obstacle to this mission. His people were not able to reflect him because of their determination to see their chosen-ness as a badge of honour rather than an awesome calling. In a similar spirit, Peter addresses the church:

Stop being hateful! Quit trying to fool people, and start being sincere. Don't be jealous or say cruel things about others. Be like

---

459   Romans 11:11-32 (selected verses).

newborn babies who are thirsty for the pure spiritual milk that will help you grow up in your salvation.[460]

A survey of the New Testament reveals that Christ's work of salvation covers three Greek tenses: past, present + future. Our salvation has a secure basis in the past, is being worked out in the present and will be secured in the future. How different to the gospel many thought they'd signed up to when they responded to an offer to 'go to heaven'!

Of the 134 references Jesus makes to heaven, 92 of them are simply references to the dwelling place of God, 33 cover those occasions when Matthew shies away from referring to the Kingdom of God and just 9 refer to it as a place of existence beyond death. Correspondingly, Jesus only speaks of hell 11 times, always as a warning to the religious. We must also balance these handful of scriptures with the 47 references Jesus makes to the Kingdom of God, which he says is in our midst now and can be entered and participated in before death. To be saved, therefore, is to be reconciled to God so that we can participate in the Kingdom of God now and thereby enjoy God for ever.

You have already found out how good the Lord really is. Come to Jesus Christ. He is the living stone that people have rejected, but which God has chosen and highly honoured.[461]

As above, we are meant to recall who it was that rejected Jesus.

And now you are living stones that are being used to build a spiritual house. You are also a group of holy priests, and with the help of Jesus Christ you will offer sacrifices that please God. It is just as God says in the Scriptures, "Look! I am placing in Zion a choice and precious cornerstone. No one who has faith in that one will be disappointed.[462]

Note where the stone is placed: Zion. This establishes a continuity with the Old Testament record of God's dealings with Israel.

You are followers of the Lord, and that stone is precious to you.

460   1 Peter 2:1-2 (CEV).

461   1 Peter 2:3-4 (CEV).

462   1 Peter 2:5-6 (CEV).

But it isn't precious to those who refuse to follow him. They are the builders who tossed aside the stone that turned out to be the most important one of all. They disobeyed the message and stumbled and fell over that stone, because they were doomed. But you are God's chosen and special people. You are a group of royal priests and a holy nation. God has brought you out of darkness into his marvellous light. Now you must tell all the wonderful things that he has done. The Scriptures say, "Once you were nobody. Now you are God's people. At one time no one had pity on you. Now God has treated you with kindness.[463]

It is as if Peter is pleading with his readers: "Is the message still not clear?" as he borrows the dominant image of the early verses of John's gospel and uses it to highlight the purpose of our being chosen: we are people of the light in order to tell all the wonderful things that God has done. Just like his first-chosen people refused to do. In Exodus 20 God's people refused the invitation to draw near to God and they were thus unable to shine with his radiance.

A number of years ago I was on a trip to Belarus, the one I referred to in the acknowledgements to this book. I recall walking through an open-air market with stalls containing thousands of beautifully painted matryoshkas: Russian nesting dolls. As I was selecting a doll to take home for my daughter Bethany it struck me that they illustrated the relationship between Father, Son and Holy Spirit: each resembled the other, were truly one and yet could also be experienced independently of each other.

As we wrestled with the creative task of preparing the graphics for this book my son Shaun saw the matryoshka as an equally powerful symbol of the relationship between a disciple and Christ. Paul loves to remind us that we are each 'In Christ', in the sense that our life and our future are wrapped up in his work on the cross and his resurrected life. There is more to it than that though.

The New Testament teaches clearly that, as we imitate Christ and the character of Christ we see in others, we are becoming formed into a likeness that is his. This is represented by the distinctive shape and the similar images on the body of each doll. But our becoming like Christ happens in such a way that none of our story or our individual identity becomes

---

463   1 Peter 2:7-10 (CEV).

lost. Thus we add our own faces to a doll that looks like Jesus - as John's drawings at the beginning of each chapter illustrate so beautifully.

Bethany's doll holds just six smaller representations of itself inside it. Christ has made many more copies of himself and he continues to do so. Each of us bear the shape of Christ whilst also telling our own story and it is God's will that we also become filled with the radiant life that is his. May his will be done and his Kingdom come on earth, as in heaven. Amen.

Bibliography

Edwin A. Abbott – *Flatland: A Romance of Many Dimensions* (New York: Dover Publications, 1992).

Kenneth Bailey – *Jesus Through Middle Eastern Eyes: Cultural Studies in the Gospels* (London: SPCK, 2008).

Joan Bakewell - *The Heart of the "Heart of the Matter"* (London: BBC Books, 1996).

William Barclay – *The Gospel of John, Volume 1. Revised Edition* (Edinburgh: Saint Andrew Press, 1982).

C. K. Barrett – *The Gospel According to St John* (London: SPCK, 1956).

Rob Bell - *The Gods Aren't Angry* DVD (Zondervan, 2008).

Rob Bell – *Everything is Spiritual* DVD (Zondervan, 2010).

Jack Bernard – *How to become a Saint: a beginners guide* (Grand Rapids: Brazos Press, 2007).

Wendell Berry – *Jayber Crow* (Washington: Counterpoint, 2000).

Wendell Berry – *Blessed are the Peacemakers: Christ's Teachings of Love, Compassion and Forgiveness* (Washington: Counterpoint, 2005).

Mike Breen and Steve Cockram – *Building a Discipling Culture* (Pawley's Island: 3DM, 2009).

Mike Breen – *Covenant and Kingdom: The DNA of the Bible* (Pawley's Island: 3DM, 2010).

Mike Breen and Alex Absalom – *Launching Missional Communities: A Field Guide* (Pawley's Island: 3DM, 2010).

Mike Breen - *Leading Missional Communities* (Pawley's Island: 3DM, 2013).

Mike and Sally Breen - *Family on Mission* (Pawley's Island: 3DM, 2014).

Marcus Brigstocke – *God Collar* (London: Bantam Press, 2011).

Brené Brown – *Daring Greatly* (London: Portfolio Penguin, 2012).

David Daube - *The New Testament and Rabbinic Judaism* (Peabody: Hendrickson, 1994).

D. Durnbaugh - *The Believers' Church: The history and character of radical Protestantism* (New York: Macmillan, 1970).

Carol Dweck – *Mindset: The New Psychology of Success* (New York: Ballantine Books, 2008).

John Eldredge – *Waking the Dead* (Nashville: Thomas Nelson, 2003).

G. R. Evans trans, Bernard of Clairvaux: *Selected Works, The Classics of Western Spirituality* (Mahwah, NJ: Paulist Press, 1987).

Andy Freeman and Pete Greig – *Punk Monk: New Monasticism and the Ancient Art of Breathing* (Ventura: Regal Books, 2007).

Kate Fox – *Watching the English* (London: Hodder and Stoughton, 2005).

Michael Frost - *Seeing God in the Ordinary: A Theology of the Everyday* (Peabody: Hendrickson, 2000).

Michael Frost – *Exiles: Living Missionally in a Post Christian Culture* (Peabody: Hendrickson, 2006).

Michael Frost and Alan Hirsch - *The Shaping of Things to Come: Innovation and Mission for the 21st Century Church* (Peabody: Hendrickson, 2006).

Michael Frost and Alan Hirsch – *ReJesus: A Wild Messiah for a Missional Church* (Peabody: Hendrickson, 2009).

Malcolm Gladwell – *Blink: The Power of Thinking Without Thinking* (London: Penguin Books, 2005).

J. Lee Grady – *What happened to the fire?* (Grand Rapids: Chosen Books, 1994).

Timothy Keller - *The Freedom of Self-Forgetfulness* (Leyland: 10Publishing,

Lisa Graham McMinn – *The Contented Soul: The art of savouring life* (Downers Grove: IVP 2006).

Greg Hawkins + Cally Parkinson – *Reveal: Where are You?* (Willow Creek Resources: Barrington, Illinois, 2007).

Greg Hawkins + Cally Parkinson – *Follow Me – What's next for you?* (Willow Creek Resources: Barrington, Illinois, 2008).

Alan Hirsch – *The Forgotten Ways: Reactivating the Missional Church* (Grand Rapids: Brazos Press, 2009).

Peter R. Holmes – *Becoming more human: exploring the interface of spirituality, Discipleship and Therapeutic Faith Community* (Milton Keynes: Paternoster, 2005).

Peter R. Holmes – *Trinity in Human Community: Exploring congregational life in the image of the Social Trinity* (Milton Keynes: Paternoster, 2006).

Peter Holmes and Susan Williams – *Becoming more like Christ* (Paternoster; Milton Keynes, 2007).

David Instone-Brewer - *The Jesus Scandals* (Oxford: Monarch, 2012).

A. J. Jacobs - *The Year of Living Biblically* (London: Arrow Books, 2009).

William James – *The Varieties of Religious Experience* (New York: Penguin, 1985).

Beresford Job – *Biblical Church* (Epping: Bethany Publishing, 2007).

Mike King - *Presence-centered Youth Ministry: Guiding Students into Spiritual Formation* (Downers Grove: IVP Books, 2006).

Stephen Kuhrt – *Tom Wright for Everyone* (London: SPCK, 2011).

C. S. Lewis – *God in the Dock: Essays on Theology and Ethics* (Glasgow: Fount, 1989).

Tanya Luhrmann – *When God Talks Back: Understanding the American evangelical relationship with God.* (New York: Vintage Books, 2012).

Rob McAlpine – *Post Charismatic?* (Eastbourne: Kingsway Communications, 2008).

James McClendon – *Doctrine: Systematic Theology volume 2* (Nashville: Abingdon Press, 1994).

Brian McLaren - *The Secret Message of Jesus,* (Nashville: Thomas Nelson, 2006).

Brian McLaren – *Naked Spirituality* (London: Hodder and Stoughton, 2011).

Brian McLaren - Video clips entitled *"Domesticated Jesus"* and *"Atheist"*.

Gerald G. May - *Addiction and Grace: Love and Spirituality in the Healing of Addictions* (New York: HarperCollins, 1991).

Stuart Murray-Williams - *Post Christendom: Church and Mission in a Strange New World* (Carlisle: Authentic Media, 2004).

Jo Nesbo – *The Redeemer* (London: Vintage, 2009).

M. Scott Peck - *Further Along the Road Less Traveled: The Unending Journey toward Spiritual Growth* (New York: Touchstone, 1993).

John Piper – *Future Grace* (Leicester: IVP, 1995).

John Rentoul - *"What on earth was Osborne thinking?"* in The Independent on Sunday. 25th March 2012.

Richard Rohr – *The Naked Now* (New York: Crossroad Publishing, 2009).

Richard Rohr – *Preparing for Christmas with Richard Rohr* (Cincinnati: Saint Anthony Messenger Press, 2008).

Richard Rohr - DVD set - *Holding the Tension: The Power of Paradox*.

Peter Scazzero – *Emotionally Healthy Spirituality: Unleash a Revolution in your Life in Christ* (Nashville: Thomas Nelson, 2006).

Rabbi Andrew Sheldrake – *Contours of Messianic Judaism* (Norwich: Adat Yeshua, 2007).

Ann Spangler and Lois Tverberg – *Sitting at the Feet of Rabbi Jesus: How the Jewishness of Jesus can Transform your Faith* (Grand Rapids: Zondervan, 2009).

John Steinbeck – *East of Eden* (New York: Penguin; 1992).

David H. Stern – *Jewish New Testament Commentary* (Clarksville: Jewish New Testament Publications, 1992).

R. Tasker – *John, Tyndale New Testament Commentary* (Leicester: IVP, 1983).

Lois Tverberg – *Walking in the Dust of Rabbi Jesus: How the Jewish Words of Jesus can Change your Life* (Grand Rapids: Zondervan, 2012).

Dorothy Walker - *Michael Craig-Martin: Landscapes* (Dublin: Douglas Hyde Gallery, 2001).

Rob Warner – *Reinventing English Evangelicalism* (Carlisle: Paternoster, 2007).

John Westerhoff and John Eusden – *The Spiritual Life* (New York: Seabury Press, 1982).

Christopher Wright - *The Mission of the People of God: A Biblical Theology of the Church's Mission.* {Grand Rapids: Zondervan, 2010),

Tom Wright – *John for Everyone Parts 1 and 2* (London: SPCK, 2003).

N. T. Wright – *Following Jesus: Biblical Reflections on Discipleship* (London: SPCK, 1994).

N. T. Wright – *The New Testament and the People of God: Christian Origins and the Question of God v. 1* (Minneapolis: Fortress Press, 1992).

N. T. Wright - *Jesus and the Victory of God: Christian Origins and the Question of God: v. 2* (London: SPCK Publishing, 1996).

N. T. Wright – *The Challenge of Jesus* (London: SPCK, 2000).

Nigel G Wright - *Disavowing Constantine: Mission, Church and the Social Order in the Theologies of John Howard Yoder and Jurgen Moltmann* (Carlisle: Paternoster, 2000).

Philip Yancey – *Reaching for the Invisible God* (Grand Rapids: Zondervan, 2000).

Lightning Source UK Ltd.
Milton Keynes UK
UKOW06f1136250915

259251UK00011B/263/P